INDIA BOOKVARSITY

L O T U S C H O I C E S

Editor: Mahendra Kulasrestha

Classics Revived
for an
Ultra-modern World

The Golden Book of
U P A N I S H A D S

Humanity's Earliest Philosophical Compositions

Isha Upanishad
Kena Upanishad
Katha Upanishad
Mundak Upanishad
Prashna Upanishad
Aitareya Upanishad
Kaushitaki Upanishad
Taittiriya Upanishad
Shvetashwatara Upanishad
Chhandogya Upanishad
Brihadaranyaka Upanishad

4735/22, Prakash Deep Building,
Ansari Road, Darya Ganj,
New Delhi- 110002

THE GOLDEN BOOK OF UPANISHADS

Eleven major Upanishads translated into easy-to understand English by the renowned Indologist

F. MAX MULLER

Introduction by the translator of sixty Upanishads in German

PAUL DEUSSEN

Lotus Press : Publishers & Distributors
Unit No. 220, 2nd Floor, 4735/22, Prakash Deep Building,
Ansari Road, Darya Ganj, New Delhi- 110002
Ph.: 41325510, 98118-38000
• E-mail : lotuspress1984@gmail.com
www.lotuspress.co.in

Source:
Sacred Books of the East
Edited by F. Max Muller
and published by
Clarendon Press, Oxford, UK
in the 1880s

The Golden Book of Upanishads

ISBN: 81-8382-012-3

Printed & Published by : **Lotus Press Publishers & Distributors,** New Delhi-02

Warmly dedicated to
SULTAN DARA SHIKOH
ANQUETIL DUPERRON
and
ARTHUR SCHOPENHAUER
to whom
goes the credit of
reviving them
in modern times

Ishavasyamidam sarvam
The Lord pervades everything.
—Isha

Prajnanam Brahma
Brahman is pure consciousness.
—Aitareya

Aham Brahmasmi
I am Brahman
—Brihadaranyaka

Tat twam asi
You are That—Brahman
—Chhandogya

Ayamatma Brahma
The Atman is Brahman
—Mandukya

Brahmaivedam vishvamidam varishtham
All this manifested universe is the supreme Brahman.
— Mundaka

Uttishthata jagrata prapya varannibodhata
Arise, awake and realise your goal.
—Katha

Editorspeak

The Research of Atman

The ill-fated elder brother of Aurangzeb, Dara Shikoh, was an admirer of the philosophy of the Upanishads, and got as many as 50 of these translated and published into Persian—a number which no Hindu in India has touched till date—in the mid-seventeenth century. Even the great Shankaracharya selected only ten for his commentary, obviously the ones which supported his philosophy of the Advaita. Persian at that time was quite well known among European scholars and the well-read, and a century later, the whole work was translated into Latin in two volumes of almost two thousand pages by Anquetil Duperron—which opened the floodgates of the spread of their glory in the West. The famous French philosopher Arthur Schopenhauer of those times, was so impressed by their high yet simple philosophy, that he became the flag-bearer of all that was ancient in Indian thought and culture.

He declared that no Western religion or theology could compare it, and so far as the efforts of Christianity towards the conversion of India were concerned, they would never succeed—a statement which was resented by many, including Max Muller, in later times. But he was also supported by many more who came to be called his spiritual ancestors. Another half century later, two translations were made in German, the first by Franz Mischel and the second by Paul Deussen, who also wrote a detailed study of the Upanishadic philosophy, which is perhaps the best on the subject penned by anyone till date. The present editor, for this reason, has thought it fit to provide a summary from this work in this book for the benefit of the readers, which, he believes, will help them understand the intricacies as well as the finer points of the otherwise complex subject in a better way. His German translation of sixty Upanishads is now available in its English rendering also, most intelligently done by V.M. Bedekar and G.B. Palsule, and published by the well known Motilal Benarsidas. Those further interested in the hoary subject are advised to consult these three valuable books. Paul Deussen visited India and lived here for a while and wrote a few other books on other aspects of Indian culture; he was an admirer of Swami Vivekananda also.

The Upanishads are many—the number fluctuates from 108 to 235 but it is a pity that not more than 11 or 12 are known to us today and the translations available in English or Hindi do not exceed this number. This particular category of scriptures is our heritage and further attention should be paid to it; even a Muslim like Dara Shikoh selected 50 from the lot for translation. The Bhagavadgita is more popular but those who know about the subject, will agree that the Upanishads are much more basic and even more pleasant to delve in about the theories of the Atman, Brahman, etc. They provide the first rays of light—the early morning Ushas light, if we may say so—of the first philosophy of the world. Like the Gita, which has been translated in so many easy-to-yet-easier versions by scholars of the world, the Upanishads also deserve a similar treatment for better understanding and use. The Bible should be the model, its new translation which serves its purpose in a most remarkable way.

The Rigveda contained the seeds of the philosophy which developed into the Upanishads in the form of Atman, Brahman, Purusha, Prakriti, Prana, Prajna, the three qualities of Satva, Rajas and Tamas, the five Koshas, the practice of Yoga leading one to the state of Samadhi, etc. To say the least, these essentially abstract concepts were related to the basic philosophy of life and its purpose, the understanding of human mind and its processes as psychology, and also the physiological analysis of human body and its functioning by conceptualising the theories of Prana and its bifurcations into sub-forms like Apana, Vyana, Udana, etc.—which helped in the early development of the science of health and medicine as Ayurveda.

It is important to underline the fact that, in view of the ancientness of those times, these concepts were most striking. It should also be noted that no other culture could compare this level of ideas, and, till the nineteenth century, when they were first taken note of by modern scholars—many of them expressed their amazement at their newness with the resultant difficulty in comprehension. Paul Deussen has been specific that similar ideas were next expressed by the Greeks and yet later by the German philosopher Emannuel Kant. There is in both the cases a gap of many centuries. Where religions such as the Jew, Christianity and Islam are concerned, they in no case did philosophise the problem of existence, being content with the easier idea of God as the cause as well as purpose of everything, which in all these cases remained cheerfully vague. The last chapter of the

Bible tries to picture his status to an extent that it creates more fury and fire than light and understanding. The presentations regarding God in the Old Testament also are not very soothing—a fact noted by Christian scholars also. Knowledge and epistemology are the special characteristics of the Upanishads and related writings and, they are quite remarkable.

Max Muller is of the view that the ease of life in India would have been the reason of the growth of basic thought in the country, and that may well be so. The difficult hilly and desert areas of western Asia gave rise to the one powerful God-centred train of religions, starting with the Jew religion of Moses. The Old Testament tells the story in a most vivid manner, and in quite some details, The history of the Jews till the present times, through the horrors of Hitler as well as the lifelong wanderings of the whole race all over the world, does establish the necessity of a strong belief in a God for sheer survival of people fated to live in difficult circumstances. Though it also leads us to the superiority of Fate, or Destiny, over God—but that is another question to be tackled perhaps in the 21st century.

There is no doubt that India should be proud of the Upanishads, and for these should be grateful to her special Fate or Destiny. Hers is one culture which though `wounded' could not be destroyed, in harsh medieval ages. Once again is she rising and trying to walk, after a long long time. This writer believes that she, her people, the educated, including the Indiaspora, should see, read, study, understand her achievements, revive them if needed, and transcend them for further human benefit. A great leap in world living and culture has already started taking shape and we have to make our contribution by providing new, yet bolder ideas in the realms of philosophy.

Atman, Prana, and Prajna are the three micro concepts contributed by the Upanishads to world culture, and that too at that most ancient period of history. These eminently stand to reason and can be further developed scientifically in modern times. Brahman and Karman are the other two concepts which, though quite attractive intellectually, may only be part truths of reality, mere extensions of fantasy or intelligent thinking. In any case, in comparison to other world religions, these are highly commendable and pride-worthy. There are many other ideas, such as the relating of sleep and dreams to Brahman, as discussed in the larger Brihadaranyaka and Chhandogya Upanishads, which sound funny to modern knowledge, but they do establish India's status as a community of investigators.

The Upanishads—as also other religio-philosophical literature of various kinds—should be read for the sake of knowledge, if not as a matter of belief. It also helps comparison, so much needed for devising a final, or almost final, philosophy and religion for the whole humanity in the third millennium now started with the 21st century. At a time when Christianity is fast losing ground, as so remarkably discussed by Karen Armstrong in her famous work *History of God*, and Islam tottering courtesy its overstress on terrorism, despite its several very strong beneficial concepts—such as that of Zakat, which, in the present writer's view, is and can be an important instrument of relieving poverty—such an effort, again, as pointed out by dear Karen, is not only the need of the hour, but a distinct possibility.

Amen, Peace, Shanti.

Paul Deussen

The Birth of Philosophy Upanishads the First

The philosophy of the Upanishads forms the culminating point of the Indian doctrine of the universe. It had been already reached in Vedic times, and in philosophical significance has been surpassed by none of the later development of thought upto the present day. The Upanishads were called Vedanta, the last part of the Vedas, and became for India a permenent and characteristic spiritual atmosphere, which pervades all the products of the later literature. A remarkable and at first sight perplexing feature in this evolution of thought, through pantheism, cosmogonism, theism, atheism (Sankhya), and deism (Yoga), etc., is the persistence with which the original idealism holds its ground, not anulled or set aside by the pantheistic and theistic developments that grew out of it. On the contrary, it remains a living force, the influence of which may be more or less directly traced everywhere.

The Vedic literature has been classified into four principal parts, corresponding to the four priestly offices at the Soma sacrifice: the Rig, Yajur, Sama and Atharva, each of which comprises a Samhita, Brahmana and a Sutra. The Brahmana is then further divided into three orders, closely connected with and even overlapping each other—Vidhi, Arthavada and Vedanta or Upanishad. All these of all the four Vedas have been preserved not separately, but in several often numerous forms, as each Veda was taught in different

Shakhas (branches or schools), which in treatment of the common subject matter varied so considerably from one another that, in course of time, distinct works were produced, the contents of which nevertheless remained the same.

Each of the three ancient Vedas comprises not one Brahmana but several, and, similarly, there exists for each Veda not one but several Upanishads. The link between the Upanishad and the Brahmana with its very different spirit is as a rule not direct, but established ordinarily by means of an Aranyaka or 'forest book', to the close of which the Upanishad is attached, or in which it is included.

The name is given either because on account of its mysterious character it should be imparted to the student not in the village but outside of it in the jungle, or because from the very beginning it was "a Brahmin appointed to the vow of the anchorite", according to Sayana. The contents of the Aranyakas perhaps favour rather the latter conception, so far as they consist mainly of all kinds of explanations of the ritual and allegorical speculations therein. This is only what might be expected in the life of the forest as a substitute for the actual sacrificial observances, which for the most part no longer practicable; and they form a natural transition to the speculations of the Upanishads, altogether emancipated as these are from the limitations of a formal cult.

According to Shankara, the Upanishads were so named because they "destroy" inborn ignorance, or because they "conduct" to Brahman. The word is usually explained by Indian writers by *rahasyam* or secret doctrine. The word Upanishad, derived as a substantive form from the root *sad,* to sit, can denote a sitting; and the preposition *upa,* nearby, indicates, in contrast to *parishad, samsad* (assembly), a confidential secret sitting, we may assume that this name was used also in course of time to denote the purpose of this sitting, i.e., "secret instruction".

Research of Brahman and Atman

All the thoughts of the Upanishads move around two

fundamental ideas: the Brahman and the Atman. As a rule these terms are used synonymously: where a difference reveals itself, Brahman appears as the older and less intelligible expression; Atman as the later and more significant; Brahman as the unknown that needs to be explained, Atman as the known through which the other unknown finds its explanation; Brahman as the first principle so far as it is comprehended in the universe, Atman so far as it is known in the inner self of man. The difference between Brahman and Atman emerges where they appear side by side with one another, in brief sayings like 'truly the Brahman is the Atman' (in Brihadaranyak Upanishad).

If we hold to this distinction of the Brahman as the cosmical principle of the universe, and Atman as the psychical, the fundamental thought of the entire Upanishad philosophy may be expressed by the simple equation:

Brahman = Atman

That is to say, the Brahman, the power which presents itself to us materialised in all existing things, which creates, sustains, preserves, and receives back into itself again all worlds, this eternal, infinite, divine power is identical with the Atman, with that which, after stripping off everything external we discover in ourselves as our real most essential being, our individual self, the soul. **This identity of the Brahman and the Atman with God and the soul, is the fundamental thought of the entire doctrine of the Upanishads.** It is briefly expressed by the great saying *"tat tvam asi"*, "that art thou" and *"aham Brahma asmi"*, "I am Brahman"; and in the compound word *'Brahma-Atma-aikyam'*, "unity of the Brahman and the Atman" is described as the fundamental dogma of the Vedanta system.

If we strip this thought of the various forms, figurative to the highest degree and not seldom extravagant, under which it appears in the Vedanta texts, and fix our attention upon it solely in its philosophical simplicity as the identity of God and the Soul, the Brahman and the Atman, it will be found to possess a significance reaching far beyond the Upanishads, their time and country; nay, we claim for it an inestimable value for the whole race or mankind. We are unable to look into the future, we do not know what revelations and discoveries are in store for the restlessly enquiring human spirit, but one thing we may assert with confidence—**whatever new and unwanted paths the philosophy of the future may strike out, this principle will remain permanently unshaken, and from it no deviation can possibly take place.**

If ever a general solution is reached of the great riddle, which presents itself to the philosopher in the nature of things all the more clearly the further our knowledge extends, the key can only be found where alone the secret of nature lies open to us from within, that is to say, in our innermost self.

It is here that for the first time the original thinkers of the Upanishads, to their immortal honour found it when they recognised our Atman, our inmost individual being, as the Brahman, the inmost being of universal nature and of all her phenomena.

Greek Philosophy and Kant

There have been three occasions as far as we know on which philosophy has advanced to a clearer comprehension of its recurring task, and of the solution demanded: first in India in the Upanishads, again in Greece in the philosophy of Parmenides and Plato and finally, at a most recent time, in the philosophy of Kant and Schopenhauer. Greek philosophy reached its climax in the teachings of Parmenides and Plato, that the entire universe of change is, as Parmenides describes it, merely phenomenal, or in Plato's words, a world of shadows; and how both philosophers endeavoured through it to grasp the essential reality, that which Plato, in an expression that recalls the doctrine of the Upanishads no less than the phraseology of Kant describes as the *abro* (Atman).

We shall then see further how this same thought, obscured for a time under the influence of Aristotle and throughout the Middle Ages, was taken up again in quite a different way, and shone forth more clearly than ever before in the philosophy founded by Kant, adopted and perfected by his great successor Schopenhauer. Here we have to do with the Upanishads, and the worldwide historical significance of these documents cannot, in our judgement, be more clearly indicated than by showing how the deep fundamental conception of Plato and Kant was precisely that which already formed the basis of Upanishad teaching.

The objects which lie around us on every side in infinite space, and to which by virtue of our corporeal nature we ourselves belong, are, according to Kant, not things in themselves but only apparitions. According to Plato, they are not the true realities, but merely shadows of them. And according to the doctrine of the Upanishads, they are not the Atman, the real 'Self' of the things but mere 'Maya'—that is to say, a sheer deceit, an illusion. All worldly objects and relationships are, as Yajnavalkya says in Brihadaranyak Upanishad, of no value for their own sake but for the sake of the Atman, nay, they exist solely in the Atman, and that man is utterly and hopelessly undone who knows them 'apart from the self'. This Atman is the Brahman, the entire universe. **All religions unconsciously depend on the fundamental dogma of the Kantian philosophy, which in a less definite form was already laid down in the Upanishads.**

Kshatriyas Developed the Concept

The doctrines of the Upanishads were fostered in the homes of the Kshatriyas, though the conceptions may have originated with the Brahmins, who were engrossed with the fire rituals. There are many indications to point to the fact that the Upanishadic doctrine of the sole reality of the Atman, of its evolution as the universe, the identity with the soul, and so forth, may have originated from the Brahmins such as Yajnavalkya, yet in the earliest times met with acceptance rather in Kshatriya circles than among the Brahmins, and it was only later that they were adopted by them and interwoven with the ritual on the lines of allegorical interpretation. In the beginning these may even be partly despised by them, so it was the fourth Atharvaveda which opened its arms to the late born or rejected children of the Atman research.

The consequence of this generosity was that in course of time everything which appeared in the shape of Upanishad, that is, a mystical text, whether it were the expression merely of the religious-philosophical consciousness of a limited circle or even an individual thinker, was credited to the Atharvaveda, or by later collectors was included in it without further hesitation. There are pure Vedanta Upanishads, Yoga Upanishads, Sanyasa Upanishads, and Shiva and Vishnu Upanishads, over 200 in number, but to us it seems that nearly 60 of them would have met with general recognition.

It is very striking that the texts of the Upanishads frequently trace back some of their most important doctrines to Kshatriya kings. In Chhandogya Upanishad five learned Brahmins request from Uddalaka Aruni instruction concerning the Atman Vaishvanara, but the Brahmin Uddalaka distrusts his ability to explain everything to them, and all the six therefore take themselves to the King Ashvapati Kaikeya, and receive from him the true instruction.

In the Brihadaranyaka and Kaushitaki Upanishads the far-famed Vedic scholar Gargya Balaki volunteers to expound the Brahman to King Ajatashatru of Kashi, and propounds twelve erroneous explanations; whereupon to him the King exhibits the Brahman as the Atman under the figure of a deep-sleeper, prefacing his exposition with the remark, 'Though this is a reversal of the rule, for a Brahmin to betake himself as a pupil to a Kshatriya in order to have the Brahman expounded to him; I proceed to instruct you." In this narrative, preserved by two different Vedic schools, it is expressly declared that the knowledge of the Brahman as Atman, is possessed by the King, and is not possessed by the Brahmin 'famed as a Vedic scholar.'

In Chhandogya Upanishad two Brahmins are instructed by the King Pravahana Jaivali concerning the Akasha as the ultimate substation of all things, of which they are ignorant. Similarly, the same Upanishad contains the teaching given by Sanat Kumara, the god of war, to the Brahmin Narada. Here the former pronounces inadequate the comprehensive Vedic learning of the Brahmin with the words, 'All that you have studied is merely name.'

Finally, the leading text of the doctrine of the soul's transmigration which is extant in three different recensions, is propounded in the form of an instruction given to Aruni by the King Pravahana Jaivali, in which he says to the Brahmin, 'Because as you have told me, O Gautama, this doctrine has never upto the present time been in circulation among the Brahmins, therefore in all the worlds the government has remained in the hands of the warrior caste.' These words are said in the Kaushitaki Upanishad, which in the Chhandagya and Brihadaranyaka are as follows: 'As surely as I wish that you, like your ancestors, may remain well disposed to us, so surely upto the present day this knowledge has never been in the possession of a Brahmin.'

The fact that the Brahmins during a long period had not attained to the possession of this knowledge, for which they nevertheless display great eagerness, is most simply explained on the supposition that this teaching was studiously withheld from them; that it was transmitted in a narrow circle among the Kshatriyas; that, in a word, it was *upanishad*, secret doctrine. **The Brahmins rather eagerly adopted the doctrine of the Atman though it was fundamentally opposed to the Vedic cult of the the gods and the system of ritual.** But they combined it by the help of allegorical interpretation with the ritualistic tradition and attached it to the curriculum of their schools. The Upanishads thus became the end of Vedas.

Then another thing happened. Soon the Brahmins started laying claim to the new teaching as their exclusive privilege.

They were able to point to princes and leaders, as Janaka, Janashruti, etc., who were said to have gone for instructions to the Brahmins. Authorities on the ritual like Shandilya and Yajnavalkya were transformed into originators and upholders of the ideas of the Upanishads, and the Atman doctrine was made to presuppose the tradition of the Veda: 'Only he who knows the Veda comprehends the great omnipresent Atman.'

Expansion of the Ideas

After the Upanishad ideas had been adopted by the Vedic schools, they passed through a varied expansion and development under the hands of their teachers. To begin with, they were brought into accord with the ritual tradition by interpreting the latter in the Aranyakas in the spirit of the Atman doctrine, and thus the adherents of the Rigveda brought it into connection with the Uktham (hymn), those of the Samaveda with the Saman (song) and those of the Yajurveda with the sacrifice, expecially the horse-sacrifice as being its highest form.

The new doctrine also further developed in a manner which altogether transcended the traditional cult, with which indeed, it often found itself in open contradiction. Definitions which by the one were highly regarded, failed to meet with acceptance with another.

Texts appear with some variations in the different Vedic schools. This rich mental life may not improbably have lasted for centuries, and the fundamental thought of the doctrine of the Atman have attained an ever complete development by means of the reflection of individual thinkers in familiar intercourse before a chosen circle of pupils, and probably also by public discussions at royal courts. The oldest Upanishads preserved to us are to be regarded as the final result of this mental process. The Brihadaranyaka and Chhandogya are not only the richest in content, but also the oldest of the extant Upanishads.

On the rise of the new teaching an attempt was made to preserve the traditional heirlooms of the ritual, while transforming them into symbols of the Atman doctrine. For example, for the four priests—*hotar, adhvaryu, udgatar* and *brahmin*—the four cosmical and the corresponding psychical phenomenal forms of the Atman are substituted—as fire and speech, sun and eye, wind and breath, moon and *manas*—and instead of the usual rewards there was introduced union with the Atman as realised in the universe. Similarly, instead of the Brahmin his *manas* is introduced, and instead of the *hotar* and *adhvaryu*, the *vach* embodied in them. Similarly, the Agnihotram is replaced by the Prana-Agnihotram.

Later on, the Brahman comes to be described as Sachchidanand, *sat* (being), *chit* (mind) and *ananda* (bliss)—this name does not appear in any except the latest of the Upanishads.

The Upanishads are radically opposed to the entire Vedic sacrificial cult, and the older they are the more markedly does this opposition declare itself. The Brihadaranyaka says: 'He who worships another deity other than the Atman, and says, "It is one and I am another," is not wise. But he is like a house-dog of the gods. Just, then, as many house-dogs are of use to men, so each individual man is useful to the gods. If one house-dog only is stolen, it is disagreeable, how much more if many! Therefore, it is not pleasing to them that men should know this.'

No satisfactory chronology of the Upanishads can be framed, since each of the principal Upanishads contains earlier and later texts side by side with one another.

F. Max Muller

Discovery of the Upanishads in Modern Times

The ancient Vedic literature, the foundation of the whole literature of India, which has been handed down in that country in an unbroken succession from the earliest times within the recollection of man to the present day, became known for the first time beyond the frontiers of India through the Upanishads. **The Upanishads were first translated from Sanskrit into Persian by, or, it may be, for Dara Shikoh, the eldest son of Shah Jehan, an enlightened prince, who openly professed the liberal religious tenets of the great Emperor Akbar, and even wrote a book intended to reconcile the religious doctrines of Hindus and Mohammedans.** He seems first to have heard of the Upanishads during his stay in Kashmir in 1640. He afterwards invited several Pandits from Benares to Delhi, who were to assist him in the work of translation. The translation was finished in 1657. Three years after the accomplishment of this work, in 1659, **the prince was put to death by his brother Aurangzeb, in reality, no doubt, because he was the eldest son and legitimate successor of Shah Jehan, but under the pretext that he was an infidel, and dangerous to the established religion of the empire.**

When the Upanishads had once been translated from Sanksrit into Persian, at that time the most widely read language of the East and understood likewise by many

European scholars, they became generally accessible to all who took an interest in the religious literature of India. It is true that under Akbar's reign (1556-1586) similar translations had been prepared, but neither those nor the translations of Dara Shikoh attracted the attention of European scholars till the year 1775. In that year Anquetil Duperron, the famous traveller and discoverer of the Zend-avesta, received one MS. of the Persian translation of the Upanishads, sent to him by M. Gentil, the French resident at the court of Shiya-ud-daula, and brought by M. Bernier. **After receiving another MS., Anquetil Duperron collated the two, and translated the Persian translation into French (not published), and into Latin.** That Latin translation was published in 1801 and 1802, in 2 volumes.

This translation, though it attracted considerable interest among scholars, was written in so utterly unintelligible a style, that it required the lynxlike perspicacity of an intrepid philosopher, such as Schopenhauer, to discover a thread through such a labyrinth. Schopenhauer, however, not only found and followed such a thread, but he had the courage to proclaim to an incredulous age the vast treasures of thought which were lying buried beneath that fearful jargon.

Schopenhauer not only read this translation carefully, but **he makes no secret of it, that his own philosophy is powerfully impregnated by the fundamental doctrines of the Upanishads.** He dwells on it again and again, and it seems both fair to Schopenhauer's memory and highly important for a true appreciation of the philosophical value of the Upanishads, to put together what that vigorous thinker has written on those ancient rhapsodies of truth :

> 'If the reader has also received the benefit of the Vedas, the access to which by means of the Upanishads is in my eyes the greatest privilege which this still young century (1818) may claim before all previous centuries, (for I anticipate that the influence of Sanskrit literature will not be less profound than the revival of Greek in

the fourteenth century)—if then the reader, I say, has received his initiation in primeval Indian wisdom, and received it with an open heart, he will be prepared in the very best way for hearing what I have to tell him. It will not sound to him strange, as to many others, much less diagreeable; for I might, if it did not sound conceited, contend that every one of the detached statements which constitute the **Upanishads, may be deduced as a necessary result from the fundamental thoughts which I have to enunciate, though those deductions themselves are by no means to be found there.**

'If I consider, that Sultan Mohammed Dara Shikoh, the brother of Aurangzeb, was born and bred in India, was a learned, thoughtful, and enquiring man, and therefore probably understood his Sanskrit about as well as we our Latin, that moreover he was assisted by a number of the most learned Pandits, **all this together gives me at once a very high opinion of his translation of the Vedic Upanishads into Persian.** If, besides this, I see with what profound and quite appropriate reverence Anquetil Duperron has treated that Persian translation, rendering it in Latin word by word, retaining, in spite of Latin grammar, the Persian syntax, and all the Sankskrit words which the Sultan himself had left untranslated, though explaining them in a glossary, I feel the most perfect confidence in reading that translation, and that confidence soon receives its most perfect justification. For how entirely does the Oupnekhat (Upanishads) breathe throughout the holy spirit of the Vedas! How is every one who by a diligent study of its Persian Latin has become familiar with that incomparable book, stirred by that spirit to the very depth of his soul! How does every line display its firm, definite, and throughout harmonious meaning! From every sentence deep, original, and sublime thoughts arise, and the whole is pervaded by a high and holy and earnest spirit. Indian air surrounds us, and original thoughts of kindred spirits. And oh, how thoroughly is the mind here washed clean of all early engrafted Jewish superstitions, and of all philosophy that cringes before those superstitions! **In the whole world there is no study, except that of the originals, so beneficial and so elevating as that of the Oupnekhat.** It has been the solace of my life, it will be the solace of my death!'

Rammohun Roy

Greater, however, than the influence exercised on the philosophical thought of modern Europe, has been the impulse which these same Upanishads have imparted to the religious life of modern India. In about the same year (1774 or 1775) when the first MS. of the Persian translation of the Upanishads was received by Anquetil Duperron, Rammohun Roy was born in India, the reformer and reviver of the ancient religion of the Brahmins. A man who in his youth could write a book *Against the Idolatry of all Religions,* and who afterwards expressed in so many exact words his 'belief in the divine authority of Christ,' was not likely to retain anything of the sacred literature of his own religon, unless he had perceived in it the same divine authority which he recognised in the teaching of Christ. He rejected the Puranas, he would not have been swayed in his convictions by the authority of the Laws of Manu, or even by the sacredness of the Vedas. He was above all that. But he discovered in the Upanishads and in the so-called Vedanta something different from all the rest, something that ought not to be thrown away, something that, if rightly understood, might supply the right native soil in which alone the seeds of true religion, aye, of true Christianity, might spring up again and prosper in India, as they had once sprung up and prospered from the philosophies of Origen or Synesius. European scholars have often wondered that Rammohun Roy, in his defence of the Veda, should have put aside the Samhitas and the Brahmanas, and laid his finger on the Upanishads only, as the true kernel of the whole Veda.

Rammohun Roy, like Buddha and other enlightened men before him, perceived that the time for insisting on all that previous discipline with its minute prescriptions and superstitous observances was gone, while the knowledge conveyed in the Upanishads or the Vedanta, enveloped though it may be in strange coverings, should henceforth form the foundation of a new religious life. He would tolerate nothing idolatrous, not even in his mother, poor woman, who after joining his most bitter opponents, confessed to her son, before she set out on her last pilgrimage to Jagannath, where she died, that 'he was right, but that she was a weak woman, and grown too old to give up the observances which were a comfort to her.' It was not therefore from any regard of their antiquity or their sacred character that Rammohun Roy clung to the Upanishads, that he translated them into Bengali, Hindi, and English, and published them at his own expense. It was because he recognised in them seeds of eternal truth, and was bold enough to distinguish between what was essential in them and what was not.

'In India,' Schopenhauer writes, 'our religion will now and never strike root: the primitive wisdom of the human race will never be pushed aside there by the events of Galilee. On the contrary, Indian wisdom will flow back upon Europe, and produce a thorough change in our knowing and thinking.'

My real love for Sanskrit literature was first kindled by the Upanishads. It was in the year 1844, when attending Schelling's lectures at Berlin, that my attention was drawn to those ancient theosophic treatises, and I still possess my collations of Sanskrit MSS. which had then just arrived at Berlin, the Chambers collection, and my copies of commentaries, and commentaries on commentaries, which I made at that time. Some of my translations which I left with Schelling, I have never been able to recover, though to judge from others which I still possess, the loss of them is of small consequence. Soon after leaving Berlin, when continuing my Sanksrit studies at Paris under Burnouf, I put aside the Upanishads, convinced that for a true appreciation of them it was necessary to study, first of all, the earlier periods of Vedic literature, as represented by the hymns and the Brahmanas of the Vedas.

In returning, after more than thirty years, to these favourite studies, I find that my interest in them, though it has changed in character, has by no means diminished.

It is true, no doubt, that the stratum of literature which contains the Upanishads is later than the Samhitas, and later than the Brahmanas, but the first gems of Upanishad doctrines go back at least as far as the Mantra period, which provisionally has been fixed between 1000 and 800 B.C. Conceptions corresponding to the general teaching of the Upanishads occur in certain hymns of the Rigveda Samhita, they must have existed therefore before that collection was finally closed. One hymn in the Samhita of the Rigveda (I, 191) was designated by Katyayana, the author of the *Sarvanukramanika,* as an Upanishad. Here, however, Upanishad means rather a secret charm than a philosophical doctrine. Verses of the hymns have often been incorporated in the Upanishads, and among the Oupnekhats translated into Persian by Dara Shikoh we actually find the Purusha Sukta, the 90th hymn of the tenth book of the Rigveda, forming the greater portion of the Bark'heh Soukt. In the Samhita of the Yajurveda, however, in the Vajasaneyi Sakha, we meet with a real Upanishad, the famous Isa or Isavasya Upanishad, while the Sivasamkalpa, too, forms part of its thirty-fourth book.

The number of Upanishads translated by Dara Shikoh amounts to 50; their number, as given in the *Mahavakya Muktavali* and in the Muktika Upanishad, is 108. Professor Weber thinks that their number, so far as we know at present, may be reckoned at 235.

How Upanishad became the recognised name of the philosophical treatises contained in the Veda is difficult to explain. Most European scholars are agreed in deriving Upanishad from the root *sad,* to sit down, preceded by the two prepositions *ni,* down, and *upa,* near, so that it would express the idea of session, or assembly of pupils sitting down near their teacher to listen to his instruction. In the Trikandasesha, Upanishad is explained by *samipasadana,* sitting down near a person.

Native philosophers seem never to have thought of deriving Upanishad from *sad,* to sit down. They derive it either from the root *sad,* in the sense of destruction, supposing these ancient treatises to have received their name because they were intended to destroy passion and ignorance by means of divine revelation, or from the root *sad,* in the sense of approaching, because a knowledge of Brahman comes near to us by means of the Upanishads, or because we approach Brahman by their help. Another explanation proposed by Sankara in his commentary on the Taittiriya Upanishad *param sreyo' syam nishannam.*

The Upanishads, no doubt, were meant to destroy ignorance and passion, and nothing seemed more natural therefore than their etymological meaning should be that of destroyers.

The history and the genius of the Sanksrit language leave little doubt that Upanishad meant originally session, particularly a session consisting of pupils, assembled at a respectful distance round their teacher.

Contents

1

Isha Upanishad
God Pervades Everything

This short but valuable Upanishad provides excellent glimpses into the basic ideas of the Vedanta philosophy. It describes the nature and characteristics of Atman, the ethical conduct of one who knows it as well as a view of the beyond. Its unequivocal declaration that the Lord pervades the whole universe and allied beings, one should not covet others' goods and try to live within one's means and help the needy, may be taken as a commandment to human beings.

All this, whatsoever moves on earth, is to be hidden in the Lord. When thou hast surrendered all this, then thou mayest enjoy. Do not covet the wealth of any man!

Though a man may wish to live a hundred years, performing works, it will be thus with him; but not in any other way: work will thus not cling to a man.

There are the worlds of the Asuras covered with blind darkness. Those who have destroyed their self (who perform works, without having arrived at a knowledge of the true Self), go after death to those worlds.

That one, the Self, though never stirring, is swifter than thought. The Devas (senses) never reached it, it walked before them. Though standing still, it overtakes the others who are running. Matarishvan 'the wind, the moving spirit' bestows powers on it.

It strirs and it stirs not; it is far, and likewise near. It is inside of all this, and it is outside of all this.

And he who beholds all beings in the Self, and the Self in all beings, he never turns away from it.

When to a man who understands, the Self has become all things, what sorrow, what trouble can there be to him who once beheld that unity?

He 'the Self' encircled all, bright, incorporeal, scatheless, without muscles, pure, untouched by evil; a seer, wise, omnipresent, self-existent, he disposed all things rightly for eternal years.

All who worship what is not real knowledge (good works), enter into blind darkness: those who delight in real knowledge, enter, as it were, into greater darkness.

One thing, they say, is obtained from real knowledge; another, they say, from what is not knowledge. Thus we have heard from the wise who taught us this.

He who knows at the same time both knowledge and not-knowledge, overcomes death through not-knowledge, and obtains immortality through knowledge.

All who worship what is not the true cause, enter into blind darkness: those who delight in the true cause, enter, as it were, into greater darkness.

One thing, they say, is obtained from knowledge of the cause; another, they say, from knowledge of what is not the cause. Thus we have heard from the wise who taught us this.

He who knows at the same time both the cause and the destruction (the perishable body), overcomes death by destruction (the perishable body), and obtains immortality through knowledge of the true cause.

The door of the True is covered with a golden disk. Open that, O Pushan, that we may see the nature of the True.

O Pushan, only seer, Yama (Judge), Surya (sun), son

of Prajapati, spread thy rays and gather them! The light which is thy fairest form, I see it. I am what He is, the person in the sun.

Breath to air, and to the immortal! Then this my body ends in ashes. Om! Mind, remember! Remember thy deeds! Mind, remember! Remember thy deeds!

Agni, lead us on to beatitude by a good path, thou, O God, who knowest all things! Keep far from us crooked evil, and we shall offer thee the fullest praise!

2

Kena Upanishad

Who gave us eyes, ears and speech...

Who—Kena—gave us speech, makes us see and hear—are the questions answered in this short and beautiful Upanishad. Divided into two parts, the first in verse and the second in prose, it discusses the worship of Brahman, the Supreme power, with and without attributes. The concept of Brahman is India's contribution to philosophy, and its attainment the goal of human beings. The Upanishad provides insights into the subject.

1

The Pupil asks: 'At whose wish does the mind sent forth proceed on its errand? At whose command does the first breath go forth? At whose wish do we utter this speech? What god directs the eye, or the ear?'

The Teacher replies: 'It is the ear of the ear, the mind of the mind, the speech of speech, the breath of breath, and the eye of the eye. When freed 'from the senses' the wise, on departing from this world, become immortal.

'The eye does not go thither, nor speech, nor mind. We do not know, we do not understand, how any one can teach it.

'It is different from the known, it is also above the unknown, thus we have heard from those of old, who taught us this.

'That which is not expressed by speech and by which speech is expressed, that alone know as Brahman, not that which people here adore.

'That which does not think by mind, and by which, they say, mind is thought, that alone know as Brahman, not that which people here adore.

'That which does not see by the eye, and by which one sees the work of the eyes, that alone know as Brahman, not that which people here adore.

'That which does not hear by the ear, and by which the ear is heard, that alone know as Brahman, not that which people here adore.

'That which does not breathe by breath, and by which breath is drawn, that alone know as Brahman, not that which people here adore.'

2

The Teacher says: 'If thou thinkest I know it well, then thou knowest surely but little, what is that form of Brahman known, it may be, to thee?'

The Pupil says: 'I do not think I know it well, nor do I know that I do not know it. He among us who knows this, he knows it, nor does he know that he does not know it.

'He by whom the Brahman is not thought, by him it is thought; he by whom it is thought, knows it not. It is not understood by those who understand it, it is understood by those who do not understand it.

'It is thought to be known as if by awakening, and then we obtain immortality indeed. By the Self we obtain strength, by knowledge we obtain immortality.

'If a man know this here, that is the true end of life; if he does not know this here, then there is great destruction (new births). The wise who have thought on all things and recognised the Self in them become immortal, when they have departed from this world.'

3

Brahman obtained the victory for the Devas. The Devas became elated by the victory of Brahman, and they thought, this victory is ours only, this greatness is ours only.

Brahman perceived this and appeared to them. But they did not know it, and said: 'What sprite (Yaksha) is this?'

They said to Agni (fire): 'O Jatavedas, find out what sprite this is.' 'Yes,' he said.

He ran towards it, and Brahman said to him: 'Who are you?' He replied: 'I am Agni, I am Jatavedas.'

Brahman said: 'What power is in you?' Agni replied: 'I could burn all whatever there is on earth.'

Brahman put a straw before him, saying: 'Burn this.' He went towards it with all his might, but he could not burn it. Then he returned thence and said: 'I could not find out what sprite this is.'

Then they said to Vayu (air): 'O Vayu, find out what sprite this is.' 'Yes,' he said.

He ran towards it, and Brahman said to him: 'Who are you?' He replied: 'I am Vayu, I am Matarisvan.'

Brahman said: 'What power is in you?' Vayu replied: 'I could take up all whatever there is on earth.'

Brahman put a straw before him, saying: 'Take it up.' He went towards it with all his might, but he could not take it up. The he returned thence and said: 'I could not find out what sprite this is.'

Then they said to Indra: 'O Maghavan, find out what sprite this is.' He went towards it, but it disappeared from before him.

Then in the same space he came towards a woman, highly adorned: it was Uma, the daughter of Himavat. He said to her: 'Who is that sprite?'

4

She replied: 'It is Brahman. It is through the victory of Brahman that you have thus become great. After that he knew that it was Brahman.

Therefore these Devas, Agni, Vayu, and Indra, are as it were, above the other gods, for they touched the Brahman nearest.

And therefore Indra is, as it were, above the other gods, for he touched it nearest, he first knew it.

This is the teaching of Brahman, with regard to the gods (mythological): It is that which now flashes forth in the ligtning, and now vanishes again.

And this is the teaching of Brahman, with regard to the body (psychological): It is that which seems to move as mind, and by it imagination remembers again and again.

That Brahman is called Tadvana, by the name of Tadvana it is to be meditated on. All beings have a desire for him who knows this.

The Teacher: 'As you have asked me to tell you the Upanishad, the Upanishad has now been told you. We have told you the Brahmi Upanishad.

'The feet on which that Upanishad stands are penance, restraint, sacrifice; the Vedas are all its limbs, the True is its abode.

'He who knows this Upanishad, and has shaken off all evil, stands in the endless, unconquerable world of heaven, yea, in the world of heaven.'

3

Katha Upanishad

I will go to death

The Katha formed a school of the Black Yajurveda, which had developed five varieties of yajnas, or fire-ceremonies, one of which, the Nachiketas, was bestowed on him by Yama, the god of death, whom he pleased with his devotion. The Upanishad relates the interesting story as well as the ceremony, which ensures the attainment of an imperishable world which lies on the other side of the sun. It deals with the Atman as the subject of knowledge.

1

Vajashravasa, desirous of heavenly rewards, surrendered at a sacrifice all that he possessed. He had a son of the name of Nachiketas.

When the promised presents were being given to the priests, faith entered into the heart of Nachiketas, who was still a boy, and he thought:

'Unblessed, surely, are the worlds to which a man goes by giving as his promised present at a sacrifice cows which have drunk water, eaten hay, given their milk, and are barren.'

He knowing that his father had promised to give up all that he possessed, and therefore his son also said to his father: 'Dear father, to whom wilt thou give me?'

He said it a second and a third time. Then the father replied angrily: 'I shall give thee unto Death.'

(The father, having once said so, though in haste, had to be true to his word and to sacrifice his son.)

The son said: 'I go as the first, at the head of many who have still to die; I go in the midst of many who are now dying. What will be the work of Yama, the ruler of the departed, which today he has to do unto me?

'Look back how it was with those who came before, look forward how it will be with those who come hereafter. A mortal ripens like corn, like corn he springs up again.'

(Nachiketas enters into the abode of Yama Vaivasvata, and there is no one to receive him. Thereupon one of the attendants of Yama is supposed to say:)

'Fire enters into the houses, when a Brahmin enters as a guest. That fire is quenched by this peace-offering;—bring water, O Vaivasvata!

'A Brahamin that dwells in the house of a foolish man without receiving food to eat, destroys his hopes and expectations, his possessions, his righteousness, his sacred and his good deeds, and all his sons and cattle.'

(Yama, returning to his house after an absence of three nights, during which time Nachiketas had received no hospitality from him, says:)

'O Brahmin, as thou, a venerable guest, hast dwelt in my house three nights without eating, therefore choose now three boons. Hail to thee! and welfare to me!'

Nachiketas said: 'O Death, as the first of the three boons I choose that Gautama, my father, be pacified, kind, and free from anger towards me; and that he may know me and greet me, when I shall have been dismissed by thee.'

Yama said: 'Through my favour Auddalaki Aruni, thy father, will know thee, and be again towards thee freed from the mouth of death.'

Nachiketas said: 'In the heaven-world there is no fear; thou art not there, O Death, and no one is afraid on account of old age. Leaving behind both hunger and thirst, and out of the reach of sorrow, all rejoice in the world of heaven.'

'Thou knowest, O Death, the fire-sacrifice which leads us to heaven; tell it to me, for I am full of faith. Those who live in the heaven-world reach immortality,—this I ask as my second boon.'

Yama said: 'I tell it thee, learn it from me, and when though understandest that fire-sacrifice which leads to heaven, know, O Nachiketas, that it is the attainment of the endless worlds, and their firm support, hidden in darkness.'

Yama then told him that fire-sacrifice, the beginning of all the worlds, and what bricks are required for the altar, and how many, and how they are to be placed. And Nachiketas repeated all as it had been told to him. The Mrityu, being pleased with him, said again:

The generous, being satisfied, said to him :'I give thee now another boon; that fire-sacrifice shall be named after thee, take also this many-coloured chain.'

'He who has three times performed this Nachiketa rite, and has been united with the three father, mother, and teacher', and has performed the three duties study, sacrifice, almsgiving' overcomes birth and death. When he has learnt and understood this fire, which knows or makes us know all that is born of Brahman, which is venerable and divine, then he obtains everlasting peace.

'He who knows the three Nachiketa fires, and knowing the three, piles up the Nachiketa sacrifice, he, having first thrown off the chains of death, rejoices in the world of heaven, beyond the reach of grief.'

'This, O Nachiketas, is thy fire which leads to heaven, and which thou hast chosen as thy second boon. That fire all men will proclaim. Choose now, O Nachiketas, thy third boon.'

Nachiketas said: 'There is that doubt, when a man is dead,—some saying, he is; others, he is not. This I should like to know, taught by thee; this is the third of my boons.'

Death said: 'On this point even the gods have doubted formerly; it is not easy to understand. That subject is subtle. Choose another boon, O Nachiketas, do not press me, and let me off that boon.'

Nachiketas said: 'On this point even the gods have doubed indeed, and thou, Death, hast declared it to be not easy to understand, and another teacher like thee is not to be found:—surely no other boon is like unto this.'

Death said: 'Choose sons and grandsons who shall live a hundred years, herds of cattle, elephants, gold, and horses. Choose the wide abode of the earth, and live thyself as many harvests as thou desirest.'

'If you can think of any boon equal to that, choose wealth and long life. Be king, Nachiketas, on the wide earth. I make thee the enjoyer of all desires.

'Whatever desires are difficult to attain among mortals, ask for them according to thy wish;—these fair maidens with their chariots and musical instruments,— such are indeed not to be obtained by men,—be waited on by them whom I give to thee, but do not ask me about dying.'

Nachiketas said: 'These things last till tomorrow, O Death, for they wear out this vigour of all the senses. Even the whole of life is short. Keep thou thy horses, keep dance and song for thyself.

'No man can be made happy by wealth. Shall we possess wealth, when we see thee? Shall we live, as long as thou rulest? Only that boon which I have chosen is to be chosen by me.'

'What mortal, slowly decaying here below, and knowing, after having approached them, the freedom from decay enjoyed by the immortals, would delight in a long life, after he has pondered on the pleasures which arise from beauty and love?'

'No, that on which there is this doubt, O Death, tell us what there is in that great Hereafter. Nachiketas does not choose another boon but that which enters into the hidden world.'

•

Death said: 'The good is one thing, the pleasant another; these two, having different objects, chain a man. It is well with him who clings to the good; he who chooses the pleasant, misses his end.

'The good and the pleasant approach man: the wise goes round about them and distinguishes them. Yea, the wise prefers the good to the pleasant, but the fool chooses the pleasant through greed and avarice.

'Thou, O Nachiketas, after pondering all pleasures that are or seem delightful, hast dismissed them all. Thou hast not gone into the road that leadeth to wealth, in which many men perish.

'Wide apart and leading to different points are these two, ignorance, and what is known as wisdom. I believe Nachiketas to be one who desires knowledge, for even many pleasures did not tear thee away.

'Fools dwelling in darkness, wise in their own conceit, and puffed up with vain knowledge, go round and round, staggering to and from, like blind men led by the blind.

'The Hereafter never rises before the eyes of the careless child, deluded by the delusion of wealth. "This is the world," he thinks, there is no other;"—thus he falls again and again under my sway.

'He the Self of whom' many are not even able to hear, whom many, even when they hear of him, do not comprehend; wonderful is a man, when found, who is able to teach him the Self; wonderful is he who comprehends him, when taught by an able teacher.

'That Self, when taught by an inferior man, is not easy to be known, even though often thought upon; unless it be taught by another, there is no way to it, for it is inconceivably smaller than what is small.

'That doctrine is not to be obtained by argument, but when it is declared by another, then, O dearest, it is easy to understand. Thou hast obtained it now; thou art truly a man of true resolve. May we have always an inquirer like thee!'

Nachiketas said: 'I know that what is called a treasure is transient, for that eternal is not obtained by things which are not eternal. Hence the Nachiketa fire-sacrifice has been laid by me first; then, by means of transient things, I have obtained what is not transient (the teaching of Yama).'

Yama said: 'Though thou hadst seen the fulfilment of all desires, the foundation of the world, the endless rewrds of good deeds, the shore where there is no fear, that which is magnified by praise, the wide abode, the rest, yet being wise thou hast with firm resolve dismissed it all.

'The wise who, by means of meditation on his Self, recognises the Ancient, who is difficult to be seen, who has entered into the dark, who is hidden in the cave, who dwells in the abyss, as God, he indeed leaves joy and sorrow far behind.

'A mortal who has heard this and embraced it, who has separated from it all qualities, and has thus reached the subtle Being, rejoices, becauses he has obtained what is a cause for rejoicing. The house of Brahman is open, I believe, O Nachiketas.'

Naichketas said: 'That which thou seest as neither this nor that, as neither effect nor cause, as neither past nor future, tell me that.'

Yama said: 'That word or place which all the Vedas record, which all penances proclaim, which men desire when they live as religious students, that word I tell thee briefly, it is Om.

'That imperishable syllable means Brahman, that syllable means the highest Brahmin; he who knows that syllable, whatever he desires, is his.

'This is the best support, this is the highest support; he who knows that support is magnified in the world of Brahma.

'The knowing Self is not born, it dies not; it sprang from nothing, nothing sprang from it. the Ancient is unborn, eternal, everlasting; he is not killed, though the body is killed.

'If the killer thinks that he kills, if the killed thinks that he is killed, they do not understand; for this one does not kill, nor is that one killed.

'The Self, smaller than small, greater than great, is hidden in the heart of that creature. A man who is free from desires and free from grief, sees the majesty of the Self by the grace of the Creator.

'Though sitting still, he walks far; though lying down, he goes everywhere. Who, save myself, is able to know that god who rejoices and rejoices not?

'The wise who knows the Self as bodiless within the bodies, as unchanging among changing things, as great and omnipresent, does never grieve.

'That Self cannot be gained by the Veda, nor by undestanding, nor by much learning. He who the Self chooses, by him the Self can be gained. The Self chooses him 'his body' as his own.

'But he who has not first turned away from his wickedness, who is not tranquil, and subdued, or whose mind is not at rest, he can never obtain the Self even or by knowledge.

'Who then knows where He is, He to whom the Brahmins and Kshatriyas are as it were, but food, and death itself a condiment?'

•

'There are the two, drinking their reward in the world of the own works, entered into the cave of the heart, dwelling on the highest summit the ether in the heart. Those who know Brahman call them shade and light; likewise, those householders who perform the Trinachiketa sacrifice.

'May we be able to master that Nachiketa rite which is a bridge for sacrificers; also that which is the highest, imperishable Brahman for those who wish to cross over to the fearless shore.

'Know the Self to be sitting in the chariot, the body to be the chariot, the intellect (*buddhi*) the charioteer, and the mind the reins.

'The senses they call the horses, the objects of the senses their roads. When he 'the Highest Self' is in union with the body, the senses, and the mind, then wise people call him the Enjoyer.

'He who has no understanding and whose mind 'the reins' is never firmly held, his senses 'horses' are unmanageable, like vicious horses of a charioteer.

'But he who has understanding and whose mind is always firmly held, his senses are under control, like good horses of a charioteer.

'He who has no understanding, who is unmindful and always impure, never reaches that place, but enters into the round of births.

'But he who has understanding, who is mindful and always pure, reaches indeed that place, from whence he is not born again.

'But who has understanding for his charioteer, and who holds the reins of the mind, he reaches the end of his journey, and that is the highest place of Vishnu.

'Beyond the senses there are the objects, beyond the objects there is the mind, beyond the mind there is the intellect, the Great Self is beyond the intellect.

'Beyond the Great there is the Undeveloped, beyond the Undeveloped there is the Person (Purusha). Beyond the Person there is nothing—this is the goal, the highest road.

'That Self is hidden in all beings and does not shine forth, but it is seen by subtle seers through their sharp and subtle intellect.

'A wise man should keep down speech and mind; he should keep them within the Self which is knowledge; he should keep knowledge within the Self which is the Great; and he should keep the Great within the Self which is the Quiet.

'Rise, awake! having obtained your boons, understand them! The sharp edge of a razor is difficult to pass over; thus the wise say the path to the Self is hard.

'He who had perceived that which is without sound,

without touch, without form, without decay, without taste, eternal, without smell, without beginning, without end, beyond the Great, and Unchangeable, is freed from the jaws of death.

'A wise man who has repeated or heard the ancient story of Nachiketas told by Death, is magnified in the field of Brahman.

'And he who repeats this greatest mystery in an assembly of Brahmins, or full of devotion at the time of the Sraddha sacrifice, obtains thereby infinite rewards.'

2

Death said: 'The Self-existent pierced the openings of the senses so that they turn forward : therefore man looks forward, not backward into himself. Some wise man, however, with his eyes closed and wishing for immortality, saw the Self behind.

'Children follow after outward pleasures, and fall into the snare of widespread death. Wise men only, knowing the nature of what is immortal, do not look for anything stable here among things unstable.

'That by which we know form, taste, smell, sounds, and loving touches, by that also we know what exists besides. This is that which thou hast asked for.

'The wise, when he knows that that by which he perceives all objects in sleep or in waking is the great omnipresent Self, grieves no more.

'He who knows this living soul which eats honey (preceives objects) as being the Self, always near, the Lord of the past and the future, henceforward fears no more. This is that.

'He who knows him who was born first from the brooding heat for he was born before the water, who, entering into the heart, abides therein, and was perceived from the elements. This is that.

'He who knows Aditi also, who is one with all deities,

who arises with Prana (breath or Hiranyagarbha), who, entering into the heart, abides therein, and was born from the elements. This is that.

'There is Agni (fire), the all-seeing, hidden in the two fire-sticks, well-guarded like a child in the womb by the mother, day after day to be adored by men when they awake and bring oblations. This is that.

'And that whence the sun rises, and whither it goes to set, there all the Devas are contained, and no one goes beyond. This is that.

'What is here visible in the world, the same is there invisible in Brahman; and what is there, the same is here. He who sees any difference here between Brahman and the world, goes from death to death.

'Even by the mind this Brahman is to be obtained, and then there is no difference whatsoever. He goes from death to death who sees any difference here.

'The Person Purusha, of the size of a thumb, stands in the middle of the Self, as lord of the past and the future, and henceforward fears no more. This is that.

'That Person, of the size of a thumb, is like a light without smoke, lord of the past and the future, he is the same today and tomorrow. This is that.

'As rain-water that has fallen on a mountain-ridge runs down the rocks on all sides, thus does he, who sees a difference between qualities, run after them on all sides.

'As pure water poured into pure water remains the same, thus, O Gautama, is the Self of a thinker who knows.'

•

'There is a town with eleven gates belonging to the Unborn Brahman, whose thoughts are never crooked. He who approaches it, grieves no more, and liberated from all bonds of ignorance becomes free. This is that.

The Brahman is the swan (sun), dwelling in the bright heaven; he is the Vasu air, dwelling in the sky, he is the sacrificer (fire), dwelling on the hearth; he is the guest, Soma, dwelling in the sacrificial jar; he dwells in men, in gods (*vara*), in the sacrifice (*rita*), in heaven; he is born in the water, on earth, in the sacrifice (*rita*), on the mountains; he is the True and the Great.

'The Brahman it is who sends up the breath (Prana), and who throws back the breath (Apana). All the Devas (senses) worship him, the adorable, or the dwarf, who sits in the centre.'

'When that Brahman, who dwells in the body, is torn away and freed from the body, what remains then? This is that.

'No mortal lives by the breath that goes up and by the breath that goes down. We live by another, in whom these two repose.

'Well then, O Gautama, I shall tell thee this mystery, the old Brahmin, and what happens to the Self, after reaching death.

'Some enter the womb in order to have a body, as organic beings, others go into inorganic matter, according to their work and according to their knowledge.

'He, the highest Person, who is awake in us while we are asleep, shaping one lovely sight after another, that indeed is the Bright, that is Brahman, that alone is called the Immortal. All worlds are contained in it, and no one goes beyond. This is that.

'As the one fire, after it has entered the world, though one, becomes different according to whatever it burns, thus the one Self within all things becomes different, according to whatever it enters, and exists also without.

'As the one air, after it has entered the world, though one, becomes different according to whatever it enters, thus the one Self within all things becomes different, according to whatever it enters, and exists also without.

'As the sun, the eye of the whole world, is not contaminated by the external impurities seen by the eyes, thus the one Self within all things is never contaminated by the misery of the world, being himself without.

'There is one ruler, the Self within all things, who makes the one form manifold. The wise who perceive him within their Self, to them belongs eternal happiness, not to others.

'There is one eternal thinker, thinking non-eternal thoughts, who, though one, fulfils the desires of many. The wise who perceive him within their Self, to them belongs eternal peace, not others.

'They perceive that highest indescribable pleasure, saying, This is that. How then can I undersand it? Has it its own light, or does it reflect light?

'The sun does not shine there, nor the moon and the stars, nor these lightnings, and much less this fire. When he shines, everyithing shines after him; by his light all this is lighted.'

•

'There is that ancient tree, whose roots grow upward and whose branches grow downward;—that indeed is called the Bright, that is called Brahman, that alone is called the Immortal. All worlds are contained in it, and no one goes beyond. This is that.

'Whatever there is, the whole world, when gone forth from the Brahman, trembles in its breath. That Brahman is a great terror, like a drawn sword. Those who know it become immortal.

'From terror of Brahman fire burns, from terror the sun burns, from terror Indra and Vayu, and Death, as the fifth, run away.

'If a man could not understand it before the falling asunder of his body, then he has to take body again in the worlds of creation.

'As in a mirror, so Brahman may be seen clearly here in this body; as in a dream, in the world of the Fathers; as in the water, he is seen about in the world of the Gandharvas; as in light and shade, in the world of Brahma.

'Having understood that the senses are distinct from the Atman, and that their rising and setting, their waking and sleeping, belongs to them in their distinct existence and not to the Atman, a wise man grieves no more.

'Beyond the senses is the mind, beyond the mind is the highest created Being, higher than that Being is the Great Self, higher than the Great, the highest Undeveloped.

'Beyond the Undeveloped is the Person, the all-pervading and entirely imperceptible. Every creature that knows him is liberated, and obtains immortaility.

'His form is not to be seen, no one beholds him with the eye. He is imagined by the heart, by wisdom, by the mind. Those who know this, are immortal.

'When the five instruments of knowledge stand still together with the mind, and when the intellect does not move, that is called the highest state.

'This, the firm holding back of the senses, is what is called Yoga. He must be free from thoughtlessness then, for Yoga comes and goes.

'He, the Self, cannot be reached by speech, by mind, or by the eye. How can it be apprehended except by him who says: "He is?"

'By the words "He is," is he to be apprehended, and by admitting the reality of both, the invisible Brahman and the visible world, as comming from Brahman. When he has been apprehended by the words "He is," then his reality reveals itself.

'When all desires that dwell in his heart cease, then the mortal becomes immortal, and obtains Brahman.

'When all the ties of the heart are severed here on earth, then the mortal becomes immortal— here ends the teaching.

'There are a hundred and one arteries of the heart, one of them penetrates the crown of the head. Moving upwards by it, a man at his death reaches the Immortal; the other arteries serve for departing in different directions.

'The Person not larger than a thumb, the inner Self, is always settled in the heart of men. Let a man draw that Self forth from his body with steadiness, as one draws the pith from reed. Let him know that Self as the Bright, as the Immortal; yes, as the Bright, as the Immortal.'

He having received this knowledge taught by Death and the whole rule of Yoga, Nachiketa became free from passion and death, and obtained Brahman. Thus it will be with another also who knows thus what relates to the Self.

May He protect us both! May He enjoy us both! May we acquire strength together! May our knowledge become bright! May we never quarrel! Om! Peace! peace! peace!

4

Mundaka Upanishad

From him is born breath, mind . . .

'Mundaka' means the monks who have shaven their heads clean—and as such the Upanishad is believed to have belonged to them, but it has been one of the most popular Upanishad. It is liked on account of the purity with which it presents the old Vedanta doctrine, and the beauty of its verses. It deals with the preparatory stages of the knowledge of Brahman, its doctrine and the way to attain it.

1

Brahma was the first of the Devas, the maker of the universe, the preserver of the world. He told the knowledge of Brahman, the foundation of all knowledge, to his eldest son Atharvan.

Whatever Brahma told Atharvan, that knowledge of Brahman Atharvan formerly told to Angir; he told it to Satyavaha Bharadvaja, and Bharadvaja told it in succession to Angiras.

Shaunaka, the great householder, approached Angiras respectfully and asked: 'Sir, what is that through which, if it is known, everything else becomes known?'

He said to him: 'Two kinds of knowledge must be known, this is what all who know Brahman tell us, the higher and the lower knowledge.

'The lower knowledge is the Rigveda, Yajurveda,

Samaveda, Atharvaveda, Shiksha (phonetics), Kalpa (ceremonial), Vyakarana (grammar), Nirukta (etymology), Chhandas (metre), Jyotisha (astronomy); but the higher knowledge is that by which the Indestructible Brahman is apprehended.

'That which cannot be seen, nor seized, which has no family and no caste, no eyes nor ears, no hands nor feet, the eternal, the omnipresent, allpervading, infinitesimal, that which is imperishable, that it is which the wise regard as the source of all beings.

'As the spider sends forth and draws in its thread, as plants grow on the earth, as from every man hairs spring forth on the head and the body, thus does everything arise here from the Indestructible.

'The Brahman swells by means of brooding (Tapa) hence is produced matter (food); from matter breath, mind, the true (Satya), the worlds (seven), and from the works formed by men in the worlds, the immortal, the eternal effects, rewards, and punishments of works.

'From him who perceives all and who knows all, whose brooding consists of knowledge, from the highest Brahman is born that Brahman, name, form, and matter (food).

•

This is the truth: the sacrificial works which the poets saw in the hymns of the Veda have been performed in many ways in the Treta age. Practise them diligently, ye lovers of truth, this is your path that leads to the world of good works!

When the fire is lighted and the flame flickers, let a man offer his oblations between the two portions of melted butter, as an offering with faith.

If a man's Agnihotra sacrifice is not followed by the new-moon and full-moon sacrifices, by the four-months' sacrifices, and by the harvest sacrifice, if it is unattended, by guests, not offered at all, or without the Vaishvadeva ceremony, or not offered according to rule, then it destroys his seven worlds.

Kali (black), Karali (terrific), Manojava (swift as

thought), Sulohit (very red), Sudhumravarna (purple), Sphulingini (sparkling), all these playing about are called the seven tongues of fire.

If a man performs his sacred words when these flames are shining, and the oblations follow at the right time, then they lead him as sun-rays to where the one Lord of the Devas dwells.

Come hither, come hither! the brilliant oblations say to him, and carry the sacrificer on the rays of the sun, while they utter pleasant speech and praise him, saying: 'This is thy holy Brahma-world (Svarga), gained by thy good works.'

But frail, in truth, are those boats, the sacrifices, the eighteen, in which this lower ceremonial has been told. Fools who praise this as the highest good, are subject again and again to old age and death.

Fools dwelling in darkness, wise in their own conceit, and puffed up with vain knowledge, go round and round staggering to and fro, like blind men led by the blind.

Children, when they have long lived in ignorance, consider themselves happy. Because those who depend on their good works are, owing to their passions, improvident, they fall and become miserable when their life in the world which they had gained by their good works is finished.

Considering sacrifice and good works as the best, these fools know no higher good, and having enjoyed their reward on the height of heaven, gained by good works, they enter again this world or a lower one.

But those who practice penance and faith in the forest, tranquil, wise, and living on alms, depart free from passion through the sun to where that immortal Person dwells whose nature is imperishable.

Let a Brahmin, after he has examined all thsse worlds which are gained by works, acquire freedom from all desires. Nothing that is eternal (not made) can be gained by what is not eternal (made). Let him, in order to understand this, take fuel in his hand and approach a Guru who is learned and dwells entirely in Brahman.

To that pupil who has approached him respectfully, whose thoughts are not troubled by any desires, and who has obtained perfect peace, the wise teacher truly told that knowledge of Brahman through which knows the eternal and true Person.

2

This is the truth. As from a blazing fire sparks, being like unto fire, fly forth a thousandfold, thus are various beings brought forth from the Imperishable, my friend, and return thither also.

That heavenly Person is without body, he is both without and within, not produced, without breath and without mind, pure, higher than the high, Imperishable.

From him when entering on creation, is born breath, mind, and all organs of sense, ether, air, light, water, and the earth, the support of all.

Fire (the sky) is his head, his eyes the sun and the moon, the quarters his ears, his speech the Vedas disclosed, the wind his breath, his heart the universe; from his feet came the earth; he is indeed the inner Self of all things.

From his comes Agni (fire), the sun being the fuel; from the moon (Soma) comes rain (Parjanya); from the earth herbs; and man gives seed unto the woman. Thus many beings are begotten from the Person (Purusha).

From him come the Rik, the Saman, the Yajus, the Diksha (initiatory rites), all sacrifices and offerings of animals, and the fees bestowed on priests, the year too, the sacrificer, and the worlds, in which the moon shines brightly and the sun.

From him the many Devas too are begotten, the Sadhyas (genii), men, cattle, birds, the up and down breathings, rice and corn for sacrifices, penance, faith, truth, abstinence, and law.

The seven senses (Prana) also spring from him, the seven lights (acts of sensation), the seven kinds of fuel (objects by which the senses are lighted), the seven sacrifices results of sensation, these seven worlds (the places of the senses, the worlds determined by the senses) in which the senses move, which rest in the cave of the heart, and are placed there seven and seven.

Hence come the seas and all the mountains, from him flow the rivers of every kind; hence come all herbs and the juice through which the inner Self subsists with the elements.

The Person is all this, sacrifice, penance, Brahman, the highest immortal; he who knows this hidden in the cave of the heart, he, O friend, scatters the knot of ignorance here on earth.

•

Manifest, near, moving in the cave of the heart is the great Being. In it everything is centred which ye know as moving, breathing, and blinking, as being and not-being, as adorable, as the best, that is beyond the understanding of creatures.

That which is brilliant, smaller than small, that on which the worlds are founded and their inhabitants, that is the indestructible Brahman, that is the breath, speech, mind; that is the true, that is the immortal. that is to be hit. Hit it, O friend!

Having taken the Upanishad as the bow, as the great weapon, let him place on it the arrow, sharpened by devotion! Then having drawn it with a thought directed to that which is, hit the mark, O friend, that which is the Indestructible!

Om is the bow, the Self is the arrow, Brahman is called its aim. It is to be hit by a man who is not thoughtless; and then, as the arrow becomes one with the target, he will become one with Brahman.

In him the heaven, the earth, and the sky are woven, the mind also with all the senses. Know him alone as the Self, and leave off other worlds! He is the bridge of the Immortal.

He moves about becoming manifold within the heart

where the arteries meet, like spokes fastened to the nave. Meditate on the Self as Om! Hail to you, that you may cross beyond the sea of darkness!

He who understands all and who knows all, he to whom all this glory in the world belongs, the Self, is placed in the ether, in the heavenly city of Brahman 'the heart'. He assumes the nature of mind, and becomes the guide of the body of the senses. He subsists in food, in close proximity to the heart. The wise who understand this, behold the Immortal which shines forth full of bliss.

The fetter of the heart is broken, all doubts are solved, all his works and their effects perish when He has been beheld who is high and low (cause and effect).

In the highest golden sheath there is the Brahman without passions and without parts. That is pure, that is the light of lights, that is it which they know who know the Self.

The sun does not shine there, nor the moon and the stars, nor these lightnings, and much less this fire. When he shines, everything shines after him; by his light all this is lighted.

That immortal Brahman is right and left. It has gone forth below and above; Brahman alone is all this, it is the best.

3

Two birds, inseparable friends, cling to the same tree. One of them eats the sweet fruit, the other looks on without eating.

On the same tree man sits grieving, immersed, bewildered by his own impotence (Anisa). But when he sees the other lord (Isa) contented and knows his glory, then his grief passes away.

When the seer sees the brilliant maker and lord of the world as the Person who has his source in Brahman, then he is wise, and shaking off good and evil, he reaches the highest oneness, free from passions.

For he is the Breath shining forth in all beings, and he who understands this becomes truly wise, not a talker only. He revels in the Self, he delights in the Self, and having performed his works, truthfulness, penance, meditation, etc., he rests, firmly established in Brahman, the best of those who know Brahman.

By truthfulness, indeed, by penance, right knowledge, and abstinence must that Self be gained; the Self whom spotless anchorites gain is pure, and like a light within the body.

The true prevails, not the untrue; by the true the path is laid out, the way of the gods, Devayana, on which the sages, satisfied in their desires, proceed to where there is that highest place of the True One. That true Brahman shines forth grand divine, inconceivable, smaller than small; it is far beyond what is far and yet near here, it is hidden in the cave of the heart among those who see it even here.

He is not apprehended by the eye, nor by speech, nor by the other senses, not by penance or good works. When a man's nature has become purified by the serene light of knowledge, then he sees him, meditating on him as without parts.

That subtle Self is to be known by thought (Chetas) there where breath has entered fivefold; for every thought of men is interwoven with the senses, and when thought is purified, then the Self arises.

Whatever state a man whose nature is purified imagines, and whatever desires he desires for himself or for others, that state he conquers and those desires he obtains. Therefore let every man who desires happiness worship the man who knows the Self.

•

He the knower of the Self knows that highest home of Brahman, in which all is contained and shines brightly. The wise who without desiring happiness, worship that Person, transcend this seed, they are not born again.

He who forms desires in his mind, is born again through his desires here and there. But to him whose desires are fulfilled and who is conscious of the true Self within himself all desires vanish, even here on earth.

That Self cannot be gained by the Veda, nor by understanding, nor by much learning. He whom the Self chooses, by him the Self can be gained. The Self chooses him 'his body' as his own.

Nor is that Self to be gained by one who is destitute of strength, or without earnestness, or without right meditation. But if a wise man strives after it by those means by strength, earnestness, and right meditation, then his Self enters the home of Brahman.

When they have reached him, the Self, the sages become satisfied through knowledge, they are conscious of their Self, their passions have passed away, and they are tranquil. The wise, having reached Him who is ominipresent everywhere, devoted to the Self, enter into him wholly.

Having well ascertained the object of the knowledge of the Vedanta, and having purified their nature by the Yoga of renunciation, all anchorites, enjoying the highest immortality, become free at the time of the great end 'death' in the worlds of Brahma.

Their fifteen parts enter into their elements, their Devas the senses, into their corresponding Devas. Their deeds and their Self with all his knowledge become all one in the highest Imperishable.

As the flowing rivers disappear in the sea, losing their name and their form, thus a wise man, freed from name and form, goes to the divine Person, who is greater than the great.

He who knows that highest Brahman, becomes even Brahman. In his race no one is born ignorant of Brahman. He overcomes grief, he overcomes evil; free from the fetters of the heart, he becomes immortal.

And this is declared by the follwing Rik verse: 'Let a

man tell this science of Brahman to those only who have performed all necessary acts, who are versed in the Vedas, and firmly established in the lower Brahman, who themselves offer as oblation the one Rishi (Agni), full of faith, and by whom the rite of carrying fire on the head has been perfomed, according to the rule of the Atharvanas.'

The Rishi Angiras formerly told this true science to Saunaka; a man who has not performed the proper rites, does not read it. Adoration to the highest Rishis! Adoration to the highest Rishis!

5

Prashna Upanishad
Everything is fixed in Prana

This interesting Upanishad deals in six questions put by six seekers of Brahman to the sage Pippalada: origin of matter and the life of Prajapati; the role of Prana in activating life forces; Prana in human beings; aspects of sleep, light and deep meditation on Om; and the parts of human beings. The concepts of Pitriyana and Devayana are also presented. The ideas are unique to Indian thought.

First Question

Adoration to the Highest Self! Harih, Om!

Sukeshas Bharadvaja, and Shaivya Satyakama, and Sauryayanin Gargya, and Kausalya Ashvalayana, and Bhargava Vaidarbhi, and Kabandhin Katyayana, these were devoted to Brahman, firm in Brahman, seeking for the Highest Brahman. They thought that the venerable Pippalada could tell them all that, and they therefore took fuel in their hands like pupils, and approached him.

That Rishi said to them : 'Stay there a year longer, with penance, abstinence, and faith; then you may ask questions according to your pleasure, and if we know them, we shall tell you all.'

Then 'after the year was over' Kabandhin Katyayana approached him and asked: 'Sir, from whence may these creatures be born?'

He replied: 'Prajapati 'the lord of creatures' was desirous of creatures. He performed penance, and having performed penance, he produces a pair, matter (*rayi*) and spirit (Prana), thinking that they together should produce creatures for him in many ways.

'The sun is spirit, matter is the moon. All this, what has body and what has no body, is matter, and therefore body indeed is matter.

'Now Aditya, the sun, when he rises, goes toward the East, and thus receives the Eastern spirits into his rays. And when he illuminates the South, the West, the North, the Zenith, the Nadir, the intermediate quarters, and everything, he thus receives all spirits into his rays.

'Thus he rises, as Vaishvanara, belonging to all men, assuming all forms, as spirit, as fire. This has been said in the following verse:

'They knew him who assumes all forms, the golden, who knows all things, who ascends highest, alone in his splendours, and warms us; the thousand-rayed, who abides in a hundred places, the spirit of all creatures, the Sun, rises.

'The year indeed is Prajapati, and there are two paths thereof, the Southern and the Northern. Now those who here believe in sacrifices and pious gifts as work done, gain the moon only as their future world, and return again. Therefore the Rishis who desire offspring, go to the South, and that path of the Fathers is matter (*rayi*).

'But those who have sought the Self by penance, abstinence, faith, and knowledge, gain by the Northern path Aditya, the sun. This is the home of the spirits, the immortal, free from danger, the highest. From thence they do not return, for it is the end. Thus says the Shloka:

'Some call him the father with five feet (the five seasons), and with twelve shapes (the twelve months), the giver of rain in the highest half of heaven; others again say that the sage is placed in the lower half, in the chariot with seven wheels and six spokes.

'The month is Prajapati; its dark half is matter, its bright half spirit. Therefore some Rishis perform sacrifice in the bright half, others in the other half.

'Day and Night are Prajapati; its day is spirit, its night matter. Those who unite in love by day waste their spirit, but to unite in love by night is right.

'Food is Prajapati. Hence proceeds seed, and from it these creatures are born.

'Those therefore who observe this rule of Prajapati, produce a pair, and to them belongs this Brahma-world here. But those in whom dwell penance, abstinence, and truth,

'To them belongs that pure Brahma-world, to them, namely, in whom there is nothing crooked, nothing false, and no guile.'

Second Question

Then Bhargava Vaidarbhi asked him: 'Sir, How many gods keep what has thus been created, how many manifest this, and who is the best of them?'

He replied: 'The ether is that god, the wind, fire, water, earth, speech, mind, eye, and ear. These, when they have manifested their power, contend and say: We each of us support this body and keep it.

'Then Prana, breath, spirit, life, as the best, said to them : Be not deceived, I alone, dividing myself fivefold, support this body and keep it.

'They were incredulous; so he, from pride, did as if he were going out from above. Thereupon, as he went out, all the others went out, and as he returned, all the others returned. As bees go out when their queen goes out, and return when she returns, thus did speech, mind, eye, and ear; and, being satisfied, they praise Prana, saying:

'He is Agni (fire), he shines as Surya (sun), he is Parjanya (rain), the powerful (Indra), he is Vayu (wind), he is the earth, he is matter, he is God—he is what is and what is not, and what is immortal.

'As spokes in the nave of a wheel, everything is fixed in Prana, the verses of the Rigveda, Yajurveda, Samaveda the sacrifice, the Kshatriyas, and the Brahmins.

'As Prajapati, lord of creatures, thou movest about in the womb, thou indeed art born again. To thee, the Prana, these creatures bring offerings, to thee who dwellest with the other Pranas the organs of sense.

'Thou art the best carrier for the Gods, thou art the first offering to the Fathers. Thou art the true work of the Rishis, of the Atharvangiras.

'O Prana, thou art Indra by thy light, thou art Rudra, as a protector; thou movest in the sky, thou art the sun, the lord of lights.

'When thou showerest down rain, then, O Prana, these creatures of thine are delighted, hoping that there will be food, as much as they desire.

'Thou art a Vratya, O Prana, the only Rishi, the consumer of everything, the good lord. We are the givers of what thou hast to consume, thou, O Matarisva, art our father.

'Make propitious that body of thine which dwells in speech, in the ear, in the eye, and which pervades the mind; do not go away!

'All this is in the power of Prana, whatever exists in the three heavens. Protect us like a mother her sons, and give us happiness and wisdom.'

Third Question

Then Kausalya Ashvalayana asked: 'Sir, whence is that Prana (spirit) born? How does it come into this body? And how does it abide, after it has divided itself? How does it go out? How does it support what is without, and how what is within?'

He replied: 'You ask questions more difficult, but you

are very fond of Brahman, therefore I shall tell it to you.

'This Prana is born of the Self. Like the shadow thrown on a man, this Prana is spread out over the Brahman. By the work of the mind does it come into this body.

'As a king commands officials, saying to them: Rule these villages or those, so does that Prana dispose the other Pranas, each for their separate work.

'The Apana (the down-breathing) in the organs of excreation and generation; the Prana himself dwells in eye and ear, passing through mouth and nose. In the middle is the Samana (the onbreathing); it carries what has been sacrificed as food equally over the body, and the seven lights proceed from it.

'The Self is in the heart. There are the 101 arteries, and in each of them there are a hundred smaller veins, and for each of these branches there are 72,000. In these the Vyana, the backbreathing, moves.

'Through one of them, the Udana, the out-breathing leads us upwards to the good world by good work, to the bad world by bad work, to the world of men by both.

'The sun rises as the external Prana for it assists the Prana in the eye. The deity that exists in the earth, is there in support of man's Apana, downbreathing. The ether between sun and earth is the Samana onbreathing, the air is Vyana, backbreathing.

'Light is the Udana, outbreathing, and therefore he whose light has gone out comes to a new birth with his senses absorbed in the mind.

'Whatever his thought at the time of death, with that he goes back to Prana, united with light, together with the Jivatma leads on to the world, as deserved.

'He who, thus knowing, knows Prana, his offspring does not perish, and he becomes immortal. Thus says the Shloka:

'He who has known the origin, the entry, the place, the fivefold distribution, and the internal state of the Prana, obtains immortality, yes, obtains immortality.'

Fourth Question

Then Sauryayanin Gargya asked: 'Sir, What are they that sleep in this man, and what are they that are awake in him? What power (deva) is it that sees dreams? Whose is the happiness? On what do all these depend?'

He replied: 'O Gargya, As all the rays of the sun, when it sets, are gathered up in that disc of light, and as they, when the sun rises again and again, come forth, so is all this (all the senses) gathered up in the highest faculty deva, the mind. Therefore at that time that man does not hear, see, smell, taste, touch, he does not speak, he does not take, does not enjoy, does not evacuate, does not move about. He sleeps, that is what people say.

'The fires of the Pranas are, as it were, awake in that town (the body). The Apana is the Garhapatya fire, the Vyana the Anvaharyapachana fire; and because it is taken out of the Garhapatya fire, which is fire for taking out, therefore the Prana is the Ahavaniya fire.

'Because it carries equally these two oblations, the outbreathing and the inbreathing, the Saman is he, the Hotri priest. The mind is the sacrificer, the Udana is the reward of the sacrifice, and it leads the sacrificer every day in deep sleep to Brahman.

'There that god, the mind, enjoys in sleep greatness. What has been seen, he sees again; what has been heard, he hears again; what has been enjoyed in different countries and quarters, he enjoys again; what has been seen and not seen, heard and not heard, enjoyed and not enjoyed, he sees it all; he, being all, sees.

'And when he is overpowered by light, then that god sees no dreams, and at that time that happiness arises in his body.

'And, O friend, as birds go to a tree to roost, thus all this rests in the Highest Atman,—

'The earth and its subtile elements, the water and its

subtile elements, the light and its subtile elements, the air and its subtile elments, the ether and its subtile elements; the eye and what can be seen, the ear and what can be heard, the nose and what can be smelled, the taste and what can be tasted, the skin and what can be touched, the voice and what can be spoken, the hands and what can be grasped, the feet and what can be walked, the mind and what can be perceived, intellect (Buddhi) and what can be conceived, personality and what can be personified, thought and what can be thought, light and what can be lighted up, the Prana and what is to be supported by it.

'For he it is who sees, hears, smells, tastes, perceives, conceives, acts, he whose essence is knowledge, the Person, and he dwells in the highest, indestructible Self,—

'He who knows that indestructible being, obtains what is the highest and indestructible, he without a shadow, without a body, without colour, bright,—yes, O friends, he who knows it, becomes all-knowing, becomes all. On this there is this Shloka:

'He, O friend, who knows that indestructible being wherein the true knower, the vital spirits (Pranas), together with all the powers (deva), and the elements rest, he being all-knowing, has penetrated all.'

Fifth Question

Then Shaivya Satyakama asked him: 'Sir, if some one among men should meditate here until death on the syllable Om, what would he obtain by it?'

He replied: 'O Satyakama, the syllable Om (AUM) is the highest and also the other Brahman; there he who knows it arrives by the same means at one of the two.

'If he meditate on one Matra (the A), then, being enlightened by that only, he arrives quickly at the earth. The Rik verses lead him to the world of men, and being endowed there with penance, abstinence, and faith, he enjoys greatness.

'If he meditate with two Matras (A+U) he arrives at the Manas, and is led up by the Yajus verses to the sky, to the Soma world. Having enjoyed greatness in the Soma world, he returns again.

'Again, he who meditates with this syllable AUM of three Matras, on the Highest Person, he comes to light and to the sun. And as a snake is freed from its skin, so is he freed from evil. He is led up by the Saman verses to the Brahma-world; and from him, full of life, Hiranyagarbha, the lord of the Satya-loka, he learns to see the all-pervading, the Highest Person. And there are these two Shlokas:

'The three Matras (A+U+M), if employed separate, and only joined one to another, are mortal; but in acts, external, or intermediate, if well performed, the sage trembles not.

'Through the Rik verses he arrives at this world, through the Yajus verses at the sky, through the Saman verses at that which the poets teach,—he arrives at this by means of the Onkara; the wise arrives at that which is at rest, free from decay, from death, from fear,—the Highest.'

Sixth Question

Then Sukeshas Bharadvaja asked him saying: 'Sir, Hiranyanabha, the prince of Kosala, came to me and asked this question: Do you know the person of sixteen parts, O Bharadvaja? I said to the prince: I do not know him; if I knew him how should I not tell you? Surely, he who speaks what is untrue withers way to the very root; therefore I will not say what is untrue. Then he mounted his chariot and went away silently. Now I ask you, where is that person?'

He replied: 'Friend, that person is here within the body, he in whom these sixteen parts arise.

'He reflected: What is it by whose departure I shall depart, and by whose staying I shall stay?

'He sent forth Prana; from Prana Sraddha (faith), ether, air, light, water, earth, sense, mind, food; from food came vigour, penance, hymns, sacrifice, the worlds, and in the worlds the name also.

'As these flowing rivers that go towards the ocean, when they have reached the ocean, sink into it, their name and form are broken, and people speak of the ocean only, exactly thus these sixteen parts of the spectator that go towards the Person (Purusha), when they have reached the Person, sink into him, their name and form are broken, and people speak of the Person only, and he becomes without parts and immortal. On this there is this verse:

'That person who is to be known, he in whom these parts rest, like spokes in the nave of a wheel, you know him, lest death should hurt you.'

Then Pippalada said to them: 'So far do I know this Highest Brahman, there is nothing higher than it.'

And they praising him, said: 'You, indeed, are our father, you who carry us from our ignorance to the other shore.'

Adoration to the highest Rishis!
Adoration to the highest Rishis!
Tat sat. Harih, Om!

6

Aitareya Upanishad

Knowledge is Brahman

The Aitareyas were a school of the Rigveda and the Upanishad is regarded to have been produced by Mahidasa Aitareya, an unloved son of a Rishi. It describes the creation of the worlds by Atman which existed alone in the beginning. It first created the four spheres, then eight world guardians, then the primeval man, the Purusha. The creation of food gave them sustenance. The Atman is also regarded as Brahman.

1

Adoration to the Highest Self.

Verily, in the beginning all this was Atman, one only; there was nothing else blinking whatsoever.

He thought: 'Shall I send forth worlds?' He sent forth these worlds,

Ambha, Marichi, Mara, and Ap.

That Ambha (floods) is above the heaven, and it is heaven, the support. The Marichis (the lights) are the sky. The Mara (mortal) is the earth, and the waters under the earth are the Ap world.

He thought: 'There are these worlds; shall I send forth guardians of the worlds?'

He then formed the Purusha (the Person), taking him forth from the water.

He brooded on him and when that person had thus been brooded on a mouth burst forth like an egg. From the mouth proceeded speech, from speech Agni (fire).

Nostrils burst forth. From the nostrils proceeded scent (Prana), from scent Vayu (air).

Eyes burst forth. From the eyes proceeded sight, from sight Aditya (sun).

Ears burst forth. From the ears proceeded hearing, from hearing the Dish, quarters of the world.

Skin burst forth. From the skin proceeded hairs, sense of touch, from the hairs shrubs and trees.

The heart burst forth. From the heart proceeded mind, from mind Chandramas (moon).

The navel burst forth. From the navel proceeded the Apana, the down-breathing, from Apana death.

The generative organ burst forth. From the organ proceeded seed, from seed water.

•

Those deities, Agni and the rest, after they had been sent forth, fell into this great ocean.

Then he, the Self, besieged him, the person with hunger and thirst.

The deities then, tormented by hunger and thirst, spoke to him, the Self: Allow us a place in which we may rest and eat food.'

He led a cow towards them. They said: 'This is not enough.' He led a horse towards them. They said: 'This is not enough.'

He led man towards them. Then they said: 'Well done, indeed.' Therefore man is well done.

He said to them: 'Enter, each according to his place.'

Then Agni (fire), having become speech, entered the mouth. Vayu (air), having become scent, entered the nostrils. Aditya (sun), having become sight, entered the eyes. The Dish, regions, having become hearing, entered the ears. The shrubs and trees, having become hairs, entered the skin. Chandramas, the moon, having become mind, entered the heart. Death, having become downbreathing, entered the navel. The waters, having become seed, entered the generative organ.

Then Hunger and Thirst spoke to the Self: 'Allow us to a place.' He said to them: 'I assign you to those very deities there, I make you co-partners with them.' Therefore to whatever deity an oblation is offered, hunger and thirst are co-partners in it.'

•

He thought: 'There are these worlds and the guardians of the worlds. Let me send forth food for them.'

He brooded over the water. From the water thus brooded on, matter was born. And that matter which was born, that verily was food.

When this food (the object matter) had thus been sent forth, it wished to flee, crying and turning away. He (the subject) tried to grasp it by speech. He could not grasp it by speech. If he had grasped it by speech, man would be satisfied by naming food.

He tried to grasp it by scent (breath). He could not grasp it by scent. If he had grasped it by scent, man would be satisfied by smelling food.

He tried to grasp it by the eye. He could not grasp it by the eye. If he had grasped it by the eye, man would be satisfied by seeing food.

He tried to grasp it by the ear. He could not grasp it by the ear. If he had grapsed it by the ear, man would be satisfied by hearing food.

He tried to grasp it by the skin. He could not grasp it by the skin. If he had grasped it by the skin, man would be satisfied by touching food.

He tried to grasp it by the mind. He could not grasp it by the mind. If he had grapsed it by the mind, man would be satisfied by thinking food.

He tried to grasp it by the generative organ. He could not grasp it by the organ. If he had grasped it by the organ, man would be satisfied by sending forth food.

He tried to grasp it by the downbreathing (the breath which helps to swallow food through the mouth and to carry it off through the rectum, the Payvindriya). He got it.

Thus it is Vayu (the getter) who lays hold of food, and the Vayu is verily Annayu (he who gives life or who lives by food).

He thought: 'How can all this be without me?'

And then he thought: 'By what way shall I get there?'

And then he thought: 'If speech names, if scent smells, if the eye sees, if the ear hears, if the skin feels, if the mind thinks, if the off-breathing digests, if the organ sends forth, then what am I?'

Then opening the suture of the skull, he got in by that door.

That door is called the Vidriti (tearing asunder), the Nandana (the place of bliss).

There are three dwelling-places for him, three dreams; this dwelling-place (the eye), this dwelling-place (the throat), this dwelling-place (the heart).

When born (when the Highest Self had entered the body) he looked through all things, in order to see whether anything wished to proclaim here another, Self. He saw this person only, himself, as the widely spread Brahman. 'I saw it,' thus he said;

Therefore he was Idam-dra (seeing this).

Being Idamdra by name, they call him Indra mysteriously. For the Devas love mystery, yea, they love mystery.

2

Let the women who are with child move away!

Verily, from the beginning he (the self) is in man as a germ, which is called seed.

This seed, which is strength gathered from all the limbs of the body, he, the man, bears as self in his self, body. When he commits the seed to the woman, then he, the father, causes it to be born. That is his first birth.

That seed become the self of the woman, as if one of her own limbs. Therefore it does not injure her.

She nourishes her husband's self, the son, within her. She who nourishes, is to be nourished.

The woman bears the germ. The father elevates the child even before the birth, and immediately after.

When he thus elevates the child both before and after his birth, he really elevates his own self,

For the continuation of these worlds (men). For thus are these worlds continued.

The son, being his self, is then placed in his stead for the performance of all good works.

But his other self, the father, having done all he has to do, and having reached the fulll measure of his life, departs.

And departing from hence he is born again. That is his third birth.

And this has been declared by a Rishi (Rv. IV, 27, I):

'While dwelling in the womb, I discovered all the births of these Devas. A hundred iron strongholds kept me, but I escaped quickly down like a falcon.'

Vamadeva, lying in the womb, has thus declared this.

And having this knowledge he stepped forth. After this dissolution of the body, and having obtained all his desires in that heavenly world, became immortal, yea, he became immortal.

3

Let the women go back to their place.

Who is he whom we meditate on as the Self? Which is the Self?

That by which we see (form), that by which we hear (sound), that by which we perceive smells, that by which we utter speech, that by which we distinguish sweet and not sweet, and what comes from the heart and the mind, namely, perception, command, understanding, knowledge, wisdom, seeing, holding, thinking, considering, readiness (or suffering), remembering, conceiving, willing, breathing, loving, desiring?

No, all these are various names only of knowledge, the true Self.

And that Self, consisting of knowledge, is Brahman, it is Indra, it is Prajapati. All these Devas, these five great elements, earth, air, ether, water, fire, these and those which are, as it were, small and mixed, and seeds of this kind and that kind, born from germs, horses, cows, men, elephants, and whatsoever breathes, whether walking or flying, and what is immoveable—all that is produced by the Self.

It rests on the Self. The world is led produced by knowledge, the Self. Knowledge is its cause.

Knowledge is Brahman.

Vamadeva, having by this conscious self stepped forth from this world, and having obtained all desires in that heavenly world, became immortal, yea, he became immortal. Thus it is.

My speech rests in the mind, my mind rests in speech. Appear to me thou, the Highest Self! You speech and mind are the two pins that hold the wheels of the Veda. May what I have learnt not forsake me. I join day and night with what I have learnt. I shall speak of the real, I shall speak the true. May this protect me, may this protect the teacher! May this protect me, may it protect the teacher, yea, the teacher!

Next follows the Upanishad of the Samhita.

The former half is the earth, the latter half the heaven, their union the air, thus says Mandukeya; their union is the ether, thus did Makshavya teach it.

That air is not considered independent, therefore I do not agree with Manduka's son.

Verily, the two are the same, therefore air is considered independent, thus says Agastya. For it is the same, whether they say air or ether.

So far with reference to deities (mythologically); now with reference to the body (physiologically):

The former half is speech, the latter half is mind, their union breath (Prana), thus says Shuravira Mandukeya.

But his eldest son said: The former half is mind, the latter half speech. For we first conceive with the mind indeed, and then we utter with speech. Therefore the former half is indeed mind, the latter half speech, but their union is really breath.

Verily, it is the same with both, the father and the son.

This meditation, joined with mind, speech, and breath, is like a chariot drawn by two horses and one horse between them.

And he who thus knows this union, becomes united with offspring, cattle, fame, glory of countenance, and the world of Svarga. He lives his full age.

Now all this comes from the Mandukeyas.

•

Next comes the meditation as taught by Sakalya.

The first half is the earth, the second half heaven, their uniting the rain, the uniter Parjanya.

And so it is when Parjanya rains thus strongly, without ceasing, day and night.

Then they say also in ordinary language, 'Heaven and earth have come together.'

So much with regard to the deities; now with regard to the body:—

Every man is indeed like an egg. There are two halves of him, thus they say : 'This half is the earth, that half heaven.' And there between them is the ether, the space of the mouth, like the ether between heaven and earth. In this ether there in the mouth the breath is fixed, as in that other ether the air is fixed. And as there are those three luminaries 'in heaven', there are these three luminaries in man.

As there is that sun in heaven, there is this eye in the head. As there is that lightning in the sky, there is this heart in the body; as there is that fire on earth, there is this seed in the member.

Having thus represented the self, body, as the whole world, Shakalya said: This half is the earth, that half heaven.

He who thus knows this union, becomes united with offspring, cattle, fame, glory of countenance, and the world of Svarga. He lives his full age.

•

Next come the reciters of the Nirbhuja.

Nirbhuja abides on earth, Pratrinna in heaven, the Ubhayamantarena in the sky.

Now, if any one should chide him who recites the Nirbhuja, let him answer: 'Thou art fallen from the two lower places.' If any one should chide him who recites the Pratrinna, let him answer: 'Thou art fallen from the two higher places.' But he who recites the Ubhayamantarena, there is no chiding him.

For when he turns out the Sandhi (the union of words), that is the form of Nirbhuja; and when he pronounces two syllables pure (without modification), that is the form of Pratrinna. This comes first. By the Ubhayamantarena, what is between the two, both are fulfilled, the sandhi and the pada.

Let him who wishes for proper food say the Nirbhuja; let him who wishes for Svarga, say the Pratrinna; let him who wishes for both say the Ubhayamantarena.

Now if another man, and enemy, should chide him who says the Nirbhuja, let him say to him: 'Thou hast offended the earth, the deity; the earth, the deity, will strike thee.'

If another man should chide him who says the Pratrinna, let him say to him: 'Thou hast offended heaven, the deity; heaven, the deity, will strike thee.'

If another man should chide him who says the Ubhayamantarena, let him say to him : 'Thou hast offended the sky, the deity; the sky, the deity, will strike thee.'

And whatever the reciter shall say to one who speaks to him or does not speak to him, depend upon it, it will come to pass.

But to a Brahmin let him not say anything except what is auspicious.

Only he may curse a Brahmin in excessive wealth.

Nay, not even in excessive wealth should he curse a Brahmin, but he should say, 'I bow before Brahmins,'—thus says Shuravira Mandukeya.

•

Next follow the imprecations.

Let him know that breath is the beam on which the whole house of the body rests.

If any one, a Brahmin or another man, should chide him, who by meditation has become that breath as beam, then, if he thinks himself strong, he says: 'I grasped the breath, the beam, well; thou dost not prevail against me who have grasped the breath as the beam.' Let him say to him: 'Breath, the beam, will forsake thee.'

But if he thinks himself not strong, let him say to him: 'Thou couldst not grasp him who wishes to grasp the breath as the beam. Breath, the beam, will forsake thee.'

And whatever the reciter shall say to one who speaks to him or does not speak to him, depend upon it, it will come to pass. But to a Brahmin let him not say anything except what is auspicious. Only he may curse a Brahmin in excessive wealth. Nay, not even in excessive wealth should he curse a Brahmin, but he should say, 'I bow before Brahmins,'—thus says Shuravira Mandukeya.

•

Now those who repeat the Nirbhuja say:

'The former half is the first syllable, the latter half the second syllable, and the space between the first and second halves is the Samhita (union).'

He who thus knows this Samhita (union), becomes united with offspring, cattle, fame, glory of countenance, and the world of Svarga. He lives his full age.

Now Hrasva Mandukeya says: 'We reciters of Nirbhuja say, "Yes, the former half is the first syllable, and the latter half the second syllable, but the Samhita is the space between the first and second halves in so far as by it one turns out the union (sandhi), and knows what is the accent and what is not, and distinguishes what is the mora and what is not."

He who thus knows this Samhita (union), becomes united with offspring, cattle, fame, glory of countenance, and the world of Svarga. He lives his full age.

Now his middle son, the child of his mother Pratibodhi, says: 'One pronounces these two syllable letter by letter, without entirely separating them, and without entirely uniting them. Then that mora between the first and Second halves, which indicates the union, that is the Saman (evenness, sliding). I therefore hold Saman only to be the Samhita (union).'

This has also been declared by a Rishi (Rv. II, 23, 16):—

'O Brihaspati, they know nothing higher than Saman.'

He who thus knows this Samhita (union), becomes united with offspring, cattle, fame, glory of countenance, and the world of Svarga. He lives his full age.

•

Tarukshya said: 'The Samhita (union) is formed by means of the Brihat and Rathantara Samans.'

Verily, the Rathantara Saman is speech, the Brihat Saman is breath. By both, by speech and breath, the Samhita is formed.

For this Upanishad, for acquiring from his teacher the knowledge of this Samhita of speech and breath, Tarukshya guards his teacher's cows a whole year.

For it alone Tarukshya guards his teacher's cows a whole year.

This has also been declared by a Rishi (Rv. X, 181, 1; and Rv. X, I8I, 2):—

'Vasishtha carried hither the Rathantara;' 'Bharadvaja brought higher the Brihat of Agni.'

He who thus knows this Samhita (union), becomes united with offspring, cattle, fame, glory of countenance, and the world of Svarga. He lives his full age.

Kauntharavya said: 'Speech is united with breath, breath with the blowing air, the blowing air with the Vishvedevas, the Vishvedevas with the heavenly world, the heavenly world with Brahman. That Samhita is called the gradual Samhita.'

He who knows this gradual Samhita (union), becomes united with offspring, cattle, fame, glory of countenance, and the world of Svarga, in exactly the same manner as this Samhita, i.e., gradually.

If that worshipper, whether for his own sake or for that of another, recites the Samhita, let him know when he is going to recite, that this Samhita went up to heaven, and that it will be even so with those who by knowing it become Devas. May it always be so!

He who thus knows this Samhita (union), becomes united with offspring, cattle, fame, glory of countenance, and the world of Svarga. He lives his full age.

Panchalachanda said: 'The Samhita (union, composition) is speech.'

Verily, by speech the Vedas, by speech the metres are composed. Friends unite through speech, all beings unite through speech; therefore speech is everything here.

With regard to this view of speech being more than breath, it should be borne in mind that when we thus repeat the Veda or speak, breath is absorbed in speech; speech swallows breath. And when we are silent or sleep, speech is absorbed in breath; breath swallows speech. The two swallow each other. Verily, speech is the mother, breath the son.

This has been declared also by a Rishi (Rv. X, 114, 4):—

'There is one bird; as wind he has entered the sky; as breath or living soul he saw this whole world. With my ripe mind I saw him close to me in the heart; the mother licks or absorbs him (breath), and he absorbs the mother (speech).'

He who thus knows this Samhita (union), becomes united with offspring, cattle, fame, glory of countenance, and the world of Svarga. He lives his full age.

Next follows the Prajapati Samhita.

The former half is the wife, the latter half the man; the result of their union the son; the act of their union the begetting; that Samhita is Aditi, indestructible.

For Aditi, indestructible, is all this whatever there is, father, mother, son, and begetting.

This has also been declared by a Rishi (Rv. I, 189, 10):—

'Aditi is mother, is father, is son.'

He who thus knows this Samhita (union), becomes united with offspring, cattle, fame, glory of countenance, and the world of Svarga. He lives his full age.

5

Sthavira Shakalya said that breath is the beam, and as the other beams rest on the house-beam, thus the eye, the ear, the mind, the speech, the senses, the body, the whole self rests on this breath.

Of that self the breathing is like the sibilants, the bones like the mutes, the marrow like the vowels, the fourth part, flesh, blood, and the rest, like the semivowels,—so said Hrasava Mandukeya.

To us it was said to be a triad only.

Of that triad, viz. bones, marrow, and joints, there are 360 parts on this side, the right, and 360 on that side the left. They make 720 together, and 720 are the days and nights of the year. Thus that self which consists of sight, hearing, metre, mind, and speech is like unto the days.

He who thus knows this self, which consists of sight, hearing, metre, mind, and speech, as like unto the days, obtains union, likeness, or nearness with the days, has sons and cattle, and the lives his full age.

•

Next comes Kauntharavya:

There are 360 syllables (vowels), 360 sibilants (consonants), 360 groups.

What we called syllables are the days, what we called sibilants are the nights, what we called groups are the junctions of days and nights. So far with regard to the gods, the days.

Now with regard to the body. The syllables which we explained mythologically, are physiologically the bones; the sibilants which we explained mythologically, are physiologically the marrow.

Marrow is the real breath (life), for marrow is seed, and without life, it will decay, it will not grow.

The groups which we explained mythologically, are physiologically the joints.

Of that triad, bones, marrow, and joints, there are 540 parts on the right, and 540 on the left. They make 1080 together, and 1080 are the rays of the sun. They make the Brihati verses and the day of the Mahavrata.

Thus that self which consists of sight, hearing, metre,

mind, and speech is like unto the syllables.

He who knows this self which consists of sight, hearing, metre, mind, and speech, as like unto the syllables.

He who knows this self which consists of sight, hearing, metre, mind, and speech, as like unto syllables, obtains union, likeness, or nearness with the syllables, has sons and cattle, and lives his full age.

•

Badhva says, there are four persons to be meditated on and worshipped.

The person of the body, the person of the metres, the person of the Veda, and the Great person.

What we call the person of the body is this corporeal self. Its essence is the incorporeal conscious self.

What we call the person of the metres is this collection the Veda. Its essence is the vowel a.

What we call the person of the Veda is the mind by which we know the Vedas, the Rigveda, Yajurveda, and Samaveda. Its essence is Brahman.

Therefore let one chose a Brahmin priest who is full of Brahman (the Veda), and is able to see any flaw in the sacrifice.

What we call the Great person is the year, which causes some beings to fall together, and causes others to grow up. Its essence in yonder sun are both one and the same. Therefore the sun appears to every man singly and differently.

This has also been declared by a Rishi (Rv. I, 115, I):—

'The bright face of the gods arose, the eye of Mitra, Varuna, and Agni; it filled heaven and earth and the sky,—the sun is the self of all that rests and moves.'

'This I think to be the regular Samhita as conceived by me,' thus said Badhva.

For the Bahvrikas consider him, the self, in the great hymn (*mahad uktha*), the Adhvaryus in the sacrificial fire, the Chhandogyas in the Mahavrata ceremony. Him they see in this earth, in heaven, in the air, in the ether, in the water, in herbs, in trees, in the moon, in the stars, in all beings. Him alone they call Brahman.

That self which consists of sight, hearing, metre, mind, and speech is like unto the year.

He who recites to another that self which consists of sight, hearing, metre, mind, and speech, and is like unto the year.

•

To him the Vedas yield no more milk, he has no luck in what he has learnt from his Guru; he does not know the path of virtue.

This has also been declared by a Rishi (Rv. X, 71, 6):—

'He who has forsaken the Veda, that knows his friends, in his speech there is no luck. Though he hears, he hears in vain, for he does not know the path of virtue.'

Here it is clearly said that he has no luck in what he has learnt, and that he does not know the path of virtue.

Therefore let no one who knows this, lay the sacrificial fire belonging to the Mahavrata for another, let him not sing the Samans of the Mahavrata for another, let him not recite the Sastras of that day for another.

However, let him willingly do this for a father or for an Acharya; for that is done really for himself.

We have said that the incorporeal conscious self and the sun is seen as if it were the moon; no rays spring from it; the sky is red like madder; the patient cannot retain the wind, his head smells bad like a raven's nest :—let him know then that his self in the body is gone, and that he will not live very long.

Then whatever he thinks he has to do, let him do it, and let him recite the following hymns: *Yad anti yach cha durake* (Rv. IX, 67, 21-27); *Ad it pratnasya retasah* (Rv. IX, 113, 6-11); *Ud vayam tamasas pari* (Rv. I, 50, 10).

Next, when the sun is seen pierced, and seems like the nave of a cart-wheel, when he sees his own shadow pierced, let him know then that it is so (as stated before, i.e., that he is going to die soon).

Next, when he sees himself in a mirror or in the water with a crooked head, or without a head, or when his pupils are seen inverted or not straight, let him know then that it is so.

Next, let him cover his eyes and watch, then threads are seen as if falling together. But if he does not see them, let him know then that it is so.

Next, let him cover his ears and listen, and there will be a sound as if of a burning fire or of a carriage. But if he does not hear it, let him know then that it is so.

Next, when fire looks blue like the neck of a peacock, or when he sees lightning in a cloudless sky, or no lightning in a clouded sky, or when he sees as it were bright rays in a dark cloud, let him know then that it is so.

Next, when he sees the ground as if it were burning, let him know that it is so.

These are the visible signs.

Next come the dreams.

If he sees a black man with black teeth, and that man kills him; or a boar kills him; a monkey jumps on him; the wind carries him along quickly; having swallowed gold he spits it out; he eats honey; he chews stalks; he carries a red lotus; he drives with asses and boars; wearing a wreath of red flowers he drives a black cow with a black calf, facing the south.

If a man sees any one of these dreams, let him fast, and cook a pot of milk, sacrifice it, accompanying each oblation with a verse of the Ratri hymn (Rv. X, 127), and then, after having fed the Brahmins, with other food prepared at his house eat himself the rest of the oblation.

Let him know that the person within all beings, not heard here, not reached, not thought, not subdued, not seen, not understood, not classed but, hearing, thinking, seeing, classing, sounding, understanding, knowing, is his Self.

•

Now next the Upanishad of the whole speech. True

all these are Upanishads of the whole speech, but this they call so.

The mute consonants represent the earth, the sibilants the sky, the vowels heaven.

The mute consonants represent Agni (Fire), the sibilants air, the vowels the sun.

The mute consonants represent the Rigveda, the sibilants the Yajurveda, the vowels the Samaveda.

The mute consonants represent the upbreathing, the sibilants the downbreathing, the vowels the backbreathing.

Next comes this divine lute the human body, made by the gods. The lute made by man is an imitation of it.

As there is a head of this, so there is a head of that lute, made by man. As there is a stomach of this, so there is the cavity in the board of that. As there is a tongue of this, so there is a tongue in that. As there are fingers of this, so there are strings of that. As this is endowed with sound and firmly strung, so that is endowed with sound and firmly strung. As this is covered with a hairy skin, so that is covered with a hairy skin.

Verily, in former times they covered a lute with a hairy skin.

He who knows this lute made by the Devas and meditates on it, is willingly listened to, his glory fills the earth, and wherever they speak Aryan languages, there they know him.

Next follows the verse, called Vagrasa, the essence of speech. When a man reciting or speaking in and assembly does not please, let him say this verse:

'May the queen of all speech, who is covered, as it were, by the lips, surrounded by teeth, as if by spears who is a thunderbolt, help me to speak well.' This is the Vagrasa, the essence of speech.

•

Next Krishna-Harita confided this Brahmin concerning speech to him (his pupil):

Prajapati, the year, after having sent forth all creatures,

burst. He put himself together again by means of Chhandas (Vedas). Because he put himself together again by means of Chhandas, therefore the text of the Veda is called Samhita, put together.

Of that Samhita the letter *n* is the strength, the letter *sh* the breath and self (atman).

He who knows the Rik verses and the letters *n* and *sh* for every Samhita, he knows the Samhita with strength and breath. Let him know that this is the life of the Samhita.

If the pupil asks, 'Shall I say it with the letter *n* or without it?' let the teacher say, 'With the letter *n*. And if he asks, 'Shall I say it with the letter *sh* or without it?' let the teacher say, 'With the letter *sh*.'

Hrasva Mandukeya said: 'If we here recite the verses according to the Samhita (attending to the necessary changes of *n* and *s* into *n* and *sh*), and if we say the adhyaya of Mandukeya (Ait. Ar. III, I), then the letters *n* and *sh* (strength and breath) have by this been obtained for us.'

Sthavira Shakalya said: 'If we recite the verses according to the Samhita, and if we say the adhyaya of Mandukeya, then the letters *n* and *sh* have by this been obtained for us.'

Here the Rishis, the Kavasheyas, knowing this, said: 'Why should we repeat the Veda, why should we sacrifice? We offer as a sacrifice breath in speech, or speech in breath. What is the end of the other.'

Let no one tell these Samhitas to one who is not a resident pupil, who has not been with his teacher at least one year, and who is not himself to become an instructor. Thus say the teachers, yea, thus say the teachers.

7

Taittiriya Upanishad
From food are produced all creatures

This interesting Upanishad is divided into three clearcut parts. The first 'Shiksha Valli', which means instructions in general, provides instructions in pronunciation and accent in particular; the second 'Ananda Valli' presents beautiful evidences of the ancient Indian's absorption into the mysteries of nature; and the third 'Bhrigu Valli' is devoted to the Bhargavi Varuni Vidya—the teaching acquired by Bhrigu from his father Varuna—the doctrine of Brahman as to how it can be recognised. The importance of Food is underlined in this remarkable Upanishad.

1

On Shiksha (Pronunciation)

Harih, Om! May Mitra be propitious to us, and Varuna, Aryaman also, Indra, Brihaspati, and the wide-striding Vishnu.

Adoration to Brahman! Adoration to thee, O Vayu (Air)! Thou indeed art the visible Brahman. I shall proclaim thee alone as the visible Brahman. I shall proclaim the right. I shall proclaim the true.

May it protect me! May it protect the teacher! yes, may it protect me, and may it protect the teacher! Om! Peace! peace! peace!

•

Om! Let us explain Shiksha, the doctrine of pronunciation, letter, accent, quantity, effort in the formation of letters, modulation and union of letters (*sandhi*). This is the lecture on Shiksha.

•

May glory come to both of us, teacher and pupil, together! May Vedic light belong to both of us!

Now let us explain the Upanishad (the secret meaning) of the union (samhita), under five heads, with regard to the worlds, the heavenly lights, knowledge, offspring, and self (body). People call these the great Samhitas.

First, with regard to the worlds. The earth is the former element, heaven the latter, ether their union;

That union takes place through Vayu (air). So much with regard to the worlds.

Next, with regard to offspring. The mother is the former element, the father the latter, offspring their union. That union takes place through procreation. So much with regard to offspring.

Next, with regard to the body. The lower jaw is the former element, the upper jaw the latter, speech their union. that union takes place through speech. So much with regard to the Self.

These are the great Samhitas. He who knows these Samhitas (unions), as here explained, becomes united with offspring, cattle, Vedic light, food, and with the heavenly world.

•

May he who is the strong bull of the Vedas, assuming all forms, who has risen from the Vedas, from the Immortal, may that lord Indra strengthen me with wisdom! May I, O God, become an upholder of the Immortal!

May my body be able, my tongue sweet, may I hear much with my ears! Thou Om art the shrine of Brahman, covered by wisdom. Guard what I have learnt.

She (Sri, happiness) brings near and spreads,

And makes, without delay, garments for herself, cows, food, and drink at all times; therefore bring that Sri (happiness) higher to me, the woolly, with her cattle! Svaha! May the Brahmin students come to me, Svaha! May they come from all sides, Svaha! may they come forth to me, Svaha! May they practise restraint, Svaha! May they enjoy peace, Svaha!

May I be a glory among men, Svaha! May I be better than the richest, Svaha! May I enter into thee, O treasure, Om, Svaha! Thou, O treasure, enter into me, Svaha! In thee, consisting of a thousand branches, in thee, O treasure, I am cleansed, Svaha! As water runs downward, as the months go to the year, so, O preserver, of the world, may Brahmin students always come to me from all sides, Svaha!

Thou art a refuge! Englighten me! Take possession of me!

•

Bhu, bhuvas, Suvas, these are the three sacred interjections (Vyahriti). Mahachamasya taught a fourth, viz., Mahas which is Brahman, which is the Self. The others (devatas) are its members.

Bhu is this world, Bhuvas is the sky, Suvas is the other world.

Mahas is the sun. All the worlds are increased by the sun. Bhu is Agni (fire), Bhuvas is Vayu (air), Suvas is Aditya (sun). Mahas is the moon. All the heavenly lights are increased by the moon.

Bhu is the Rik verses, Bhuvas is the Saman verses, Suvas is the Yajus verses.

Mahas is Brahman. All the Vedas are increased by the Brahman.

Bhu is Prana (upbreathing), Bhuvas is Apana (downbreathing), Suvas is Vyana (backbreathing). Mahas is food. All breathings are increased by food.

Thus there are these four times four, the four and four sacred interjections. He who knows these,

Knows the Brahman. All Devas bring offerings to him.

•

There is the ether within the heart, and in it there is the Person (Purusha) consisting of mind, immortal, golden.

Between the two palates there hangs the uvula, like a nipple—that is the starting-point of Indra the, lord. Where the root of the hair divides, there he opens the two sides of the head, and saying Bhu, he enters Agni (the fire); saying Bhuvas, he enters Vayu (air);

Saying Suvas, he enters Aditya (sun); saying Mahas, he enters Brahman. He there obtains lordship, he reaches the lord of the mind. He becomes lord of speech, lord of sight, lord of hearing, lord of knowledge. Nay, more than this. There is the Brahman whose body is ether, whose nature is true, rejoicing in the senses (Prana), delighted in the mind, perfect in peace, and immortal.

Worship thus, O Prachinayogya!

•

The earth, the sky, heaven, the four quarters, and the intermediate quarters,—'Agni (fire), Vayu (air), Aditya (sun), Chandramas (moon), and the stars,—'so much with reference to material objects.

Now with reference to the self, the body: Prana (upbreathing), Apana (downbreathing), Vyana (backbreathing), Udana (outbreathing), and Samana (onbreathing),'—'The skin, flesh, muscle, bone, and marrow. Having dwelt on this fivefold arrangement of the worlds, the gods, beings, breathings, senses, and elements of the body, a Rishi said: 'Whatever exists is fivefold.'

By means of the one fivefold set, that referring to the body, he completes the other fivefold set.

•

1. Om means Brahman. 2. Om means all this. 3. Om means obedience. When they have been told, 'Om, speak,' they speak. 4. After Om they sing Samans. 5. After Om they recite hymns. 6. After Om the Adhvaryu gives the response. 7. After Om the Brahmin priest gives orders. 8. After Om

the sacrificer allows the performance of the Agnihotra. 9. When a Brahmin is going to begin his lecture, he says, 10. 'Om, may I acquire Brahman (the Veda).' He thus acquires the Veda.

•

What is necessary? The right, and learning and practising the Veda. The true, and learning and practising the Veda. Penance, and learning and practising the Veda. Restraint, and learning and practising the Veda. Tranquillity, and learning and practising the Veda. The fires (to be consecrated), and learning and practising the Veda. The Agnihotra sacrifice, and learning and practising the Veda. Guests to be entertained, and learning and practising the Veda. Man's duty, and learning and practising the Veda. Children, and learning and practising the Veda. Marriage, and learning and practising the Veda. Children's children, and learning and practising the Veda.

Satyavachas Rathitara thinks that the true only is necessary. Taponitya Paurashishti thinks that penance only is necessary. Naka Maudgalya thinks that learning and practising the Veda only are necessary,—for that is penance, that is penance.

•

1. 'I am he who shakes the tree, i.e., the tree of the world, which has to be cut down by knowledge. 2. May glory is like the top of a mountain. 3. I, whose pure light of knowledge has risen high, am that which is truly immortal, as it resides in the sun. 4. I am the brightest treasure. 5. I am wise, immortal, imperishable.' 6. This is the teaching of the Veda, by the poet Trishanku.

•

After having taught the Veda, the teacher instructs the pupil: 'Say what is true! Do thy duty! Do not neglect the study of the Veda! After having brought to thy teacher his proper reward, do not cut off the line of children! Do not swerve from the truth! Do not swerve from duty! Do not neglect what is useful! Do not neglect greatness! Do not neglect the learning and teaching of the Veda!

'Do not neglect the sacrificial works due to the Gods and Fathers! Let thy mother be to thee like unto a god! Let thy father be to thee like unto a god! Let thy teacher be to thee like unto a god! Let thy guest be to thee like unto a god! Whatever actions are blameless, those should be regarded, not others. Whatever good works have been performed by us, those should be observed by thee,—

'Not others. And there are some Brahmins better than we. They should be comforted by thee by giving them a seat. Whatever is given should be given with faith, not without faith,—with joy, with modesty, with fear, with kindness. If there should be any doubt in thy mind with regard to any sacred act or with regard to conduct,—

'In that case conduct thyself as Brahmins who possess good judgment conduct themselves therein, whether they be appointed or not, as long as they are not too severe, but devoted to duty. And with regard to things that have been spoken against, as Brahmins who possess good judgment conduct themselves therein, whether they be appointed or not, as long as they are not too severe, but devoted to duty,

Thus conduct thyself. 'This is the rule. This is the teaching. This is the true purport (Upanishad) of the Veda. This is the command. Thus should you observe. Thus should this be observed.'

•

May Mitra be propitious to us, and Varuna, Aryaman also, Indra, Brihaspati, and the widestriding Vishnu! Adoration to Brahman! Adoration to thee, O Vayu! Thou indeed art the visible Brahman. I proclaimed thee alone as the visible Brahman.

I proclaimed the right. I proclaimed the true. It protected me. It protected the teacher. Yes, it protected me, it protected the teacher. Om! Peace! peace! peace!

2

On Ananda (Bliss)

Harih, Om! May the Brahman protect us both, teacher and pupil! May it enjoy us both! May we acquire strength together! may our knowledge become bright! May we never quarrel!

•

He who knows the Brahman attains the highest Brahman. On this the following verse is recorded:

'He who knows Brahman, which is the cause, not effect, which is conscious, which is without end, as hidden in the depth of the heart, in highest ether, enjoys all blessings, at one with the omniscient Brahman.

From that Brahman sprang ether, akasa, through which we hear; from ether air, through which we hear and feel; from air fire, through which we hear, feel, and see; from fire water, through which we hear, feel, see, and taste; from water earth, through which we hear, feel, see, taste, and smell. From earth herbs, from herbs food, from food seed, from seed man. Man thus consists of the essence of food. This is his head, this his right arm, this his left arm, this his trunk (atman), this the seat, the support.

On this there is also the following Shloka :

•

'From food are produced all creatures which dwell on earth. Then they live by food, and in the end they return to food. For food is the oldest of all beings, and therefore it is called panacea, Sarvaushadha, i.e. consisting of all herbs, or quieting the heat of the body of all beings.'

They who worship food as Brahman, obtain all food. For food is the oldest of all beings, and therefore it is called panacea. From food all creatures are produced; by food, when born, they grow. Because it is fed on, or because it feeds on beings, therefore it is called food (Anna).

Different from this, which consists of the essence of food, is the other, the inner Self, which consists of breath. The former is filled by this. It also has the shape of man. Like the human shape of the former is the human shape of the latter. Prana (upbreathing) is its head. Vyana (back-breathing) is its right arm. Apana (downbreathing) is its left arm. Ether is its trunk. the earth the seat, the support.

On this there is also the following Shloka:

•

'The devas breathe after Prana, so do men and cattle. Breath is the life of beings, therefore it is called Sarvayusha, all-enlivening.'

They who worship breath as Brahman, obtain the full life. For breath is the life of all beings, and therefore it is called Sarvayusha. The embodied Self of this, consisting of breath, is the same as that of the former, consisting of food.

Different from this, which consists of breath, is the other, the inner Self, which consists of mind. The former is filled by this. It also has the shape of man. Like the human shape of the former is the human shape of the latter. Yajus is its head. Rik is its right arm. Saman is its left arm. The doctrine (*adesa*, i.e., the Brahmana) is its trunk. The Atharvangiras (Atharvahymns) the seat, the support.

On this there is also the following Shloka:

•

'He who knows the bliss of that Brahman, from whence all speech, with the mind, turns away unable to reach it, he never fears.' The embodied Self of this, consisting of mind, is the same as that of the former, consisting of breath.

Different from this, which consists of mind, is the other, the inner Self, which consists of understanding. The former is filled by this. It also has the shape of man. Like the human shape of the former is the human shape of the latter. Faith is its head. What is right is its right arm. What is true is its left arm. Absorption (yoga) is its trunk. The great intellect is the seat (the support).

On this there is also the following Shloka:

●

'Understanding performs the sacrifice, it performs all sacred acts. All Devas worship understanding as Brahman, as the oldest. If a man knows understanding as Brahman, and if he does not swerve from it, he leaves all evils behind in the body, and attains all his wishes.' The embodied Self of this, consisting of understanding, is the same as that of the former, consisting of mind.

Different from this, which consists of understanding, is the other inner Self, which consists of bliss. The former is filled by this. It also has the shape of man. Like the human shape of the former is the human shape of the latter. Joy is its head. Satisfaction its right arm. Great satisfaction is its left arm. Bliss is its trunk. Brahman is the seat, the support.

On this there is also the following Shloka:

●

'He who nows the Brahman as non-existing, becomes himself non-existing. He who knows the Brahman as existing, him we know himself as existing.' The embodied Self of this biliss is the same as that of the former, understanding.

Thereupon follow the questions of the pupil:

'Does any one who knows not, after he has departed this life, ever go to that world? Or does he who knows, after he has departed, go to that world?'

The answer is: He wished, may I be many, may I grow forth. He brooded over himself, like a man performing penance. After he had thus brooded, he created all, whatever there is. Having sent forth, he entered into it. Having entered it, he became *sat* what is manifest, and *tyat,* what is not manifest, defined and undefined, supported and not supported, endowed with knowledge and without knowledge (as stones), real and unreal. The satya (true) became all this whatsover, and therefore the wise call the Brahman Sat-tya (the true).

On this there is also this Shloka:

•

'In the beginning this was non-existent, not yet defined by form and name. From it was born what exists. That made itself its Self, therefore it is called the Self-made. That which is Self-made is a flavour, can be tasted, for only after perceiving a flavour can any one perceive pleasure. Who could breathe, who could breathe forth, if that bliss, Brahman, existed not in the ether, in the heart? For he alone causes blessedness.

When he finds freedom from fear and rest in that which is invisible, incorporeal, undefined, unsupported, then he has obtained the fearless. For if he makes but the smallest distinction in it, there is fear from him. But that fear exists only for one who thinks himself wise, not for the true sage.

On this there is also this Shloka:

•

'From terror of the Brahman the wind blows, from terror the sun rises; from terror of its Agni and Indra, yea Death runs as the fifth.'

Now this is an examination of what is meant by Bliss (Ananda):

Let there be a noble young man, who is well read in the Veda, very swift, firm, and strong, and let the whole world be full of wealth for him, that is one measure of human bliss.

On hundred times that human bliss is one measure of the bliss of human Gandharvas, and likewise of a great sage learned in the Vedas who is free from desires.

One hundred times that bliss of human Gandharvas is one measure of the bliss of divine Gandharvas, and likewise of a great sage who is free from desires.

One hundred times that bliss of divine Gandharvas is one measure of the bliss of the Fathers, enjoying their long estate, and likewise of a great sage who is free from desires.

One hundred times that bliss of the Fathers is one measure of the bliss of the Devas, born in the Ajana heaven through the merit of their lawful works, and likewise of a great sage who is free from desires.

One hundred times that bliss of the Devas born in the Ajana heaven is one measure of the biss of the sacrificial Devas, who go to the Devas by means of their Vedic sacrifices, and likewise of a great sage who is free from desires.

One hundred times that bliss of the sacrificial Devas is one measure of the bliss of the thirty-three Devas, and likewise of a great sage who is free from desires.

One hundred times that bliss of the thirty-three Devas is one measure of the bliss of Indra, and likewise of a great sage who is free from desires.

One hundred times that bliss of Indra is one measure of the bliss of Brihaspati, and likewise of a great sage who is free from desires.

One hundred times that bliss of Brihaspati is one measure of the bliss of Prajapati, and likewise of a great sage who is free from desires.

One hundred times that bliss of Prajapati is one measure of the bliss of Brahman, and likewise of a great sage who is free from desires.

He who is this Brahman in man, and he who is that Brahman in the sun, both are one.

He who knows this, when he has departed this world, reaches and comprehends the Self which consists of food, the Self which consists of breath, the Self which consists of mind, the Self which consists of understanding, the Self which consists of bliss.

On this there is also this Shloka:

•

'He who knows the bliss of that Brahman, from whence all speech, with the mind, turns away unable to reach it, he fears nothing.'

He does not distress himself with the thought, Why did I not do what is good? Why did I do what is bad? He who thus knows both, frees himself. This is the Upanishad.

3

Of Bhrigu

Harih, Om! May the Brahman protect us both! May it enjoy us both! May we acquire strength together! May our knowledge become bright! May we never quarrel! Peace! peace! peace!

•

Bhrigu Varuni went to his father Varuna, saying: Sir, teach me Brahman. He told him this, Food, breath, the eye, the ear, mind, speech.

Then he said again to him: That from whence these beings are born, that by which, when born, they live, that into which they enter at thier death, try to know that. This is Brahman.

He performed penance. Having performed penance—

•

He perceived that food is Brahman, for from food these beings are produced; by food, when born, they live; and into food they enter at their death.

Having perceived this, he went again to his father Varuna, saying: Sir, teach me Brahman. He said to him: Try to know Brahman by penance, for penance is the means of knowing Brahman.

He performed penance. Having performed penance —

•

He perceived that breath is Brahman, for from breath these beings are born; by breath, when born, they live; into breath they enter at their death.

Having perceived this, he went again to his father Varuna, saying: 'Sir, teach me Brahman.' He said to him: Try to know Brahman by penance, for penance is the means of knowing Brahman.

He performed penance. Having performed penance—

•

He perceived that mind (manas) is Brahman, for from mind these beings are born; by mind, when born, they live; into mind they enter at their death.

Having perceived this, he went again to his father Varuna, saying: Sir, teach me Brahman. He said to him : 'Try to know Brahman by penance, for penance is the means of knowing Brahman.'

He performed penance. Having performed penance—

•

He perceived that understanding (Vijnana) was Brahman, for from understanding these beings are born; by understanding, when born, they live; into understanding they enter at their death.

Having perceived this, he went again to his father Varuna, saying: Sir, teach me Brahman. He said to him: Try to know Brahman by penance, for penance is the means of knowing Brahman.

He performed penance. Having performed penance—

•

He perceived that bliss is Brahman, for from bliss these beings are born; by bliss, when born, they live; into bliss they enter at their death.

This is the knowledge of Bhrigu and Varuna, exalted in the highest heaven (in the heart). He who knows this becomes exalted, becomes rich in food, and able to eat (be healthy), food becomes great by offspring, cattle, and the splendour of his knowledge of Brahman, great by fame.

•

Let him never abuse food, that is the rule.

Breath is food, the body eats the food. The body rests on breath, breath rests on the body. This is the food resting on food. He who knows this food resting on food, rests exalted, becomes rich in food, and able to eat (be healthy), food becomes great by offspring, cattle, and the splendour of his knowledge of Brahman, great by fame.

•

Let him never shun food, that is the rule. Water is food, the light eats the food. The light rests on water, water rests on light. This is the food resting on food. He who knows this food resting on food, rests exalted, becomes rich in food, and able to eat healthy food becomes great by offspring, cattle, and the splendour of his knowledge of Brahman, great by fame.

•

Let him acquire much food, that is the rule. Earth is food, the ether eats the food. The ether rests on the earth, the earth rests on the ether. This is the food resting on food. He who knows this food resting on food, rests exalted, becomes rich in food, and able to eat healthy food becomes great by offspring, cattle, and the splendour of his knowledge of Brahman, great by fame.

•

Let him never turn away a stranger from his house, that is the rule. Therefore a man should by all means acquire much food, for good people say to the stranger. There is food ready for him. If he gives food amply, food is given to him amply. If he gives food fairly, food is given to him fairly. If he gives food meanly, food is given to him meanly.

He who knows this, recognises and worships Brahman, as possession in speech, as acquisition and possession in up-breathing (Prana) and downbreathing (Apana); as action in the hands; as walking in the feet; as voiding in the anus. These are the human recognitions of Brahman as manifested in human actions. Next follow the recognitions of Brahman with reference to the Devas, as satisfaction in rain; as power in lightning;

As glory in cattle; as light in the stars; as procreation, immortality, and bliss in the member; as everything in the ether. Let him worship that Brahman as support, and he becomes supported. Let him worship that Brahman as greatness, and he becomes great. Let him worhsip that Brahman as mind, and he becomes endowed with mind.

Let him worship that Brahman as adoration, and all desires fall down before him in adoration. Let him worhsip that Brahman as Brahman. Let him worship this as the absorption of the gods in Brahman, and the enemies who hate him will die all around him, all around him will die the foes whom he does not love.

He who is this Brahman in man, and he who is that Brahman in the sun, both are one.

He who knows this, when he has departed this world, after reaching and comprehending the Self which consists of food, the Self which consists of breath, the Self which consists of mind, the Self which consists of understanding, the Self which consists of bliss, enters and takes possession of these worlds, and having as much food as he likes, and assuming as many forms as he likes, he sits down singing this Saman of Brahman: 'Havu, havu, havu!

'I am food (object), I am food, I am food! I am the

eater of food (subject), I am the eater of food, I am the eater of food! I am the poet who joins the two together, I am the poet, I am the poet! I am the first-born of the Right (*rita*). Before the Devas I was in the centre of all that is immortal. He who gives me away, he alone preserves me: him who eats food, I eat as food.

I overcome the whole world, I, endowed with golden light. He who knows this, attains all this. This is the Upanishad.

8

Kaushitaki Upanishad

Without Prajna, the senses do not work

The Upanishad belonged to the school of Kaushitakians of the Rigveda. Divided into four chapters, the first provides the Paryanka Vidya—the doctrine of the bedstead of rest — because the soul attaining to the yonder world appears before the bedstead or couch or throne of Brahman to be tested by him. The second discusses the Prana Vidya and the third and fourth the Atma Vidya. These doctrines are regarded as esoteric, which may even frighten people, but in any case, worthy of being practised with dedication.

1

Chitra Gangyayani, forsooth, wishing to perfrom a sacrifice, chose Aruni Uddalaka to be his chief priest. But Aruni sent his son, Shvetaketu, and said: 'Perform the sacrifice for him.' When Shvetaketu had arrived, Chitra asked him: 'Son of Gautama' is there a hidden place in the world where you are able to place me, or is it the other way, and are you going to place me in the world to which it, that other way, leads?'

He answered and said: 'I do not know this. But, let me ask the master.' Having approached his father, he asked: 'Thus has Chitra asked me; how shall I answer?'

Aruni said: 'I also do not know this. Only after having

learnt the proper portion of the Veda in Chitra's on dwelling, shall we obtain what knowledge other give us. Come, we will both go.'

Having said this he took fuel in his hand, like a pupil, and approached Chitra Gangyayani, saying: 'May I come near to you?' He replied: 'You are worthy to know Brahman, O Gautama, because you were not led away by pride. Come hither, I shall make you know clearly.'

And Chitra said: 'All who depart from this world or this body go to the moon. In the former, the bright half, the moon delights in their spirits; in the other, the dark half, the moon sends them on to be born again. Verily, the moon is the door of the Svarga, the heavenly world. Now, if a man objects to the moon, if one is not satisfied with life there, the moon sets him free. But if a man does not object, then the moon sends him down as rain upon this earth. And according to his deeds and according to his knowledge he is born again here as a worm, or as an insect, or as a fish, or as a bird, or as a lion, or as a boar, or as a serpent, or as a tiger, or as a man, or as something else in different places.

'When he has thus returned to the earth, some one asks: "Who art thou?" And he should answer: "From the wise moon, who orders the seasons, when it is born consisting of fifteen parts, from the moon who is the home of our ancestors, the seed was brought. This seed, even my, they (the gods mentioned in the Panchagni Vidya) gathered up in an active man, and through an active man they brought me to a mother. Then I, growing up to be born, a being living by months, whether twelve or thirteen, was together with my father, who also lived by years of twelve or thirteen months, that I might either know the true Brahman or not know it. Therefore, O ye seasons, grant that I may attain immortality, knowledge of Brahman. By this my true saying, by this my toil, beginning with the dwelling in the moon and ending with my birth on earth, I am like a season, and the child of the seasons." "Who art thou?" the sage asks again. I am thou," he replies. Then he sets him free to proceed onward.

'He at the time of death, having reached the path of the gods, comes to the world of Agni (fire), to the world of Vayu (air), to the world of Varuna, to the world of Indra, to the world of Prajapati, to the world of Brahman (Hiranyagarbha). In that world there is the lake Ara. The moments called Yeshtiha, the river Vijara (ageless), the tree Ilya, the city Salajya, the palace Aparajita (unconquerable), the door-keepers Indra and Prajapati, the hall of Brahman, called Vibhu (built by Vibhu, egoism), the throne Vichakshana (buddhi, perception), the couch Amitaujas (endless splendour), and the beloved Manasi (mind) and her image Chakshushi (eye), who, as if taking flowers, are weaving the worlds, and the Apsaras, the Ambas (sacred scriptures), and Ambayavis (buddhi, understanding), and the rivers Ambayas (leading to the knowledge of Brahman). To this world he who knows the Paryanka Vidya approaches. Brahman says to him: "Run towards him (servants) with such worship as is due to myself. He has reached the river Vijara, he will never age."

'Then five hundred Apsaras go towards him, one hundred with garlands in their hands, one hundred with ointments in their hands, one hundred with perfumes in their hands, one hundred with garments in their hands, one hundred with fruit in their hands. They adorn him with an adornment worthy of Brahman, and when thus adorned with the adornment of Brahman, the knower of Brahman moves towards Brahman. He comes to the lake Ara, and he crosses it by the mind, while those who come to it without knowing the truth, are drowned. He comes to the moments called Yeshtiha, they flee from him. He comes to the river Vijara, and crosses it by the mind alone, and there shakes off his good and evil deeds. His beloved relatives obtain the good, his unbeloved relatives the evil he has done. And as a man, driving in a chariot, might look at the two wheels, without being touched by them, thus he will look at day and night, thus at good and evil deeds, and at all pairs (correlative things, such as light and darkness, heat and cold, etc.). Being freed from good and freed from evil he, the knower of Brahman, moves towards Brahman.

'He approaches the tree Ilya, and the odour of Brahman reaches him. He approaches the city Salajya, and the flavour of Brahman reaches him. He approaches the palace Aparajita, and the splendour of Brahman reaches him. He approaches the door-keepers Indra and Prajapati, and they run away from him. He approaches the hall Vibhu, and the glory of Brahman reaches him. He approaches the throne Vichakshana. The Saman verses, Brihad and Rathantara, are the eastern feet of that throne; the Saman verses, Shyaita and Naudhasa, its western feet; the Saman verses, Vairupa and Vairaja, its sides lengthways (south and north); the Saman verses, Shakvar and Raivata, its sides crossways (east and west). That throne is Prajna, knowledge, for by knowledge he sees clearly. He approaches the couch Amitaujas. That is Prana. The past and the future are its eastern feet; prosperity and earth its western feet; the Saman verses, Brihad and Rathantara, are the two sides lengthways of the couch (south and north); the Saman verses, Bhadra and Yajnayajniya, are its cross-sides at the head and feet (east and west); the Rik and Saman are the long sheets (east and west); the Yajus the cross-sheets (south and north); the moon-beam the cushion; the Udgitha the coverlet; prosperity the pillow. On this couch sits Brahman, and he who knows this, who knows himself one with Brahman sitting on the couch, mounts it first with one foot only. Then Brahman says to him: Who art thou?' and he shall answer:

"I am like a season, and the child of the seasons, sprung from the womb of endless space, from the light from the luminous Brahman. The light, the origin of the year, which is the past, which is the present, which is all living things, and all elements, is the Atman. Thou art the Atman. What thou art, that am I."

'Brahman says to him: "Who am I?" He shall answer: "That which is, the true (Sat-tyam)".

'Brahman asks: "What is the true?" He says to him:

"What is different from the gods and from the senses (Prana) that is Sat, but the gods and the senses are Tyam. Therefore by that name Sattya (true) is called all this whatever there is. All this thou art."

'This is also declared by a verse: "This great Rishi, whose belly is the Yajus, the head the Saman, the form the Rik, is to be known as being imperishable, as being Brahman."

'Brahman says to him: "How dost thou obtain my male names?" He should answer : "By Prana (breath)."

'Brahman asks: "How my female names?" He should answer: "By the nose." "How forms?" "By the eye." "How sounds?" "By the ear." "How flavours of food?" "By the tongue." "How actions?" "By the hands." "How pleasures and pain?" "By the body." "How joy, delight, and offspring?" "By the organ." "How journeyings?" "By the feet." "How thoughts, and what is to be known and desired?" "By knowledge (Prajna) alone."

'Brahman says to him: "Water indeed is this my world, the whole Brahman world, and it is thine."

'Whatever victory, whatever might belongs to Brahman, that victory and that might he obtains who knows this, yea, who knows this.'

2

'Prana (breath) is Brahman', thus says Kaushitaki. Of this Prana, which is Brahman, the mind (manas) is the messenger, speech the housekeeper, the eye the guard, the ear the informant. He who knows mind as the messenger of Prana, which is Brahman, becomes possessed of the messenger. He who knows speech as the housekeeper, becomes possessed of the housekeeper. He who knows the eye as the guard, becomes possessed of the guard. He who knows the ear and the informant, becomes possessed of the informant.

Now to that Prana, which is Brhaman, all these deities mind, speech, eye, ear, bring an offering, though he asks not for it, and thus to him who knows this all creatures bring an offering, though he asks not for it. For him who knows this, there is this Upanishad, 'Beg not!' As a man who has begged through a village and got nothing sits down and says, 'I shall never eat anything given by those poeple,' and as then those who formerly refused him press him to accept their alms, thus is the rule for him who begs not, but the charitable will press him and say, 'Let us give to thee.'

'Prana (breath) is Brahman', thus says Paingya. And in that Prana, which is Brahman, the eye stands firm behind speech, the ear stands firm behind the eye, the mind stands firm behind the ear, and the spirit stands firm behind the mind. To that Prana, which is Brahman, all these deities bring an offering, though he asks not for it, and thus to him who knows this, all creatures bring an offering, though he asks not for it. For him who knows this, there is this Upanishad 'Beg not!' As a man who has begged through a village and got nothing sits down and says, 'I shall never eat anything given by those people,' and as then those who formerly refused him press him to accept their alms, thus is the rule for him who begs not, but the charitable will press him and say 'Let us give to thee.'

Now follows the attainment of the highest treasure (Prana, spirit). If man meditates on that highest treasure, let him on a full moon or a new moon, or in the bright fortnight, under an auspicious Nakshatra, at one of these proper times, bending his right knee, offer oblations of ghee with a ladle, after having placed the fire, swept the ground, strewn the sacred grass, and sprinkled water. Let him say:

'The deity called Speech is the attainer, may it attain this for me from him who possesses and can bestow what I wish for. Svaha to it!'

'The deity called Prana (breath) is the attainer, may it attain this for me from him. Svaha to it!'

'The deity called the eye is the attainer, may it attain this for me from him. Svaha to it!'

'The deity called the ear is the attainer, may it attain

this for me from him. Svaha to it!'

'The deity called mind (manas) is the attainer to it, may it attain this for me from him. Svaha to it.'

'The deity called Prajna (knowledge) is the attainer of it, may it attain this for me from him. Svaha to it!'

Then having inhaled the smell of the smoke, and having rubbed his limbs with the ointment of ghee, walking on in silence, let him declare his wish, or let him send a messenger. He will surely obtain his wish.

Now follows the Daiva Smara, the desire to be accomplished by the gods. If a man desires to become dear to any man or woman, or to any men or women, then at one of the fore-mentioned times he offers, in exactly the same manner as before, oblations of ghee, saying: 'I offer thy speech in myself, Svaha.' 'I offer thy ear in myself, Svaha.' 'I offer thy mind in myself, Svaha.' 'I offer thy Prajna (knowledge) in myself, Svaha.' Then having inhaled the smell of the smoke, and having rubbed his limbs with the ointment of ghee, walking on in silence, let him try to come in contact or let him stand speaking in the wind, so that the wind may carry his words to the person by whom he desires to be loved. Surely he becomes dear, and they think of him.

Now follows the restraint, Samyamana, instituted by Pratardana: they call it the inner Agnihotra. So long as a man speaks, he cannot breathe, he offers all the while his Prana (breath) in his speech. And so long as a man breathes, he cannot speak, he offers all the while his speech in his breath. These two endless and immortal oblations he offers always, whether waking or sleeping. Whatever other oblations there are, those, of the ordinary Agnihotra, consisting of milk and other things, they have an end, for they consist of works which, like all works, have an end. The ancients, knowing this the best Agnihotra, did not offer the ordinary Agnihotra.

Uktha is Brahman, thus said Shushka Bhringara. Let him meditate on the Uktha as the same with the Rik, and all beings will praise him as the best. Let him meditate on it as the same with Yajus, and all beings will join before him as the best. Let him meditate on it as the same with the Saman, and all beings will bow before him as the best. Let him mediate on it as the same with might, let him mediate on it as the same with glory, let him mediate on it as the same with splendour. For as the bow is among weapons the mightiest, the most glorious, the most splendid, thus is he who knows this among all beings the mighties, the most glorious, the most splendid. The Adhvaryu conceives the fire of the altar, which is used for the sacrifice, to be himself. In it the Adhvaryu weaves the Yajus portion of the sacrifice. And in the Yajus portion the Hotri weaves the Rik portion of the sacrifice. And in the Rik portion the Udgatri weaves the Saman portion of the sacrifice. The Adhvaryu or Prana is the self of the threefold knowledge; he indeed is the self of Prana. He who knows this is the self of it, becomes Prana.

Next follows the three kinds of meditation of the all-conqering Kaushitaki which adores the sun when rising, having put on the sacrificial cord, having brought water, and having thrice sprinkled the water-cup, saying; 'Thou art the deliverer, deliver me from sin.' In the same manner he adores the sun when in the zenith, saying: 'Thou art the highest deliverer, deliver me fully from sin.' In the same 'Thou art the full deliverer, deliver me fully from sin.' Thus he fully removes whatever sin he committed by day and by night. And in the same manner he who knows this, likewise adores the sun, and fully removes whatever sin he committed by day and by night.

Then let him worship every month in the year at the time of the new moon, the moon as it is seen in the west in the same manner as before described with regard to the sun, or let him send forth his speech toward the moon with two green blades of grass, saying: 'O thou who art mistress of immortal joy, through that gentle heart of mine which abides in the moon, may I never weep for misfortune concerning my children.'

The children of him who thus adores the moon do not indeed die before him. Thus it is with a man to whom a son is already born.

Now for one to whom no son is born as yet. He mutters the three Rik verses. 'Increase, O Soma! may vigour come to thee' (Rv. I, 91, 16; IX, 31, 4). 'May milk, may food go to thee' (Rv. I, 91, 18); 'That ray which the Adityas gladden.'

Having muttered these three Rik verses, he says: 'Do not increase by our breath (Prana), by our offspring, by our cattle; he who hates us and whom we hate, increase by his breath, by his offspring, by his cattle. Thus I turn the turn of the god, I return the turn of Aditya.' After these words, having raised the right arm toward Soma, he lets it go again.

Then thirdly let him worship on the day of the full moon the moon as it is seen in the east in the same manner, saying: 'Thou art Soma, the king, the wise, the five-mouthed, the lord of creatures. The Brahmin is one of thy mouths; with that mouth thou eatest the kings (Kshatriyas); make me an eater of food by that mouth! The king is one of thy mouths; with that mouth thou eatest the people (Vaishyas); make me an eater of food by that mouth! The hawk is one of thy mouths; with that mouth thou eatest the birds; make me an eater of food by that mouth! Fire is one of thy mouths; with that mouth thou eatest this world; make me an eater of food by that mouth! In thee there is the fifth mouth; with that mouth thou eatest all beings; make me an eater of food by that mouth! Do not decrease by our life, by our offspring, by our cattle; he who hates us and whom we hate, decrease by his life, by his offspring, by his cattle. Thus I turn the turn of the god, I return the turn of Aditya.' After these words, having raised the right arm, he lets it go again.

Next having addressed these prayers to Soma, when being with his wife, let him stroke her heart, saying: 'O fair one, who hast obtained immortal joy by that which has entered thy heart through Prajapati, mayest thou never fall into sorrow about thy children.' Her children then do not die before her.

Next, if a man has been absent and returns home, let him

smell his son's head, saying: 'Thou springest from every limb, thou art born from the heart, thou, my son, art my self indeed, live thou a hundred harvests.' He gives him his name, saying: 'Be thou a stone, be thou an axe, be thou solid gold; thou, my son, art my self indeed, live thou a hundred harvests.' He pronounces his name. Then he embraces him, saying: 'As Prajapati, the lord of creatures, embraced his creatures for their welfare, thus I embrace thee,' (pronouncing his name.) Then he mutters into his right ear, saying: 'O thou, quick Maghavan, give to him' (Rv. III, 36, 10). 'O Indra, bestow the best wishes' (Rv. II, 21, 6), thus he shispers into his left ear. Let him then thrice smell his head, saying: 'Do not cut off the line of our race, do not suffer. Live a hundred harvests of life; I kiss thy head, O son, with thy name.' He then thrice makes a lowing sound over his head, saying: 'I low over thee with the lowing sound of cows.'

Next follows the Daiva Parimara, the dying around of the gods (the absorption of the two classes of gods, mentioned before, into Prana or Brahman). This Brahman shines forth indeed when the fire burns, and it dies when it burns not. Its splendour goes to the sun alone, the life, Prana, the moving principle, to the air.

Thus Brahman shines forth indeed when the sun is seen, and it dies when it is not seen. Its splendour goes to the moon alone, the Prana to the air.

This Brahman shines forth indeed when the moon is seen, and it dies when it is not seen. Its splendour goes to the lightining alone, its life (prana) to the air.

This Brahman shines forth indeed when the lightning flashes, and it dies when it flashes not. Its splendour goes to the air, and the Prana to the air.

Thus all these deities, fire, sun, moon, lightning, having entered the air, though dead, do not vanish; and out of the very air they rise again. So much with reference to the mythological deities. Now then with reference to the body, physiological deities.

This Brahman shines forth indeed when the lightning

flashes, and it dies when it flashes not. Its splendour goes to the air, and the Prana to the air.

Thus all these deities, fire, sun, moon, lightning, having entered the air, though dead, do not vanish; and out of the very air they rise again. So much with reference to the mythological deities. Now then with reference to the body, physiological dieties.

This Brahman shines forth indeed when one speaks with speech, and it dies when one does not speak. His splendour goes to the eye alone, the life (Prana) to breath (Prana).

This Brahman shines forth indeed when one sees with the eye, and it dies when one does not see. Its splendour goes to the ear alone, the life (Prana) to breath (Prana).

This Brahman shines forth indeed when one hears with the ear, and it dies when one does not hear. Its splendour goes to the mind alone, the life (Prana) to breath (Prana).

This Brahman shines forth indeed when one thinks with the mind, and it dies when one does not think. Its splendour goes to the breath (Prana) alone, and the life (Prana) to breath (Prana).

Thus all these deities, the senses, etc., having entered breath or life (Prana) alone, though dead, do not vanish; and out of very breath (Prana) they rise again. And if two mountains, the southern and northern, were to move forward trying to crush him who knows this, they would not crush him. But those who hate him and those whom he hates, they die around him.

Next follows the Nihsreyasa-dana, the accepting of the pre-eminence of Prana by the other gods. The deities, speech, eye, ear, mind, contending with each for who was the best, went out of this body, and the body lay without breathing, withered, like a log of wood. Then speech went into it, but speaking by speech, it lay still. Then the eye went into it, but speaking by speech, and seeing by the eye, it lay still. Then the ear went into it, but speaking by speech, seeing by the eye, hearing by the ear, it lay still. Then mind went into it, but speaking by speech, seeing by the eye, hearing by the ear, thinking by the mind, it lay still. Then Prana went into it, and thence it rose at once. All these deities, having recognised the pre-eminence in Prana, and having comprehended Prana alone as the conscious self, Prajnatman, went out of this body with all five different kinds of Prana, and resting in the air knowing that Prana had entered the air and merged in the ether (Akasa), they went to heaven. And in the same manner he who knows this, having recognised the pre-eminence in Prana, and having comprehended Prana alone as the conscious self Prajnatman, goes out of this body with all these, does not longer believe in this body, and resting in the air, and merged in the ether, he goes to heaven, he goes to where those gods, speech, etc., are. And having reached this he, who knows this, becomes immortal with that immortality which those gods enjoy.

Next follows the father's tradition to the son, and thus they explain it. The father, when going to depart, calls his son, after having strewn the house with fresh grass, and having laid the sacrifical fire, and having placed near it a pot of water with a jug full of rice, himself covered with a new cloth, and dressed in white. He places himself above his son, touching his organs with his own organs, or he may deliver the tradition to him while he sits before him. Then he delivers it to him. The father says: 'Let me place my speech in thee.' The son says: 'I take thy speech in me.' The father says: 'Let me place my Prana in thee.' The son says: 'I take thy scent in me.' The father says: 'Let me place my tastes of food in me.' The father says: 'Let me place my actions in thee.' The son says: 'I take thy actions in me.' The father says: 'Let me place my pleasure and pain in thee.' The son says: 'I take thy pleasure and pain in me.' The father says: 'Let me place happiness, joy, and offspring in thee.' The son says: 'I take thy happiness, joy, and offspring in me.' The father says: 'Let me place my walking in thee.' The son says: 'I take thy walking in me.' The father says : 'Let me place my mind in thee.' The son says: 'I take thy mind in me.' The father says: 'Let me place my knowledge in me.' But if the father is very ill, he may say shortly: 'Let me place my spirits (Pranas) in thee', and the son: 'I take thy spirits in me.

Then the son walks round his father keeping his right side towards him, and goes away. The father calls after him: 'May fame, glory of countenance, and honour always follow thee.' Then the other looks back over his left shoulder, covering himself with his hand or the hem of his garment, saying: 'Obtain the heavenly worlds and all desires.'

If the father recovers, let him be under the authority of his son, or let him wander about as an ascetic. But if he departs, then let them despatch him, as he ought to be despatched, yea, as he ought to be despatched.

3

Pratardana forsooth, the son of Divodasa, king of Kashi, came by means of fighting and strength to the beloved abode of Indra. Indra said to him: 'Pratardana, let me give you a boon to choose.' And Pratardana answered: 'Do you yourself choose that boon for me which you deem most beneficial for a man.' Indra said to him: 'No one who chooses, chooses for another; choose thyself.' Then Pratardana replied: 'Then that boon to choose is no boon for me.'

Then, however, Indra did not swerve from the truth, for Indra is truth. Indra said to him: 'Know me only; that is what I deem most beneficial for man, that he should know me. I slew the three-headed son of Tvashtri; I delivered the Arunmukhas, the devotees, to the wolves; breaking many treaties, I killed the people of Prahlada in heaven, the people of Puloma in the sky, the people of Kalakanja on earth. And not one hair of me was harmed there. And he who knows me thus, by no deed of his is his life harmed, not by the murder of his mother, not by the murder of his father, not by theft, not by the killing of a Brahmin. If he is going to commit a sin, the bloom does not depart from his face.'

Indra said: 'I am Prana, meditate on me as the conscious self, Prajnatman, as life, as immortality. Life is Prana, Prana is life. Immortality is Prana, Prana is immortality. As long as Prana dwells in this body, so long surely there is life. By Prana he obtains immortality in the other world, by knowledge true conception. He who meditates on me as life and immortality, gains his full life in this world, and obtains in the Svarga world immortality and indestructibility.'

Pratardana said: 'Some maintain here that the Pranas become one, for otherwise no one could at the same time make known a name by speech, see a form with the eye, hear a sound with the ear, thinks thought with the mind. After having become one, the Pranas perceive all these together, one by one. While speech speaks, all Pranas see after it. While the ear hears, all Pranas hear after it. While the mind thinks, all Pranas think after it. While the Prana breathes, all Pranas breathe after it.'

'Thus it is indeed,' said Indra, 'but nevertheless there is a pre-eminence among the Pranas.'

Man lives deprived of speech, for we see dumb people. Man lives deprived of sight, for we see blind people. Man lives deprived of hearing, for we see deaf people. Man lives deprived of mind, for we see infants. Man lives deprived of his arms, deprived of his legs, for we see it thus. But Prana alone is the conscious self, Prajnatman, and having laid hold of this body, it makes it rise up. Therefore it is said, Let man worship it alone as Uktha. What is Prana, that is Prajna, self-consiciousness; what is Prajna, self-consciousness, that is Prana, for together they, Prajna and Prana, lie in this body, and together they go out of it. Of that, this is the evidence, this is the understanding. When a man, being thus asleep, sees no dream whatever, he become one with that Prana alone. Then speech goes to him when he is absorbed in Prana, with all names, the eye with all forms, the ear with all sounds, the mind with all thoughts. And when he awakes, then, as from a burning fire sparks proceed in all directions, thus from that self the Pranas, speech, etc., proceed, each towards its place; from the Pranas the gods, Agni, etc., from the gods the worlds.

On this, this is the proof, this is the understanding. When a man is thus sick, going to die, falling into weakness and faintness, they say: 'His thought has departed, he hears not, he sees not, he speaks not, he thinks not.' Then he becomes one with that Prana alone. Then speech goes to him who is asorbed in Prana with all names, the eye with all forms, the ear with all sounds, the mind with all thoughts. And when he departs from this body, he departs together with all these.

Speech gives up to him who is absorbed in Prana all names, so that by speech he obtains all names. The nose gives up to him all odours, so that by scent he obtains all odours. The eye gives up to him all forms, so that by the eye he obtains all forms. The ear gives up to him all sounds, so that by the ear he obtains all sounds. The mind gives up to him all thoughts, so that by the mind he obtains all thoughts. This is the complete absorption in Prana. And what is Prana is Prajna, self-consciousness, what is Prajna, self-consciousness is Prana. For together do these two live in the body. And together do they depart.

Now we shall explain how all things become one in that Prajna, self-consciousness.

Speech is one portion taken out of Prajna self-conscious knowledge, the word is its object, placed outside. The nose is one portion taken out of it, the odour is its object, placed outside. The eye is one portion taken out of it, the form is its object, placed outside. The ear is one portion taken out of it, the sound is its object, placed outside. The tongue is one portion taken out of it, the taste of food is its object, placed outside. The two hands are one portion taken out of it, their action is their object, placed outside. The body is one portion taken out of its, its pleasure and pain are its object, placed outside. The organ is one portion taken out of it, happiness, joy, and offspring are its object, placed outside. The two feet are one portion taken out of it. Movements are their object, placed outside. Mind is one portion taken out of it, thoughts and desires are its object, placed outside.

Having by Prajna, self-conscious knowledge, taken possession of speech, he obtains by speech all words. Having by Prajna taken possession of the nose, he obtains all odours. Having by Prajna taken possession of the eye, he obtains all forms. Having by Prajna taken possession of the ear, he obtains all sounds. Having by Prajna taken possession of the tongue, he obtains all tastes of food. Having by Prajna taken possession of the two hands, he obtains all actions. Having by Prajna taken possession of the body, he obtains pleasure and pain. Having by Prajna taken possession of the organ, he obtains happiness, joy, and offspring. Having by Prajna taken possession of the two feet, he obtains all movements. Having by Prajna taken possession of mind, he obtains all thoughts.

For without Prajna, self-consciousness, speech does not make known to the self any word. 'My mind was absent,' he says, 'I did not perceive that word.' Without Prajna the nose does not make known any odour. 'My mind was absent,' he says, 'I did not perceive that odour.' Without Prajna the eye does not make known any form. 'My mind was absent,' he says, 'I did not perceive that form.' Without Prajna the ear does not make known any sound. 'My mind was absent,' he says, 'I did not perceive that sound.' Without Prajna the tongue does not make known any taste. 'My mind was absent,' he says, 'I did not perceive that taste.' Without Prajna the two hands do not make known any act. 'Our mind was absent,' they say, 'we did not perceive any act.' Without Prajna the body does not make known pleasure or pain. 'My mind was absent,,' he says, 'I did not perceive that pleasure or pain.' Without Prajna the organ does not make known happiness, joy, or offspring. 'My mind was absent,' he says, 'I did not perceive that happiness, joy, or offspring.' Without Prajna the two feet do not make known any movement. 'Our mind was absent,' they say, 'we did not perceive that movement.' Without Prajna no thought succeeds, nothing can be known that is to be known.

Let no man try to find out what speech is, let him know the speaker. Let no man try to find out what odour is, let him know him who smells. Let no man try to find out what form is, let him know the seer. Let no man try to find out what sound is, let him know the hearer. Let no man try to find out the tastes of food, let him know the knower of tastes. Let no man try to find out what action is, let him know the agent. Let no man try to find out what pleasure and pain are, let him know the knower of pleasure and pain. Let no man try to find out what happiness, joy, and offspring are, let him know the knower of happiness, joy, and offspring. Let no man try to find out what movement is, let him know the mover. Let no man try to find out what mind is, let him know the thinker.

These ten objects, what is spoken, smelled, seen, etc., have reference to Prajna, self-consicousness, the ten subjects, speech, the senses, mind etc., have reference to objects. If there were no objects, there would be no subjects; and if there were no subjects, there would be no objects. For on either side alone nothing could be achieved. But that, the self of Prajna, consciousness, and Prana, life, is not many, but one. For as in a car the circumference of a wheel is placed on the spokes, and the spokes on the nave, thus are these objects (circumference) placed on the subjects (spokes), and the subjects on the Prana. And that Prana, breath, the living and breathing power, indeed is the self of Prajna, the self-conscious self, blessed, imperishable, immortal. He does not increase by a good action, nor decrease by a bad action.

For he, the self of Prana and Prajna, makes him, whom he wishes to lead up from these worlds, do a good deed; and the same makes him, whom he wishes to lead down from these worlds, do a bad deed. And he is the guardian of the world, he is the king of the world, he is the lord of the universe,— and he is my (Indra's) self, thus let it be known, yea, thus let it be known!

4

There was formerly Gargya Balaki, famous as a man of great reading; for it was said of him that he lived among the Ushinaras, among the Satvat-Matsyas, the Kuru-Panchala, the Kashi-Videhas. Having gone to Ajatasatru, the king of Kashi, he said to him: 'Shall I tell you Brahman?' Ajatasatru said to him: 'We give a thousand cows for that speech of yours, for verily all people run away, saying, "Janaka, the king of Mithila, is our patron."

Balaki said: 'The person that is in the sun, on him I meditate as Brahman.'

Ajatasatru said to him: 'No, no! do not challenge me to a disputation on this. I meditate on him who is called great, clad in white raiment, the supreme, the head of all beings. Whoso meditates on him thus, becomes supreme, and the head of all beings.'

Balaki said: 'The person that is in the moon, on him I meditate.'

Ajatasatru said to him: 'Do not challenge me on this. I meditate on him as Soma, the king, the self, source of all food. Whoso meditates on him thus, becomes the self, source of all food.'

Ajatasatru said to him: 'Do not challenge me on this. I meditate on him as the self in light. Whoso meditates on him thus, becomes the self in light.'

Balaki said: 'The person that is in the thunder, on him I meditate.'

Ajatasatru said to him: 'Do not challenge me on this. I meditate on him as the self of sound. Whoso meditates on him thus, becomes the self of sound.'

Balaki said: 'The person that is is in the ether, on him I meditate.'

Ajatasatru said to him: Do not challenge me on this. I mediate on him as the full, quiescent Brahman. Whoso meditates on him thus, is filled with offspring and cattle. Neither he himself nor his offspring dies before the time.'

Balaki said: 'The person that is in the air, on him I meditate.'

Ajatasatru said to him: Do not challenge me on this. I meditate on him as Indra Vaikuntha, as the unconquerable army. Whoso meditates on him thus becomes victorious, unconquerable, conquering his enemies.'

Balaki said: 'The person that is in the fire, on him I meditate.'

Ajatasatru said to him: 'Do not challenge me on this. I meditate on him as powerful. Whoso meditates on him thus, becomes powerful among others.'

Balaki said: 'The person that is in the water, on him I meditate.'

Ajatasatru said to him: 'Do not challenge me on this. I meditate on him as the self of the name. Whoso meditates on him thus, becomes the self of the name.'

So far with regard to deities (mythological); now with regard to the body (physiological).

Balaki said: 'The person that is in the mirror, on him I meditate.'

Ajatasatru said to him: 'Do not challenge me on this. I meditate on him as the likeness. Whoso meditates on him thus, to him a son is bron in his family who is his likeness, not one who is not his likeness.'

Balaki said: 'The person that is in the echo, on him I meditate.'

Ajatasatru said to him: 'Do not challange me on this. I meditate on him as the second, who never goes away. Whoso meditates on him thus, he gets a second from his second his wife, he becomes doubled.'

Balaki said: 'The sound that follows a man, on that I meditate.'

Ajatasatru said to him: 'Do not challenge me on this. I meditate on him as life. Whoso meditates on him thus, neither he himself nor his offspring will faint before the time.

Balaki said: 'The person that is in the shadow, on him I meditate.

Ajatasatru said to him: 'Do not challenge me on this. I meditate on him as death. Whoso meditates on him thus, neither he himself nor his offspring will die before the time.'

Balaki said: 'The person that is embodied, on him I meditate.'

Ajatasatru said to him: 'Do not challenge me on this. I meditate on him as Lord of creatures. Whoso meditates on him thus, is multiplied in offspring and cattle.'

Balaki said: 'The Self which is conscious and by whom he who sleeps here, walks about in sleep, on him I meditate.

Ajatasatru said to him: 'Do not challenge me on this. I meditate on him as Yama the king. Whoso meditates on him thus, everything is subdued for his excellences.'

Balaki said: 'The person that is in the right eye, on him I meditate.'

Ajatasatru said to him: 'Do not challenge me on this. I meditate on him as the self of the name, as the self of fire, as the self of splendour. Whoso meditates on him thus, he becomes the self of these.'

Balaki said: 'The person that is in the left eye, on him I meditate.

Ajatasatru said to him: 'Do not challenge me on this. I meditate on him as the self of light. Whoso meditates on him thus, he becomes the self of these.'

After this Balaki became silent. Ajatasatru said to him: 'Thus far only do you know, O Balaki?'

'Thus far only', replied Balaki.

Then Ajatasatru said to him: 'Vainly did you challenge me, saying: " Shall I tell you Brahman." O Balaki, he who is the maker of those persons whom you mentioned, he of whom all this is the work, he alone is to be known.'

Thereupon Balaki came, carrying fuel in his hand, saying: 'May I come to you as a pupil.' Ajatastru said to him: 'I deem it improper that a Kshatriya should initate a Brahmin. Come, I shall make you know clearly. Then taking him by the hand, he went forth. And the two together came to a person who was asleep. And Ajatasatru called him, saying: 'Thou great one, clad in white raiment, Soma, King.' But he remained lying. Then he pushed him with a stick, and he rose at once. Then said Ajatasatru to him: 'Balaki, where did this person here sleep? Where was he? Whence came he thus back?' Balaki did not know.

And Ajatasatru said to him: 'Where this person here slept, where he was, whence he thus came back, is this: The arteries of the heart called Hita extend from the heart of the person towards the surrounding body. Small as a hair divided a thousand times, they stand full of a thin fluid of various colours, white, black, yellow, red. In these the person is when sleeping he sees no dream.

'Then he becomes one with that Prana alone. Then speech goes to him with all names, the eye with all forms, the ear with all sounds, the mind with all thoughts. And when he awakes, then, as from a burning fire, sparks proceed in all directions, thus from that self the Pranas (speech, etc.) proceed, each towards its palce, from the Pranas the gods, from the gods the worlds. And as a razor might be fitted in a razor-case, or as fire in the fire-place, even thus this conscious self enters the self of the body considers the body as himself to the very hairs and nails. And the other selfs (such as speech, etc.) follow that self, as his people follow the master of the house. And as the master feeds with his people, nay, as his people feed on the master, thus does this conscious self feed with other selfs, as a master with his people, and the other selfs follow him, as his people follow the master. So long as Indra did not understand that self, the Asuras conquered him. When he understood it, he conquered the Asuras and obtained the pre-eminence among all gods, sovereignty, supremacy. And thus also he who knows this obtains pre-eminence among all beings, sovereignty, supremacy, – yea, he who knows this.'

9

Chhandogya Upanishad

Om is greater than the great

This is the Upanishad of the Samaveda-singers and deals with the Agnihotra ceremonies, and then moves on to the glories of Prana and of Samans in their five and sevenfold forms. Perhaps the largest Upanishad in size, it provides some of the most significant religio-philosophical utterances, ideas and tales which came down to them from olden times. The nature of the Atman is being explored through various dialogues and presentations.

1

Let a man meditate on the syllable Om, called the Udgitha; for the Udgitha, a portion of the Samaveda, is sung, beginning with Om.

The full account, however, of Om is this:

The essence of all beings is the earth, the essence of the earth is water, the essence of water the plants, the essence of plants man, the essence of man speech, the essence of speech the Rigveda, the essence of the Rigveda the Samaveda, the essence of the Samaveda the Udgitha which is Om.

That Udgitha, Om, is the best of all essences, the highest, deserving the highest place, the eighth.

What then is the Rik? What is the Saman? What is the Udgitha? This is the question.

The Rik indeed is speech, Saman is breath, the Udgitha is the syllable Om. Now speech and breath, or Rik and Saman, form one couple.

And that couple is joined together in the syllable Om. When two people come together, they fulfil each other's desire.

Thus he who knowing this, meditates on the syllable Om, the Udgitha, becomes indeed a fulfiller of desires.

That syllable is a syllable of permission, for whenever we permit anything, we say Om, yes. Now permission is gratification. He who knowing this meditates on the syllable Om, the Udgitha, becomes indeed a gratifier of desires.

By that syllable does the threefold knowledge (the sacrifice, more particularly the Soma-sacrifice, as founded in the three Vedas) proceed. When the Adhvaryu priest gives an order, he says Om. When the Hotri priest recites, he says Om. When the Udgatri priest sings, he says Om—all for the glory of that syllable. The threefold knowledge, the sacrifice, proceeds by the greatness of that syllable, the vital breaths, and by its essence, the oblations.

Now therefore it would seem to follow that both he who knows the true meaning of the syllable Om, and he who does not, perform the same sacrifice. But this is not so, for knowledge and ignorance are different. The sacrifice which a man performs with knowledge, faith, and the Upanishad is more powerful. This is the full account of the syllable Om.

•

When the Devas and Asuras struggled together, both of the race of Prajapati, the Devas took the Udgitha, Om, thinking they would vanquish the Asuras with it.

They meditated on the Udgitha as the breath in the nose, but the Asuras pierced the breath with evil. Therefore we smell by the breath in the nose both what is good-smelling and what is bad-smelling. For the breath was pierced by evil.

Then they meditated on the Udgitha as speech, but the Asuras pierced it with evil. Therefore we speak both truth and falsehood. For speech is pierced by evil.

Then they meditated on the Udgitha as the eye, but

the Asuras pierced it with evil. Therefore we see both what is sightly and unsightly. For the eye is pierced by evil.

Then they meditated on the Udgitha as the ear, but the Asuras pierced it with evil. Therefore we hear both what should be heard and what should not be heard. For the ear is pierced by evil.

Then they meditated on the Udgitha as the mind, but the Asuras pierced it with evil. Therefore we conceive both what should be conceived and what should not be conceived. For the mind is pierced by evil.

Then comes this breath of life in the mouth. They meditated on the Udgitha, Om, as that breath. When the Asuras came to it, they were scattered, as a ball of earth would be scattered when hitting a solid stone.

Thus, as a ball of earth is scattered when hitting on a solid stone, will he be scattered who wishes evil to one who knows this, or who persecutes him; for he is a solid stone.

By the breath in the mouth he distinguishes neither what is good nor what is bad-smelling, for that breath is free from evil. What we eat and drink with it supports the other vital breaths, i.e., the senses, such as smell, etc. When at the time of death he does not find that breath in the mouth, through which he eats and drinks and lives, then he departs. He opens the mouth at the time of death as if wishing to eat.

Angiras meditated on the Udgitha as that breath, and people hold it to be Angiras, i.e., the essence of the members;

Therefore Brihaspati meditated on Udgitha, Om, as that breath, and people hold it to be Brihaspati, for speech is Brihati, and that breath is the lord (*pati*) of speech;

Therefore Ayasya meditated on the Udgitha, Om, as that breath, and people hold it to be Ayasya, because it comes (*ayati*) from the mouth (*asya*);

Therefore Vaka Dalbhya knew it. He was the Udgatri, singer, of the Naimishiya sacrificers, and by singing he obtained for them their wishes.

He who knows this, and meditates on the syllable Om,

the imperishable Udgitha, as the breath of life in the mouth, he obtains all wishes by singing. So much for the Udgitha as meditated on with reference to the body.

•

Now follows the meditation on the Udgitha with reference to the gods. Let a man meditate on the Udgitha as he who sends warmth, the sun in the sky. When the sun rises it sings as Udgatri for the sake of all creatures. When it rises it destroys the fear of darkness. He who knows this, is able to destroy the fear of darkness ignorance.

This, the breath in the mouth, and the sun are the same. This is hot and that is hot. This they call Svara sound, and that they call Pratyasvara reflected sound. Therefore let a man meditate on the Udgitha as breath and as sun.

Then let a man meditate on the Udgitha as Vyana indeed. If we breathe up, that is Prana, the upbreathing. If we breathe down, that is Apana, the downbreathing. The combination of Prana and Apana is Vyana, backbreathing or holding in of the breath. This Vyana is speech. Therefore when we utter speech, we neither breathe up nor down.

Speech is Rik, and therefore when a man utters a Rik verse he neither breathes up nor down.

Rik is Saman, and therefore when a man utters a Saman verse he neither breathes up nor down.

Saman is Udgitha, and therefore when a man sings the Udgitha, Om, he neither breathes up nor down.

And other works also which require strength, such as the production of fire by rubbing, running a race, stringing a strong how, are performed without breathing up or down. Therefore let a man meditate on the Udgitha as Vyana.

Let a man meditate on the syllables of the Udgitha, i.e., of the word Udgitha. *Ut* is breath (Prana), for by means of breath a man rises (*uttal tisthati*), *gi* is speech, for speeches are called *girah*. *Tha* is food, for by means of food all subsists (*sthita*).

Ut is heaven, *gi* the sky, *tha* the earth. *Ut* is the *sun*, *gi* the air, *tha* the fire. *Ut* is the Samaveda, *gi* the Yajurveda, *tha* the Rigveda. Speech yields the milk, which is the milk of speech itself, to him who thus knowing meditates on those syllables of the name of Udgitha, he becomes rich in food and able to eat food.

Next follows the fulfilment of prayers. Let a man thus meditate on the Upasaranas, i.e., the objects which have to be approached by meditation. Let the Udgatri quickly reflect on the Saman with which he is going to praise;

Let him quickly reflect on the Rik in which that Saman occurs; on the Rishi (poet) by whom it was seen or composed; on the Devata (object) which he is going to praise;

On the metre in which he is going to praise; on the tune with which he is going to sing for himself;

On the quarter of the world which he is going to praise.

Lastly, having approached himself his name, family, etc., by meditation, let him sing the hymn of praise, reflecting on his desire, and avoiding all mistakes in pronunciation, etc. Quickly will the desire be then fulfilled to him, for the sake of which he may have offered his hymn of praise, yea, for which he may have offered his hymn of praise.

•

Let a man meditate on the syllable Om, for the Udgitha is sung beginning with Om. And this is the full account of the syllable Om:

The Devas, being afraid of death, entered upon the performance of the sacrifice prescribed in the threefold knowledge, the three Vedas. They covered themselves with the metrical hymns. Because they covered (*chhad*) themselves with the hymns, therefore the hymns are called Chhandas.

Then, as a fisherman might observe a fish in the water, Death observed the Devas in the Rik, Yajus, and Saman-sacrifices. And the Devas seeing this, rose, from the Rik, Yajus, and Saman sacrifices, and entered the Svara, i.e., the Om, they meditated on the Om.

When a man has mastered the Rigveda, he says quite

loud Om; the same, when he has mastered the Saman and the Yajus. This Svara is the imperishable syllable, the immortal, free from fear. Because the Devas entered it, therefore they became immortal, and free from fear.

He who knowing this loudly pronounces that syllable, enters the same imperishable syllable, the Svara, the immortal, free from fear, and having entered it, becomes immortal, as the Devas are immortal.

•

The Udgitha is the Pranava, the Pranava is the Udgitha. And as the Udgitha is the sun, so is the Pranava, for the sun goes sounding Om.

'Him I sang praises to, therefore art thou my only one,' thus said Kaushitaki to his son. 'Do thou revolve his rays, then thou wilt have many sons,' So much in reference to the Devas.

Now with reference to the body. Let a man meditate on the Udgitha as the breath in the mouth, for he goes sounding Om.

'Him I sang praises to, therefore art thou my only son,' thus said Kaushitaki to his son. 'Do thou therefore sing praises to the breath as manifold, if thou wishest to have many sons.'

He who knows that the Udgitha is the Pranava, and the Pranava the Udgitha, rectifies from the seat of the Hotri priest any mistake committed by the Udgatri priest in performing the Udgitha, yea, in performing the Udgitha.

•

The Rik (Veda) is this earth, the Saman (Veda) is fire. This Saman (fire) rests on that Rik (earth). Therefore the Saman is sung as resting on the Rik. *Sa* is this earth, *ama* is fire, and that makes Sama.

The Rik is the sky, the Saman air. This Saman (air) rests on that Rik (sky). Therefore the Saman is sung as resting on the Rik. *Sa* is the sky, *ama* the air, and that makes Sama.

Rik is heaven, Saman the sun. This Saman (sun) rests on that Rik (heaven). Therefore the Saman is sung as resting on the Rik. *Sa* is heaven, ama the sun, and that makes Sama.

Rik is the stars, Saman the moon. This Saman (moon) rests on that Rik (stars). Therefore the Saman is sung as resting on the Rik. *Sa* is the stars, *ama* the moon, and that makes Sama.

Rik is the white light of the sun, Saman the blue exceeding darkness (in the sun). This Saman (darkness) rests on that Rik (brightness). Therefore the Saman is sung as resting on the Rik.

Sa is the white light of the sun, *ama* the blue exceeding darkness, and that makes Sama.

Now that golden person, who is seen within the sun, with golden beard and golden hair, golden altogether to the very tips of his nails,

Whose eyes are like blue lotus's, his name is *ut* for he has risen (*udita*) above all evil. He also who knows this, rises above all evil.

Rik and Saman are his joints, and therefore he is Udgitha. And therefore he who praises the *ut* is called the Ud-gatri (the out-singer). He the golden person, called ut is lord of the worlds beyong the sun, and of all the wishes of the Devas inhabiting those worlds. So much with reference to the Devas.

•

Now with reference to the body. Rik is speech, Saman breath. This Saman (breath) rests on that Rik (speech). Therefore the Saman is sung as resting on the Rik. *Sa* is speech, *ama* is breath, and that makes Sama.

Rik is the eye, Saman the self. This Saman (shadow) rests on that Rik (eye). Therefore the Saman issung as resting on the Rik. *Sa* is the eye, *ama* the self and that makes Sama.

Rik is the ear, Saman the mind. This Saman (mind) rests on that Rik (ear). Therefore the Saman is sung as resting on the Rik. *Sa* is the ear, *ama* the mind, and that makes Sama.

Rik is the white light of the eye, Saman the blue exceeding darkness. This Saman (darkness) rests on the Rik (brightness). Therefore the Saman is sung as resting on the Rik. *Sa* is the white light of the eye, *ama* the blue exceeding darkness, and that makes Sama.

Now the person who is seen in the eye, he is Rik, he is Saman, Uktha, Yajus, Brahman. The form of that person in the eye is the same as the form of the other person in the sun, the joints of the one (Rik and Saman) are the joints of the other, the name of the one (*ut*) is the name of the other.

He is lord of the worlds beneath that, the self in the eye, and of all the wishes of men. Therefore all who sing to the Vina (lyre), sing him, and from him also they obtain wealth.

He who knowing this sings a Saman, sings to both, the Adhidaivata and Adhyatma self, the person in the sun and the person in the eye, as one and the same person. He obtains through the one, yea, he obtains the worlds beyond that, and the wishes of the Devas;

And he obtains through the other the worlds beneath that, and the wishes of men.

Therefore an Udgatri priest who knows this, may say to the sacrificer for whom he officates :

'What wish shall I obtain for you by my songs?' For he who knowing this sings a Saman is able to obtain wishes through his song, yea, through his song.

•

There were once three men, well-versed in Udgitha, Shilaka Shalavatya, Chaitkitayana Dalbhya, and Pravahana Jaivali. They said: 'We are well-versed in Udgitha. Let us have a discussion on Udgitha.'

They all agreed and sat down. Then Pravahana Jaivali said: 'Sirs, do you both speak first, for I wish to hear what two Brahmanas have to say.'

Then Shilaka Shalavatya said to Chaikitayana Dalbhya:

'Let me ask you.'

'Ask,' he replied.

'What is the origin of the Saman?' 'Tone (svar),' he replied.

'What is the origin of tone?' 'Breath,' he replied.

'What is the origin of breath?' 'Food,' he replied.

'What is the origin of food?' 'Water,' he replied.

'What is the origin of water?' 'That world, heaven,' he replied.

'And what is the origin of the world?' -

He replied: 'Let no man carry the Saman beyond the world of Svarga (heaven). We recognise the Saman in the world of Svarga, for the Saman is extolled as Svarga.'

Then said Shilaka Shalavatya to Chaikitayana Dalbhya: 'O Dalbhya, thy Saman is not firmly established. And if any one were to say, Your head shall fall off if you be wrong, surely your head would now fall.'

'Well then, let me know this from you, Sir,' said Dalbhya.

'Know it,' replied Shilaka Shalavatya.

'What is the origin of that world heaven?

'This world,' he replied.

'And what is the origin of this world?' -

He replied: 'Let no man carry the Saman beyond this world as its rest. We place the Saman in this world as its rest, for the Saman is extolled as rest.'

Then said Pravahana Jaivali to Shilaka Shalavatya: 'Your Saman, the earth, O Shalavatya, has an end. And if any one were to say, Your head shall fall off if you be wrong, surely your head would now fall.'

'Well then, let me know this from you, Sir,' said Shalavatya.

'Know it,' replied Jaivali.

•

'What is the origin of this world?' 'Ether', he replied.

For all these beings take their rise from the ether, and return into the ether. Ether is older than these, ether is their rest.

'He is indeed the Udgitha (Om = Brahman), greater than great, he is without end.

'He who knowing this meditates on the Udgitha, the greater than great, obtains what is greater than great, he conquers the worlds which are greater than great.'

Atidhanvan Shaunaka, having taught this Udgitha to Udara Shandilya, said: 'As long as they will know in your family this Udgitha, their life in this world will be greater than great.

'And thus also will be their state in the other world.' He who thus knows the Udgitha, and meditates on it thus, his life in this world will be greater than great, and also his state in the other world, yea, in the other world.

•

When the Kurus had been destroyed by (hail) stones, Ushasti Chakrayana lived as a beggar with his virgin wife at Ibhyagrama.

Seeing a chief eating beans, he begged of him. The chief said: 'I have no more, except those which are put away for me here.'

Ushasti said: 'Give me to eat them.' He gave him the beans, and said: ' There is something to drink also.' Then said Ushasti: 'If I drank of it, I should have drunk what was left by another, and is therefore unclean.'

The chief said: 'Were not those beans also left over and therefore unclean?'

'No,' he replied, 'for I should not have lived, if I had not eaten them, but the drinking of water would be mere pleasure.'

Having eaten himself, Ushasti gave the remaining beans to his wife. But she, having eaten before, took them and put them away.

Rising the next morning, Ushasti said to her: 'Alas, if we could only get some food, we might gain a little wealth.

The king here is going to offer a sacrifice, he should choose me for all the priestly offices.'

His wife said to him: 'Look, here are those beans of yours.' Having eaten them, he went to the sacrifice which was being performed.

He went and sat down on the orchestra near the Udgatris, who were going to sing their hymns of praise. And he said to the Prastotri (the leader):

'Prastotri, if you, without knowing the deity which belongs to the Prastava, the hymns, etc., of the Prastotri, are going to sing it, your head will fall off.'

In the same manner he addressed the Udgatri: 'Udgatri, if you, without knowing the deity which belongs to the Udgitha, the hymns of the Udgatri, are going to sing it, your head will fall off.'

In the same manner he addressed the Pratihartri: 'Pratihartri, if you, without knowing the deity which belongs to the Pratihara, the hymns of Pratihara, are going to sing it, your head will fall off.'

They stopped, and sat down in silence.

•

Then the sacrificer said to him: 'I should like to know who you are, Sir.' He replied: 'I am Ushasti Chakrayana.'

He said: 'I looked for you, Sir, for all these sacrificial offices, but not finding you, I chose others.'

'But now, Sir, take all the sacrificial offices'.

Ushasti said: 'Very well; but let those, with my permission, perform the hymns of praise. Only as much wealth as you give to them, so much give to me also.'

The sacrificer assented.

Then the Prastotri approached him, saying: 'Sir, you said to me, "Prastotri, if you, without knowing the deity which belongs to the Prastava, are going to sing it, your head will fall off,"—which then is that deity?'

He said: 'Breath (Prana). For all these beings merge into breath alone, and from breath they arise. This is the deity belonging to the Prastava. If, without knowing that deity, you had sung forth your hymns, your head would have fallen off, after you had been warned by me.'

Then the Udgatri approached him, saying: Sir, you said to me, " Udgatri, if you, without knowing the deity which belongs to the Udgitha, are going to sing it, your head will fall off,"—which then is that deity?'

He said: 'The sun. For all these beings praise the sun when it stands on high. This is the deity belonging to the Udgitha. If, without knowing that deity, you had sung out your hymns, your head would have fallen off, after you had been warned by me.'

Then the Pratihartri approached him, saying : Sir, you said to me, "Pratihartri, if you, without knowing the deity belonging to the Pratihara, are going to sing it, your head will fall off."—which then is that deity?'

He said: 'Food (Anna). For all these beings live when they partake of food. This is the deity belonging to the Pratihara. If, without knowing that deity, you had sung your hymns, your head would have fallen off, after you had been warned by me.'

•

Now follows the Udgitha of the dogs. Vaka Dalbhya, or, as he was also called, Glava Maitreya, went out to repeat the Veda in a quiet place.

A white dog appeared before him, and other dogs gathering round him, said to him: 'Sir, sing and get us food, we are hungry.'

The white dog said to them: 'Come to me to-morrow morning.' Vaka Dalbhya, or, as he was also called, Glava Maitreya, watched.

The dogs came on, holding together, each dog keeping the tail of the preceding dog in his mouth, as the priests do when they are going to sing praises with the Vahishpavamana hymn. After they had settled down, they began to say Hin.

'Om, let us eat! Om, let us drink! Om, may the divine Varuna, Prajapati, Savitri bring us food! Lord of food, bring hither food, bring it, Om!'

•

The syllabe Hau is this world, the earth, the syllable Hai the air, the syllable Atha the moon, the syllable Iha the self, the syllable I, fire.

The syllable U is the sun, the syllable E is the Nihava or invocation, the syllable Auhoi is the Visvedevas, the syllable Hin is Prajapati, Svara (tone) is breath (Prana), the syllable Ya is food, the syllable Vag is Viraj.

The thirteenth stobha syllable, the indistinct syllable Hun, is the Undefinable, the Highest Brahman.

Speech yields the milk, which is the milk of speech itself to him who knows this Upanishad (secret doctrine) of the Samans in this wise. He becomes rich in food, and able to eat food,—yea, able to eat food.

2

Meditation on the whole of the Saman is good, and people, when anything is food, say it is Saman; when it is not good, it is not Saman.

Thus they also say, he approcached him with Saman, i.e., becomingly; and he approached him without Saman, i.e., unbecomingly.

And they also say, truly this is Saman for us, i.e., it is good for us, when it is good; and truly that is not Saman for us, when it is good; and truly that is not Saman for us, i.e., it is not good for us, when it is not good.

If any one knowing this meditates on the Saman as good, depend upon it all good qualities will approach quickly, aye, they will become his own.

•

Let a man meditate on the fivefold Saman as the five

worlds. The Hinkara is the earth, the Prastava the fire, the Udgitha the sky, the Pratihara the sun, the Nidhana heaven; so in an ascending line.

In a descending line, the Hinkara is heaven, the Prastava the sun, the Udgitha the sky, the Pratihara the fire, the Nidhana the earth.

The worlds in an ascending and in a descending line belong to him who knowing this meditates on the fivefold Saman as the worlds.

•

Let a man meditate on the fivefold Saman as rain. The Hinkara is wind, that brings the rain; the Prastava is, 'the cloud is come;' the Udgitha is, 'it rains;' the Pratihara, 'it flashes, it thunders;'

The Nidhana is, 'it stops.' There is rain for him, and he brings rain for others who thus knowing meditates on the fivefold Saman as rain.

•

Let a man meditate on the fivefold Saman in all waters. When the clouds gather, that is the Hinkara; when it rains, that is Prastava; that which flows in the east, that is the Udgitha; that which flows in the west, that is the Pratihara; the sea is Nidhana.

He does not die in water, nay, he is rich in water who knowing this meditates on the fivefold Saman as all waters.

•

Let a man meditate on the fivefold Saman as the seasons. The Hinkara is spring, the Prastava summer (harvest of yava, etc.), the Udgitha the rainy season, the Pratihara autumn, the Nidhana winter.

The seasons belong to him, nay, he is always in season (successful) who knowing this meditates on the fivefold Saman as the seasons.

Let a man meditate on the fivefold Saman in animals.

The Hinkara is goats, the Prastava sheep, the Udgitha cows, the Pratihara horses, the Nidhana man.

•

Animals belong to him, nay, he is rich in animals who knowing this meditates on the five-fold Saman as animals Let a man meditate on the fivefold Saman which is greater than great as the Pranas (senses). The Hinkara is smell (nose), the Prastava speech (tongue), the Udgitha sight (eye), the Pratihara hearing (ear), the Nidhana mind. These are one greater than the other.

What is greater than great belongs to him, nay, he conquers the worlds which are greater than great, who knowing this meditates on the fivefold Saman, which is greater than great, as the Pranas (senses).

•

Next for the sevenfold Saman. Let a man meditate on the sevenfold Saman in speech. Whenever there is in speech the syllable Hun, that is Hinkara, *pra* is the Prastava, *a* is the Adi, the first, i.e., Om.

Ud is the Udgitha, *pra* the Pratihara, *upa* the Upadrava, ni the Nidhana.

Speeh yields the milk, which is the milk of speech itself, to him who knowing this meditates on the sevenfold Saman in speech. He becomes rich in food, and able to eat food.

•

Let a man meditate on the sevenfold Saman as the sun. The sun is Saman, because he is always the same (*sama*); he is Saman because he is the same, everybody thinking he looks towards me, he looks towards me.

Let him know that all beings are dependent on him the sun. What he is before his rising, that is the Hinkara. On it animals are dependent. Therefore animals say Hin before sunrise, for they share the Hinkara of that Saman, the sun.

What he is when first risen, that is the Prastava. On it men are dependent. Therefore men love praise (Prastuti) and celebrity, for they share the Prastava of that Saman.

What he is at the time of the Sangava, that is the *adi*, the first, the Om. On it birds are dependent. Therefore birds fly about in the sky without support, holding themselves, for they share the *adi* (the Om) of that Saman.

What he is just at noon, that is the Udgitha. On it the Devas are dependent because they are brilliant. Therefore they are the best of all the descendants of Prajapati, for they share the Udgitha of that Saman.

What he is after midday and before afternoon, that is the Pratihara. On it all germs are dependent. Therefore these, having been conceived, Pratihrita, do not fall, for they share the Pratihara of that Saman.

What he is after the afternoon and before sunset, that is the Upadrava. On it the animals of the forest are dependent. Therefore, when they see a man, they run (*upadravanti*) to the forest as a safe hiding-place, for they share the *upadrava* of that Saman.

What he is when he first sets, that is the Nidhana. On it the fathers are dependent. Therefore they put them down (*nidadhati*), for they share the Nidhana of that Saman. Thus a man meditates on the sevenfold Saman as the sun.

•

Next let a man meditate on the sevenfold Saman which is uniform in itself and leads beyond death. the word Hinkara has three syllables, the word Prastava has three syllables: that is equal (Sama).

The word Adi (first, Om) has two syllables, the word Pratihara has four syllables. Taking one syllable from that over, that is equal.

The word Udgitha has three syllables, the word Upadrava has four syllables. With three and three syllables it should be equal. One syllable being left over, it becomes trisyllabic. Hence it is equal.

The word Nidhana has three syllables, therefore it is equal. These make twenty-two syllables.

With twenty-one syllables a man reaches the sun, and death, for the sun is the twenty-first from here; with the twenty-second he conquers what is beyond the sun: that is blessedness, that is freedom from grief.

He obtains here the victory over the sun (death), and there is a higher victory than the victory over the sun for him, who knowing this meditates on the sevenfold Saman as uniform in itself, which leads beyond death, yea, which leads beyond death.

•

The Hinkara is mind, the Prastava speech, the Udgitha sight, the Pratihara hearing, the Nidhana breath. That is the Gayatra Saman, as interwoven in the five Pranas.

He who thus knows this Gayatra interwoven in the Pranas, keeps his senses, reaches the full life, he lives long, becomes great with children and cattle, great by fame. The rule of him who thus meditates on the Gayatra is, 'Be not highminded.'

•

The Hinkara is, he rubs the fire-stick; the Prastava, smoke rises; the Udgitha, it burns; the Pratihara, there are glowing coals; the Nidhana, it goes down; the Nidhana, it is gone out. This is the Rathantara Saman as interwoven in fire.

He who thus knows this Rathantara interwoven in fire, becomes radiant and strong. He reaches the full life, he lives long, becomes great with children and cattle, great by fame. The rule is, 'Do not rinse the mouth or spit before the fire.'

•

Next follows the Vamadevya as interwoven in generation.

•

Rising, the sun is the Hinkara, risen, he is the Prastava,

at noon he is the Udgitha, in the afternoon he is Pratihara, setting, he is the Nidhana. That is the Brihat Saman as interwoven in the sun.

He who thus knows the Brihat as interwoven in the sun, becomes refulgent and strong, he reaches the full life, he lives long, becomes great with children and cattle, great by fame. His rule is, 'Never complain of the heat of the sun.'

•

The mists gather, that is the Hinkara; the cloud has risen, that is the Prastava; it rains, that is the Udgitha; it flashes and thunders, that is the Pratihara; it stops, that is the Nidhana. That is the Vairupa Saman, as interwoven in Parjanya, the god of rain.

He who thus knows the Vairupa as interwoven in Parjanya, obtains all kinds of cattle (Virupa), he reaches the full life, he lives long, becomes great with children and cattle, great by fame. His rule is, 'Never complain of the rain.'

•

The Hinkara is spring, the Prastava summer, the Udgitha the rainy season, the Pratihara autumn, the Nidhana winter. That is the Vairaja Saman, as interwoven in the seasons.

He who thus knows the Vairaja, as interwoven in the seasons, shines (*virajati*) through children, cattle, and glory of countenance. He reaches the full life, he lives long, becomes great with children and cattle, great by fame. His rule is, 'Never complain of the seasons.'

•

The Hinkara is the earth, the Prastava the sky, the Udgitha heaven, the Pratihara the regions, the Nidhana the sea. These are the Shakvari Samans, as interwoven in the worlds.

He who thus knows the Shakvaris, as interwoven in the worlds, becomes possessed of the worlds, he reaches the full life, he lives long, becomes great with children and cattle, great by fame. His rule is, 'Never complain of the worlds.'

•

The Hinkara is goats, the Prastava sheep, the Udgitha cows, the Pratihara horses, the Nidhana man. These are the Revati Samans, as interwoven in animals.

He who thus knows these Revatis, as interwoven in animals, becomes rich in animals, he reaches the full life, he lives long, becomes great with children and cattle, great by fame. His rule is, 'Never complain.'

•

The Hinkara is hair. the Prastava skin, the Udgitha flesh, the Pratihara bone, the Nidhana marrow. That is the Yajna-yagnia Saman, as interwoven in the members of the body.

He who thus knows the Yajnayajniya, as interwoven in the members of the body, becomes possessed of strong limbs, he is not crippled in any limb, he reaches the full life, he lives long, becomes great with children and cattle, great by fame. His rule is, ' Do not eat marrow for a year,' or ' Do not eat marrow at all.'

•

The Hinkara is fire, the Prastava air, the Udgitha the sun, the Pratihara the stars, the Nidhana the moon. That is the Rajana Saman, as interwoven in the deities.

He who thus knows the Rajana, as interwoven in the deities, obtains the same world, the same happiness, the same company as the gods, he reaches the full life, he lives long, becomes great with children and cattle, great by fame. His rule is, 'Do not speak evil of the Brahmins.'

•

The Hinkara is the threefold knowledge, the Prastava these three worlds: the Udgitha Agni (fire), Vayu (air), and Aditya (sun); the Pratihara the stars, the birds, and the rays; the Nidhana the serpents, Gandharvas, and fathers. That is the Saman, as interwoven in everything.

He who thus knows this Saman, as interwoven in everything, he becomes everything.

And thus it is said in the following verse: 'There are the fivefold three (the three kinds of sacrificial knowledge, the three worlds etc. in their fivefold form, i.e., as identified with the Hinkara, the Prastava, etc.), and the other forms of the Saman. Greater than these there is nothing else besides.'

He who knows this, knows everything. All regions offer him gifts. His rule is, 'Let him meditate on the Saman, knowing that he is everything, yea, that he is everything.'

•

The Udgitha, of which a poet said, I choose the deep sounding note of the Saman as good for cattle, belongs to Agni; the indefinite note belongs to Prajapati, the definite note to Soma, the soft and smooth note to Vayu, the smooth and strong note to Indra, the heron-like note to Brihaspati, the dull note to Varuna. Let a man cultivate all of these, avoiding, however, that of Varuna.

Let a man sing, wishing to obtain by his son immortality for the Devas. 'May I obtain by my song oblations (*svadha*) for the fathers, hope for men, fodder and water for animals, heaven for the sacrificer, food for myself,' thus reflecting on these in his mind, let a man, Udgatri priest, sing praises, without making mistakes in pronunciation, etc.

All vowels (*svara*) belong to Indra, all sibilants (*ushman*) to Prajapati, all consonants (*sparsha*) to Mrityu (death). If somebody should reprove him for his vowels, let him say, 'I went to Indra as my refuge (when pronouncing my vowels): he will answer thee.'

And if somebody should reprove him for his sibilants, let him say, 'I went to Prajapati as my refuge: he will smash thee.' And if somebody should reprove him for his consonants, let him say, 'I went to Mrityu as my refuge: he will reduce thee to ashes.'

All vowels are to be pronounced with voice (*ghosha*) and strength (*bala*), so that the Udgatri may give strength to Indra. All sibilants are to be pronounced, neither as if swallowed, nor as if thrown out, but well opened, so that the Udgatri may give himself to Prajapati. All consonants are to be pronounced slowly, and without crowding them together, so that the Udgatri may withdraw himself from Mrityu.

•

There are three branches of the law. Sacrifice, study, and charity are the first,

Austerity the second, and to dwell as Brahmacharin in the house of a tutor, always mortifying the body in the house of a tutor, is the third. All these obtain the worlds of the blessed; but the Brahmasamstha alone, he who is firmly grounded in Brahman, obtains immortality.

Prajapati brooded on the worlds. From them, thus brooded on, the threefold knowledge (sacrifice) issued forth. He brooded on it, and from it, thus brooded on, issued the three syllables, Bhuh, Bhuvah, Svah.

He brooked on them, and from them, thus brooded on, issued the Om. As all leaves are attached to a stalk, so is all speech attached to the Om (Brahma). Om is all this, yea, Om is all this.

•

The teachers of Brahman (Veda) declare, as the Pratah-savana (morning-oblation) belongs to the Vasus, the Madhyandina-savana (noon-libation) to the Rudras, the third Savana (evening-libation) to the Adityas and the Visve devas,

Where then is the world of the sacrificer? He who does not know this, how can he perform the sacrifice? He only who knows, should perform it.

Before the beginning of the Prataranuvaka (matin-chant), the sacrificer, sitting down behind the household altar and looking towards the north, sings the Saman, addressed to the Vasus:

'Open the door of the world, let us see thee, that we

may rule on earth.'

Then he sacrifices, saying: 'Adoration to Agni, who dwells on the earth, who dwells in the world! Obtain that world, for me, the sacrificer! That is the world for the sacrificer!'

'I the sacrificer shall go thither, when this life is over, Take this!' he says, in offering the libation. 'Cast back the bolt!' Having said this, he rises. For him the Vasus fulfil the morning oblation.

Before the beginning of the Madhyandina-savana, the noon-oblation, the sacrificer, sitting down behind the Agnidhriya altar, and looking towards the north, sings the Saman, addressed to the Rudras:

'Open the door of the world, the sky, let us see thee, that we may rule wide (in the sky).'

Then he sacrifices, saying: 'Adoration to Vayu (air), who dwells in the sky, who dwells in the world. Obtain that world for me, the sacrificer! That is the world for the sacrificer!'

'I the sacrificer shall go thither, when this life is over. Take this! Cast back the bolt!' Having said this, he rises. For him the Rudras fulfil the noon-oblation.

Before the beginning of the third oblation, the sacrificer, sitting down behind the Ahavaniya altar, and looking towards the north, sings the Saman, addressed to the Adityas and Visvedevas:

'Open the door of the world, the heaven, let us see thee, that we may rule supreme in heaven.' This is addressed to the Adityas.

Next the Saman addressed to the Visvedevas: 'Open the door of the world heaven, let us see thee, that we may rule supreme in heaven.'

Then he sacrifices, saying: 'Adoration to the Adityas and to the Visvedevas, who dwell in heaven, who dwell in the world. Obtain that world for me, the sacrificer!'

'That is the world for the sacrificer! I the sacrificer shall go thither, when this life is over. Take this! Cast back the bolt!' Having said this, he rises.

For him the Adityas and the Visvedevas fulfil the third oblation. He who knows this, knows the full measure of the sacrifice, yea, he knows it.

3

The sun is indeed the honey of the Devas. The heaven is the cross-beam from which the sky hangs as a hive, and the bright vapours are the eggs of the bees.

The eastern rays of the sun are the honeycells in front. The Rik verses are the bees, the Rigveda sacrifice is the flower, the water of the sacrificial libations is the nectar of the flower.

Those very Rik verses then as bees brooded over the Rigveda sacrifice the flower; and from it, thus brooded on, sprang as its essence, fame, glory of countenance, vigour, strength, and health.

That essence flowed forth and went towards the sun. And that forms what we call the red light of the rising sun.

•

The southern rays of the sun are the honeycells on the right. The Yajus verses are the bees, the Yajurveda sacrifice is the flower, the water of the sacrificial libations is the nectar of the flower.

Those very Yajus verses as bees brooded over the Yajurveda sacrifice the flower; and from it, thus brooded on, sprang as its essence, fame, glory of countenance, vigour, strength, and health.

That flowed forth and went towards the sun. And that forms what we call the white (Shukla) light of the sun.

•

The western rays of the sun are the honey-cells behind. The Saman verses are the bees, the Samaveda sacrifice is the flower, the water is the nectar.

Those very Saman verses as bees brooded over the Samaveda sacrifice; and from it, thus brooded on, sprang as its nectar essence, fame, glory of countenance, vigour, strength, and health.

That flowed forth and went towards the sun. And that forms what we call the dark (Krishna) light of the sun.

•

The northern rays of the sun are the honeycells on the left. The hymns of the Artharvangiras are the bees, the Itihasa-purana (the reading of the old stories) is the flower, the water is the nectar.

Those very hymns of the Atharvangiras as bees brooded over the Itihasa-purana; and from it, thus brooded on, sprang as its essence, fame, glory of countenance, vigour, strength, and health.

That flowed forth, and went towards the sun. And that forms what we call the extreme dark (*parah krishnam*) light of the sun.

•

The upward rays of the sun are the honeycells above. The secret doctrines are the bees, Brahman, the Om, is the flower, the water is the nectar.

Those secret doctrines as bees brooded over Brahman, the Om; and from it, thus brooded on, sprang as its essence, fame, glory of countenance, brightness, vigour, strength, and health.

That flowed forth, and went towards the sun. And that forms what seems to stir in the centre of the sun.

These different colours in the sun are the essences of the essences. For the Vedas are essences; and of them, after they have assumed the form of sacrifice these colours rising to the sun are again the essences. They are the nectar of the nectar. For the Vedas are nectar (immortal), and of them these are the nectar.

•

On the first of these nectars, the red light, which represents fame, glory of countenance, vigour, strength, health, the Vasus live, with Agni at their head. True, the Devas do not eat or drink, but they enjoy by seeing the nectar.

They enter into that red colour, and they rise from that colour.

He who thus knows this nectar, becomes one of the Vasus, with Agni at their head, he sees the nectar and rejoices. And he, having entered that colour, rises again from that colour.

So long as the sun rises in the east and sets in the west, so long does he follow the sovereign supremacy of the Vasus.

•

On the second of these nectars the Rudras live, with Indra at their head. True, the Devas do not eat or drink, but they enjoy by seeing the nectar.

They enter into that white colour, and they rise from that colour.

He who thus knows this nectar, becomes one of the Rudras, with Indra at their head, he sees the nectar and rejoices. And he, having entered that colour, rises again from that colour.

So long as the sun rises in the east and sets in the west, twice as long does it rise in the south and set in the north; and so long does he follow the sovereign supremacy of the Rudras.

•

On the third of these nectars the Adityas live, with Varuna at their head. True, the Devas do not eat or drink, but they enjoy by seeing the nectar.

They enter into that dark colour, and they rise from that colour.

He who thus knows this nectar, becomes one of the Adityas, with Varuna at their head, he sees the nectar and rejoices. And he, having entered that colour, rises again from that colour.

So long as the sun rises in the south and sets in the

north, twice as long does it rise in the west and set in the east; and so long does he follow the sovereign supremacy of the Adityas.

•

On the fourth of these nectars the Maruts live, with Soma at their head. True, the Devas do not eat or drink, but they enjoy by seeing the nectar.

They enter in that very dark colour, and they rise from that colour.

He who thus knows this nectar, becomes one of the Maruts, with Soma at their head, he sees the nectar and rejoices. And he, having entered that colour, rises again from that colour.

So long as the sun rises in the west and sets in the east, twice as long does it rise in the north and set in the south; and so long does he follow the sovereign supremacy of the Maruts.

•

On the fifth of these nectars the Sadhyas live, with Brahman at their head. True, the Devas do not eat or drink, but they enjoy by seeing the nectar.

They enter in that very dark colour, and they rise from that colour.

He who thus knows this nectar, becomes one of the Sadhyas, with Brahman at their head, he sees the nectar and rejoices. And he, having entered that colour, rises again from that colour.

So long as the sun rises in the north and sets in the south, twice as long does it rise above, and set below; and so long does he follow the sovereign supremacy of the Sadhyas.

•

When from thence he has risen upwards, he neither rises nor sets. He is alone, standing in the centre. And on this there is this verse:

'Yonder he neither rises nor sets at any time. If this is not true, ye gods, may I lose Brahman.'

And indeed to him who thus knows this Brahma Upanishad, the secret doctrine of the Veda, the sun does not rise and does not set. For him there is day, once and for all.

This doctrine Brahman (Hiranyagarbha) told to Prajapati (Viraj), Prajapati to Manu, Manu to his offspring (Ikshvaku, etc.) And the father told that doctrine of Brahman to Uddalaka Aruni.

A father may therefore tell that doctrine of Brahman to his eldest son, or to a worthy pupil.

But no one should tell it to anybody else, even if he gave him the whole sea-girt earth, full of treasure, for this doctrine is worth more than that, yea, it is worth more.

•

The Gayatri verse is everything whatsoever here exists. Gayatri indeed is speech, for speech sings forth (*gaya-ti*) and protects (*traya-te*) everything that here exists.

That Gayatri is also the earth, for everything that here exists rests on the earth, and does not go beyond.

That earth again is the body in man, for in it the vital airs (Pranas, which are everything) rest, and do not go beyond.

That body again in man is the heart within man, for in it the Pranas, which are everything, rest, and do not go beyond.

That Gayatri has four feet and is sixfold. And this is also declared by a Rik verse (Rigveda X, 90, 3):

'Such is the greatness of Brahman, under the disguise of Gayatri; greater than it is the Person (Purusha). His feet are all things. The immortal with three feet is in heaven, i.e., in himself.'

The Brahman which has been thus described, as immortal with three feet in heaven, and as Gayatri, is the same as the ether which is around us;

And the ether which is around us, is the same as the ether which is within us. And the ether which is within us;

That is the ether within the heart. That ether in the heart, as Brahman, is omnipresent and unchanging. He who knows this obtains omnipresent and unchangeable happiness.

•

For that heart there are five gates belonging to the Devas (the senses). The eastern gate is the Prana (upbreathing), that is the eye, that is Aditya the sun. Let a man meditate on that as brightness, glory of countenance, and health. He who knows this, becomes bright and health.

The southern gate is the Vyana (backbreathing), that is the ear, that is the moon. Let a man meditate on that as happiness and fame. He who knows this, becomes happy and famous.

The western gate is the Apana (downbreathing), that is speech, that is Agni (fire). Let a man meditate on that as glory of countenance and health. He who knows this, becomes glorious and healthy.

The northern gate is the Samana (inbreathing), that is mind, that is Parjanya (rain). Let a man meditate on that as celebrity and beauty. He who knows this, becomes celebrated and beautiful.

The upper gate is the Udana (outbreathing), that is air, that is ether. Let a man meditate on that as strength and greatness. He who knows this, becomes strong and great.

These are the five men of Brahman, the doorkeepers of the Svarga (heaven) world. He who knows these five men of Brahman, the doorkeepers of the Svarga world, in his family a strong son is born. He who thus knows these five men of Brahman, as the doorkeepers of the Svarga world, enters himself the Svarga world.

Now that light which shines above this heaven, higher than all, higher than everything, in the highest world, beyond which there are no other worlds, that is the same light which is within man. And of this we have this visible proof:

Namely, when we thus perceive by touch the warmth here in the body. And of it we have this audible proof: Namely, when we thus, after stopping our ears, listen to what is like the rolling of a carriage, or the bellowing of an ox, or the sound of a burning fire within the ears. Let a man meditate on this as the Brahman which is seen and heard. He who knows this, becomes conspicuous and celebrated, yea, he becomes celebrated.

•

All this is Brahman. Let a man meditate on that visible world as beginning, ending, and breathing in the Brahman.

Now man is a creature of will. According to what his will is in this world, so will he be when he has departed this life. Let him therefore have this will and belief:

The intelligent, whose body is spirit, whose form is light, whose thoughts are true, whose nature is like ether, omnipresent and invisible, from whom all works, all desires, all sweet odours and tastes proceed; he who embraces all this, who never speaks, and is never surprised,

He is my self within the heart, smaller than a corn of rice, smaller than a corn of barley, smaller than a mustard seed, smaller than a canary seed or the kernel of a canary seed. He also is my self within the heart, greater than the earth, greater than the sky, greater than heaven, greater than all these worlds.

He from whom all works, all desires, all sweet odours and tastes proceed, who embraces all this, who never speaks and who is never surprised, he, my self within the heart, is that Brahman. When I shall have departed from hence, I shall obtain that Self. He who has this faith has no doubt, thus said Shandilya, yea, thus he said.

•

The chest which has the sky for its circumference and

the earth for its bottom, does not decay, for the quarters are its sides, and heaven its lid above. That chest is a treasury, and all things are within it.

Its eastern quarter is called Juhu, its southern Sahamana, its western Rajni, its northern Subhuta. The child of those quarters is Vayu, the air, and he who knows that the air is indeed the child of the quarters, never weeps for his sons. 'I know the wind to be the child of the quarters, may I never weep for my sons.'

'I turn to the imperishable chest with such and such and such.' 'I turn to the Prana (life) with such and such and such.' 'I turn to the Bhuh with such and such and such.' 'I turn to Bhuvah with such and such and such.' 'I turn to Svah with such and such and such.'

'When I said, I turn to Prana, then Prana means all whatever exists here—to that I turn.'

'When I said, I turn to Bhuh, what I said is, I turn to the earth, the sky, and heaven.'

'When I said, I turn to Bhuvah, what I said is, I turn to Agni (fire), Vayu (air), Aditya (sun).'

'When I said, I turn to Svah, what I said is, I turn to the Rigveda, Yajurveda, and Samaveda, That is what I said, yea, that is what I said.'

•

Man is sacrifice. His first twenty-four years are morning-libation. The Gayatri has twenty-four syllables, the morning-libation is offered with Gayatri hymns. The Vasus are connected with that part of the sacrifice. The Pranas, the five senses, are the Vasus, for they make all this to abide.

If anything ails him in that early age, let him say: 'Ye Pranas, ye Vasus, extend this my morning-libation unto the midday-libation, that I, the sacrificer, may not perish in the midst of the Pranas or Vasus.' Thus he recovers from his illness, and becomes whole.

The next forty-four years are the midday-libation. The Trishtubh has forty-four syllables, the midday-libation is offered with Trishtubh hymns. The Rudras are connected with that part of it. The Pranas are the Rudras, for they make all this to cry.

If anythng ails him in that second age, let him say: 'Ye Pranas, ye Rudras, extend this my midday-libation unto the third libation, that I, the sacrificer, may not perish in the midst of the Pranas or Rudras.' Thus he recovers from his illness, and becomes whole.

The next forty-eight years are the third libation. The Jagati has forty-eight syllables, the third libation is offered with Jagati hymns. The Adityas are connected with that part of it. The Pranas are the Adityas, for they take up all this.

If anything ails him in that third age, let him say: 'Ye Pranas, ye Adityas, extend this my third libation unto the full age, that I, the sacrificer, may not perish in the midst of the Pranas or Adityas.' Thus he recovers from his illness, and becomes whole.

Mahidasa Aitareya, the son of Itara, who knew this, said addressing a disease: 'Why dost thou afflict me, as I shall not die by it?' He lived a hundred and sixteen years. He, too, who knows this lives on to a hundred and sixteen years.

•

When a man who is the sacrificer hungers, thirsts, and abstains from pleasures, that is the Diksha, initiatory rite.

When a man eats, drinks and enjoys pleasures, he does it with the Upasadas, the sacrificial days on which the sacrificer is allowed to partake of food.

When a man laughs, eats, and delights himself, he does it with the Stuta Shastras, hymns sung and recited at the sacrifices.

Penance, liberality, righteousness, kindness, truthfulness, these form his Dakshinas, gifts bestowed on priests, etc.

Therefore when they say, ' There will be a birth,' and 'there has been a birth' (words used at the Soma-scrifice, and really meaning. 'He will pour out the Soma-juice,' and 'he has poured out the Soma-juice'), that is his new birth. His death is the Avabhritha ceremony (when the sacrificial vessels are carried away to be cleansed).

Ghora Angirasa, after having communicated this view of the sacrifice to Krishna, the son of Devaki—and he never thirsted again after other knowledge—said: 'Let a man, when his end approaches, take refuge with this Triad: "Thou art the imperishable," "Thou art the unchangeable," "Thou art the edge of Prana." ' On this subject there are two Rik verses (Rigveda VIII, 6, 30):

Then they see within themselves the ever-present light of the old seed of the world, the Sat, the highest, which is lighted in the brilliant Brahman'. Rigveda I, 50, 10:

'Perceiving above the darkness of ignorance the higher light in the sun, as the higher light within the heart, the bright source of light and life among the gods, we have reached the highest light, yea, the highest light.'

•

Let a man meditate on mind as Brahman, this is said with reference to the body. Let a man meditate on the ether as Brahman, this is said with reference to the Devas. Thus both the meditation which has reference to the body, and the meditation which has reference to the Devas, has been taught.

That Brahman (mind) has four feet (quarters). Speech is one foot, breath is one foot, the eye is one foot, the ear is one foot—so much with reference to the body. Then with reference to the gods, Agni (fire) is one foot, Vayu (air) is one foot, Aditya (sun) is one foot, the quarters are one foot. Thus both the worship which has reference to the body, and the worship which has reference to the Devas, has been taught.

Speech is indeed the fourth foot of Brahman. That foot shines with Agni (fire) as its light, and warms. He who knows this, shines and warms through his celebrity, fame, and glory of countenance.

Breath is indeed the fourth foot of Brahman. That foot shines with Vayu (air) as its light, and warms. He who knows this, shines and warms through his celebrity, fame, and glory of countenance.

The eye is indeed the fourth foot of Brahman. That foot shines with Aditya (sun) as its light, and warms. He who knows this, shines and warms through his celebrity, fame and glory of countenance.

The ear is indeed the fourth foot of Brahman. That foot shines with the quarters as its light, and warms. He who knows this, shines and warms through his celebrity, fame, and glory of countenance.

•

Aditya (the sun) is Brahman, this is the doctrine, and this is the fuller account of it:

In the beginning this was non-existent. It became existent, it grew. It turned into an egg. The egg lay for the time of a year. The egg broke open. The two halves were one of silver, the other of gold.

The silver one became this earth, the golden one the sky, the thick membrane of the white the mountains, the thin membrane of the yoke the mist with the clouds, the small veins the rivers, the fluid the sea.

And what was born from it that was Aditya, the sun. When he was born shouts of hurrah arose, and all beings arose, and all things which they desired. Therefore whenever the sun rises and sets, shouts of hurrah arise, and all beings arise, and all things which they desire.

If any one knowing this meditates on the sun as Brahman, pleasant shouts will approach him and will continue, yea, they will continue.

4

There lived once upon a time Janasruti Pautrayana (the great-grandson of Janasruti), who was a pious giver, bestowing much wealth upon the people, and alway keeping open house. He built places of refuge everywhere, wishing that people should everywhere eat of his food.

One in the night some Hamsas (swans) flew over his house, and one Swan said to another: 'Hey, Bhallaksha, (short-sighted friend). The glory of Janasruti Pautrayana has spread like the sky. Do not go near, that it may not burn thee.'

The other answered him: ' How can you speak of him, being what he is (a rajanya, noble), as if he were like Raikva with the car?'

The first replied: 'How is it with this Raikva with the car of whom thou speakest?'

The other answered: 'As in a game of dice all the lower casts belong to him who has conquered with Krita cast, so whatever good deeds other people perform, belong to that Raikva. He who knows what he knows, he is thus spoken of by me.'

Janasruti Pautrayana overheard this conversation, and as soon as he had risen in the morning, he said to his door-keeper: 'Friend, dost thou speak of me, as if I were Raikva with the car (yolk-fellow)?'

He replied: ' How is it with this Raikva with the car?'

The king said: 'As in a game of dice, all the lower casts belong to him who has conquered with Krita cast, so whatever good deeds other people perform, belong to that Raikva. He who knows what he knows, he is thus spoken of by me.'

The doorkeeper went to look for Raikva, but returned saying, ' I found him not.' Then the king said: 'Alas! where a Brahmin should be searched for in the solitude of the forest, there go for him.'

The doorkeeper came to a man who was lying beneath a car and scratching his sores. He addressed him, and said: 'Sir, are you Raikva with the car?'

He answered: 'Here I am.'

Then the doorkeeper returned, and said: 'I have found him.'

•

Then Janasruti Pautrayana took six hundred cows, a necklace, and a carriage with mules, went to Raikva and said:

'Raikva, here are six hundred cows, a necklace, and a carriage with mules; teach me the deity which you worship.'

The other replied: 'Fie, necklace and carriage be thine, O Shudra, together with the cows.'

Then Janasruti Pautrayana took again a thousand cows, a necklace, a carriage with mules, and his own daughter, and went to him.

He said to him: 'Raikva, there area thousand cows, a necklace, a carriage with mules, this wife, and this village in which thou dwellest. Sir, teach me !'

He, opening her mouth, said: 'You have brought these cows and other presents, O Shudra, but only by that mouth did you make me speak.'

These are the Raikva-parna villages in the country of the Mahavrishas (Mahapunyas) where Raikva dwelt under him. And he said to him:

•

'Air (Vayu) is indeed the end of all. For when fire goes out, it goes into air. When the sun goes down it goes into air. When the moon goes down, it goes into air.

'When water dries up, it goes into air. Air indeed consumes them all. So much with reference to the Devas.

'Now with reference to the body. Breath (Prana) is indeed the end of all. When a man sleeps, speech goes into breath, so do sight, hearing, and mind. Breath indeed consumes them all.

'These are the two ends, air among the Devas, breath among the senses (Pranah).'

Once while Shaunaka Kapeya and Abhipratarin Kakshaseni were being waited on at their meal, a religious student begged of them. They gave him nothing.

He said: 'One god—who is he?—swallowed the four great ones, he, the guardian of the world. O Kapeya, mortals see him out, O Abhipratarin, though he dwells in many places. He to whom this food belongs, to him it has not been given.'

Shaunaka Kapeya, pondering on that speech, went to the student and said: 'He is the self of the Devas, the creator of all beings, with golden tusks, the eater, not without intelligence. His greatness is said to be great indeed, because, without being eaten, he eats even what is not food. Thus do we, O Brahmacharin, meditate on that Being.' Then he said: 'Give him food.'

They gave him food. Now these five (the eater Vayu (air), and his food, Agni (fire), Aditya (sun), Chandramas (moon), Ap (water) and the other five, the eater, Prana (breath), and his food (speech, sight, hearing, mind) make ten, and that is the Krita (the highest) cost (representing the ten, the eaters and the food). Therefore in all quarters those ten are food and Krita the highest cast. These are again the Viraj of ten syllables which eats the food. Through this all this becomes seen. He who knows this sees all this and becomes an eater of food, yea, he becomes an eater of food.

•

Satyakama, the son of Jabala, addressed his mother and said: 'I wish to become Brahmacharin (religious student), mother. Of what family am I?'

She said to him: 'I do not know, my child, of what family thou art. In my youth when I had to move about much as a servant waiting on the guests in my father's house, I conceived thee. I do not know of what family thou art. I am Jabala by name, thou art Satyakama. Say that thou art Satyakam Jabala.

He going to Gautama Haridrumata said to him, 'I wish to become a Brahmacharin with you, Sir. May I come to you, Sir?

He said to him: 'Of what family are you, my friend?' He replied: 'I do not know, Sir, of what family I am. I asked my mother, and she answered: "In my youth when I had to move about much as a servant, I conceived thee. I do not know of what family thou art. I am Jabala by name, thou art Satyakama," I am therefore Satyakama Jabala, Sir.'

He said to me: 'No one but a true Brahmin would thus speak out. Go and fetch fuel, friend, I shall initiate you. You have not swerved from the truth.'

Having initiated him, he chose four hundred lean and weak cows, and said: 'Tend these, friend.' He drove them out and said to himself, 'I shall not return unless I bring back a thousand.' He dwelt a number of years in the forest, and till the cows had become a thousand.

•

The bull of the herd meant for Vayu said to him: 'Satyakama!' He replied: 'Sir!' The bull said: 'We have become a thousand, lead us to the house of the teacher;

'And I will declare to you one foot of Brahman.' 'Declare it, Sir,' he replied.

He said to him: 'The eastern region is one quarter, the western region is one quarter, the southern region is one quarter, the northern region is one quarter. This is a foot of Brahman, consisting of the four quarters, and called Prakashavat, endowed with splendour.

'He who knows this and meditates on the foot of Brahman, consisting of four quarters, by the name of Prakashavat, becomes endowed with splendour in this world. He conquers the resplendent worlds, whoever knows this and meditates on the foot of Brahman, consisting of the four quarters, by the name of Prakashavat.

•

'Agni will declare to you another foot of Brahman.'

After these words of the bull, Satyakama, on the morrow, drove the cows towards the house of the teacher. And when they came towards the evening, he lighted a fire, penned the cows, laid wood on the fire, and sat down behind the fire, looking to the east.

Then Agni (the fire) said to him: 'Satyakama !' He replied: 'Sir.'

Agni said: 'Friend, I will declare unto you one foot of Brahman.'

'Declare it, Sir,' he replied.

He said to him: 'The earth is one quarter, the sky is one quarter, the heaven is one quarter, the ocean is one quarter. This is a foot of Brahman, consisting of four quarters, and called Anantavat (endless).

'He who knows this and meditates on the foot of Brahman, consisting of four quarters, by the name of Anantavat, becomes endless in the world. He conquers the endless worlds, whoever knows this and meditates on the foot of Brahman, consisting of four quarters, by the name of Anantavat.

•

'A Hamsa (swan, meant for the sun) will declare to you another foot of Brahman.'

After these words of Agni, Satyakama, on the morrow, drove the cows onward. And when they came towards the evening, he lighted a fire, penned the cows, laid wood on the fire, and sat down behind the fire, looking toward the east.

Then a Hamsa flew near and said to him: 'Satyakama.' He replied: 'Sir.'

The Hamsa said: ' Friend, I will declare unto you one foot of Brahman.'

'Declare it, Sir,' he replied.

He said to him: ' Fire is one quarter, the sun is one quarter, the moon is one quarter, lightning is one quarter. This is a foot of Brahman, consisting of four quarters, and called Jyotishmat, full of light.

'He who knows this and meditates on the foot of Brahman, consisting of four quarters, by the name of Jyotishmat, becomes full of light in this world. He conquers the worlds which are full of light, whoever knows this and meditates on the foot of Brahman, consisting of four quarters, by the name of Jyotishmat.

•

'A diver-bird (Madgu, meant for Prana) will declare to you another foot of Brahman.'

After these words of the Hamsa, Satyakama, on the morrow, drove the cows onward. And when they came towards the evening, he lighted a fire, penned the cows, laid wood on the fire, and sat down behind the fire, looking toward the east.

Then a diver flew near and said to him: 'Satyakama.' He replied: 'Sir.'

The diver said: 'Friend, I will declare unto you one foot of Brahman.'

'Declare it, Sir,' he replied.

He said to him: 'Breath is one quarter, the eye is one quarter, the ear is one quarter, the mind is one quarter. This is a foot of Brahman, consisting of four quarters, and called Ayatanavat, having a home.

'He who knows this and meditates on the foot of Brahman, consisting of four quarters, by the name of Ayatanavat, becomes possessed of a home in this world. He conquers the worlds which offer a home, whoever knows this and meditates on the foot of Brahman, consisting of four quarters, by the name of Ayatanavat.'

•

Thus he reached the house of his teacher. The teacher said to him: 'Satyakama.' He replied: 'Sir.'

The teacher said: 'Friend, you shine like one who knows Brahman. Who then has taught you?' He replied: 'Not men. But you only, Sir, I wish, should teach me;

'For I have heard from men like you, Sir, that only knowledge which is learnt from a teacher leads to real good.'

Then he taught him the same knowledge. Nothing was left out, yea, nothing was left out.

•

Upakoshala Kamalayana dwelt as Brahmacharin (religious student) in the house of Satyakama Jabala. He tended his fires for twelve years. But the teacher, though he allowed other pupils after they had learnt the sacred books to depart to their own homes, did not allow Upakoshala to depart.

Then his wife said to him: 'This student, who is quite exhausted with austerities, has carefully tended your fires. Let not the fires themselves blame you, but teach him.' The teacher, however, went away on a journey without having taught him.

The student from sorrow was not able to eat. Then the wife of the teacher said to him: 'Student, eat! Why do you not eat?' He said: 'There are many desires in this man here, which lose themselves in different directions. I am full of sorrows, and shall take no food.'

There upon the fires said among themselves: 'This student, who is quite exhausted, has carefuly tended us. Well, let us teach him.' They said to him:

'Breath is Brahman, Ka (pleasure) is Brahman, Kha (ether) is Brahman.'

He said: 'I understand that breath is Brahman, but I do not understand Ka or Kha.'

They said: 'What is Ka is Kha, what is Kha is Ka.' They therefore taught him Brahman as breath, and as the ether in the heart.

•

After that the Garhapatya fire taught him: 'Earth, fire food, and the sun are my forms, or forms of Brahman. The person that is seen in the sun, I am he, I am he indeed.

'He who knowing this meditates on him, destroys sin, obtains the world of Agni Garhapatya, reches his full age, and lives long; his descendants do not perish. We guard him in this world and in the other, whosoever knowing this meditates on him.'

•

Then the Anvaharya fire taught him: 'Water, the quarters, the stars, the moon these are my forms. The person that is seen in the moon, I am he, I am he indeed.

'He who knowing this meditates on him, destroys sin, obtains the world of Agni Anvaharya, reaches his full age, and lives long; his descendants do not perish. We guard him in this world and in the other, whosoever knowing this meditates on him.'

•

Then the Ahavaniya fire taught him: 'Breath, ether, heaven, and lightning are my forms. The person that is seen in the lightning, I am he, I am he indeed.

'He who knowing this meditates on him, destroys sin, obtains the world of Agni Ahavaniya, reaches his full age, and lives long; his descendants do not perish. We guard him in this world and in the other, whosoever knowing this meditates on him.'

•

Then they all said: 'Upakoshala, this is our knowledge, our friend, and the knowledge of the Self, but the teacher will tell you the way to another life.'

In time his teacher came back, and said to him: 'Upakoshala.' He answered: 'Sir.' The teacher said: 'Friend, your face shines like that of one who knows Brahman. Who has taught you?'

'Who should teach me, Sir?' he said. He denies, as it were. And he said pointing to the fires: ' Are these fires other than fires?'

The teacher said: 'What, my friend, have these fires told you?'

He answered: 'This' (repeating some of what they had

told him).

The teacher said: 'My friend, they have taught you about the worlds, but I shall tell you this; and as water does not cling to a lotus leaf, so no evil deed clings to one who knows it.' He said: 'Sir, tell it me.'

•

He said: 'The person that is seen in the eye, that is the Self. This is the immortal, the fearless, this is Brahman. Even though they drop melted butter or water on him, it runs away on both sides.

'They call him Samyadvama, for all blessings (*vama*) go towards him (*samyanti*). All blessings go towards him who knows this.

'He is also Vamani, for he leads (*nayati*) all blessings (*vama*). He leads all blessings who knows this.

'He is also Bhamani, for he shines (*bhati*) in all worlds. He who knows this, shines in all worlds.

'Now if one who knows this, dies, whether people perform obsequies for him or no, he goes to light, from light to day, from day to the light half of the moon, from the light half of the moon to the six months during which the sun goes to the north, from the months to the year, from the year to the sun, from the sun to the moon, from the moon to the lightning. There is a person not human,

'He leads them to Brahman. This is the path of the Devas, the path that leads to Brahman. Those who proceed on that path, do not return to the life of man, yea, they do not return.'

•

Verily, he who purifies (Vayu) is the sacrifice, for he (the air) moving along, purifies everything. Because moving along he purifies everything, therefore he is the sacrifice. Of that sacrifice there are two ways, by mind and by speech.

The Brahman priest performs one of them in his mind. The Hotri, Adhvaryu, and Udgatri priests perform the other by words. When the Brahman priest, after the Prataranuvaka ceremony has begun, but before the recitation of the Paridhaniya hymn, has to break his silence and speak.

He performs perfectly the one way only (that by words), but the other is injured. As a man walking on one foot, or a carriage going on one wheel, is injured, his sacrifice is injured, and with the injured sacrifice the sacrificer is injured; yes, having sacrificed, he becomes worse.

But when after the Prataranuvaka ceremony has begun, and before the recitation of the Paridhaniya hymn, the Brahman priest has not, to break his silence and to speak, they perform both ways perfectly, and neither of them is injured.

As a man walking on two legs and a carriage going on two wheels gets on, so his sacrifice gets on, and with the successful sacrifice the sacrificer gets on; yes, having sacrificed, he becomes better.

•

Prajapati brooded over the worlds, and from them thus brooded on he squeezed out the essences, Agni (fire) from the earth, Vayu (air) from the sky, Aditya (sun) from heaven.

He brooded over these three deities, and from them thus brooded on he squeezed out the essences, the Rik verses from Agni, the Yajus verses from Vayu, the Saman verses from Aditya.

He brooded over the threefold knowledge, the three Vedas, and from it thus brooded on the squeezed out the essences, the sacred interjection Bhus from the Rik verses, the sacred interjection Bhuvas from the Yajus verses, the sacred interjection Svar from the Saman verses.

If the sacrifice is injured from the Rigveda side, let him offer a libation in the Garhapatya fire, saying, Bhuh, Svaha! Thus does he bind together and heal, by means of the essence and the power of the Rik verses themselves, whatever break the Rik sacrifice may have suffered.

If the sacrifice is injured from the Yajurveda side, let him offer a libation in the Dakshina fire, saying, Bhuvah,

Svaha! Thus does he bind together and heal, by means of the essence and the power of the Yajus verses themselves, whatever break the Yajus sacrifice may have suffered.

If the sacrifice is injured by the Samaveda side, let him offer a libation in the Ahavaniya fire, saying, Svah, Svaha! Thus does he bind together and heal, by means of the essence and the power of the Saman verses themselves, whatever break the Saman sacrifice may have suffered.

As one binds, softens, gold by means of lavana, and silver by means of gold, and tin by means of silver, and lead by means of tin, and iron loha by means of lead, and wood by means of iron, or also by means of leather.

Thus does one bind together and heal any break in the sacrifice by means of the Vyahritis or sacrificial injerjections which are the essence and strength of the three worlds, of the deities, and of the threefold knowledge. That sacrifice is healed in which there is a Brahman priest who knows this.

That sacrifice is inclined towards the north in the right way in which there is a Brahman priest who knows this. And with regard to such a Brahman priest there is the following Gatha: 'Wherever it falls back, thither the man goes.'—viz. the Brahmin only, as one of the Ritvij priests. 'He saves the Kurus as a mare,' viz., a Brahmin priest who knows this, saves the sacrifice, the sacrificer, and all the other priests. Therefore let a man make him who knows this his Brahmin priest, not one who does not know it; who does not know it.

5

He who knows the oldest and the best becomes himself the oldest and the best. Breath indeed is the oldest and the best.

He who knows the richest, becomes himself the richest. Speech indeed is the richest.

He who knows the firm rest, becomes himself firm in

this world and in the next. The eye indeed is the first rest.

He who knows success, his wishes succeed, both his divine and human wishes. The ear indeed is success.

He who knows the home, becomes a home of his people. The mind indeed is the home.

The five senses quarrelled together, who was the best, saying, I am better, I am better.

They went to their father Prajapati and said: 'Sir, who is the best of us?' He replied: 'He by whose departure the body seems worse than worst, he is the best of you.'

The speech departed, and having been absent for a year, it came round and said: 'How have you been able to live without me?' They replied: 'Like mute people, not speaking, but breathing with the breath, seeing with the eye, hearing with the ear, thinking with the mind. Thus we lived.' Then speech went back.

The eye (sight) departed, and having been absent for a year, it came round and said: 'How have you been able to live without me?' They replied: 'Like blind people, not seeing, but breathing with the breath, speaking with the tongue, hearing with the ear, thinking with the mind. Thus we lived.' Then the eye went back.

The ear (hearing) departed, and having been absent for a year, it came round and said: 'How have you been able to live without me?' They replied: 'Like deaf people, not hearing, but breathing with the breath, speaking with the tongue, thinking with the mind. Thus we lived.' Then the ear went back.

The mind departed, and having been absent for a year, it came round and said: 'How have you been able to live without me?' They replied: 'Like children whose mind is not yet formed, but breathing with the breath, speaking with the tongue, seeing with the eye, hearing with the ear. Thus we lived.' Then the mind went back.

The breath, when on the point of departing, tore up the other senses, as a horse, going to start, might tear up the pegs to which he is tethered. They came to him and said: 'Sir, be thou our lord; thou art the best among us. Do not depart from us !'

Then the tongue said to him: 'If I am the richest, thou art the richest.' The eye said to him: 'If I am the firm rest, thou art the firm rest.'

The ear said to him: 'If I am success, thou art success.' The mind said to him: 'If I am the home, thou art the home.'

And people do not call them, the tongues, the eyes, the ears, the minds, but the breaths (Prana, the senses). For breath are all these.

•

Breath said: 'What shall be my food?' They answered: 'Whatever there is, even unto dogs and birds.' Therefore this is food for Ana (the breather). His name is clearly Ana. To him who knows this there is nothing that is not proper food.

He said: 'What shall be my dress?' They answered: 'Water.' Therefore wise people, when they are going to eat food, surround their food before and after with water.' He (Prana) thus gains a dress, and is no longer naked.

Satyakama Jabala, after he had communicated this to Goshruti Vaiyaghrapadya, said to him: 'If you were to tell this to a dry stick, branches would grow, and leaves spring from it.'

If a man wishes to reach greatness, let him perform the Diksha, preparatory rite, on the day of the new moon, and then, on the night of the full moon, let him stir a mash of all kinds of herbs with curds and honey, and let him pour ghee on the fire, saying, 'Svaha to the oldest and the best.' After that let him throw all that remains of the ghee into the mash.

In the same manner let him pour ghee on the fire, saying, 'Svaha to the richest.' After that let him throw all that remains together into the mash.

In the same manner let him pour ghee on the fire, saying, 'Svaha to the firm rest.' After that let him throw all that remains together into the mash.

In the same manner let him pour ghee on the fire, saying, 'Sivaha to success.' After that let him throw all that remains together into the mash.

Then going forward and placing the mash in his hands, he recites: 'Thou (Prana) art Ama by name, for all this together exists in thee. He is the oldest and best, the king, the sovereign. May he make me the oldest, the best, the king, the sovereign. May I be all this.'

Then he eats with the following Rik verse at every foot: 'We choose that food'—here he swallows - 'Of the divine Savitri (Prana)'—here he swallows—'The best and all-supporting food'—here he swallows—'We meditate on the speed of Bhaga (Savitri, Prana)'—here the drinks all.

Having cleansed the vessel, whether it be a Kamsa or a Kamasa, he sits down behind the fire on a skin or on the bare ground, without speaking or making any other effort. If in his dream he sees a woman, let him know this to be a sign that his sacrifice has succeeded.

On this there is a Shloka: 'If during sacrifices which are to fulfil certain wishes he sees in his dreams a woman, let him know success from this vision in a dream, yea, from this vision in a dream.'

•

Shvetaketu Aruneya went to an assembly of the Panchalas. Pravahana Jaivali said to him: 'Boy, has your father instructed you?' 'Yes, Sir,' he replied.

'Do you know to what place men go from here?' 'No, Sir,' he replied.

'Do you know how they return again?' 'No Sir,' he replied.

'Do you know where the path of Devas and the path of the fathers diverge?' 'No, Sir,' he replied.

'Do you know why that world never becomes full?' 'No, Sir,' he replied.

'Do you know why in the fifth libation water is called Man?' 'No, Sir,' he replied.

'Then why did you say you had been instructed? How could anybody who did not know these things say that he had been instructed?' Then the boy went back sorrowful to the place of his father, and said: 'Though you had not instructed me, Sir, you said you had instructed me.

'That fellow of a Rajanya asked me five questions, and I could not answer one of them.' The father said: 'As you have told me these questions of his, I do not know any one of them. If I knew these questions, how should I not have told you?'

Then Gautama went to the king's place, and when he had come to him, the king offered him proper respect. In the morning the king went out on his way to the assembly. The king said to him: 'Sir, Gautama, ask a boon of such things as men possess.' He replied: 'Such things as men possess may remain with you. Tell me the speech which you addressed to the boy.'

The king was perplexed, and commanded him, saying: 'Stay with me some time.' Then he said: 'As to what you have said to me, Gautama, this knowledge did not go to any Brahmin before you, and therefore this teaching belonged in all the worlds to the Kshatriya class alone. Then he began:

•

'The altar on which the sacrifice is supposed to be offered is that world, heaven, O Gautama; its fuel is the sun itself, the smoke his rays, the light the day, the coals the moon, the sparks the stars.

'On that altar the Devas or Pranas represented by Agni, etc., offer the Shraddha libation consisting of water. From that oblation rises Soma, the king, the moon.

•

'The altar is Parjanya, the god of rain, O Gautama; its fuel is the air itself, the smoke the cloud, the light the lighting, the coals the thunderbolt, the sparks the thunderings.

'On that altar the Devas offer Soma, the king, the moon.

From that oblation rises rain.

•

'The altar is the earth, O Gautama; its fuel is the year itself, the smoke the ether, the light the night, the coals the quarters, the sparks the intermediate quarters.

'On that altar the Devas. Prana, offer rain. From that oblation rises food.

•

'The altar is man, O Gautama; its fuel speech itself, the smoke the breath, the light the tongue, the coals the eye, the sparks the ear.

'On that altar the Devas, Prana, offer food. From that oblation rises seed.

•

'The altar is woman, O Gautama.

'On that altar the Devas, Prana, offer seed. From that oblation rises the germ.

•

'For this reason is water in the fifth oblation called Man. This germ, covered in the womb, having dwelt there ten months, or more or less is born.

'When born, he lives whatever the length of his life may be. When he has departed, his friends carry him, as appointed, to the fire of the funeral pile from whence he came, from whence he sprang.

'Those who know this, even though they still be Grihasthas, householders, and those who in the forest follow faith and austerities, the Vanaprasthas, and of the Parivrajakas, those who do not yet know the Highest Brahman go to light, from light to day, from day to the light half of the moon, from the light half of the moon to the six months when the sun goes to the north, from the six months when the sun goes to the north to the year, from the year to the sun, from the sun to the moon, from the moon the lightning. There is a person not human,

'He leads them to the conditioned Brahman. This is the path of the Devas.

'But they who living in a village practice a life of sacrifices, works of public utility, and alms, they go to the smoke, from smoke to night, from night to the dark half of the moon, from the dark half of the moon to the six months when the sun goes to the south. But they do not reach the year.

'From the months they go to the world of the fathers, from the world of the fathers to the ether, from the ether to the moon. That is Soma, the king. Here they are eaten by the Devas, yes, the Devas eat them.

'Having dwelt there, till their good works are consumed, they return again that way as they came, to the ether, from the ether to the air. Then the sacrificer, having become air, becomes smoke, having become smoke, he becomes mist.

'Having become mist, he becomes a cloud, having become a cloud, he rains down. Then he is born as rice and corn, herbs and trees, sesamum and beans. From thence the escape is beset with most difficulties. For whoever the persons may be that eat the food, and beget offspring, he henceforth becomes like unto them.

'Those whose conduct has been good, will quickly attain some good birth, the birth of a Brahmin, or a Kshatriya, or a Vaishya. But those whose conduct has been evil, will quicky attain an evil birth, the birth of a dog, or a hog, or a Chandala.

'On neither of these two ways those small creatures, flies, worms, etc., are continually returning of whom it may be said, Live and die. Theirs is a third place.

'Therefore that would never become full.

'Hence let a man take care to himself! And thus it is said in the following Shloka:

'A man who steals gold, who drinks spirits, who dishonours his Guru's bed, who kills a Brahmin, these four fall, and as fifth he who associates with them.

'But he who thus knows the five fires is not defiled by sin even though he associates with them. He who knows this, is pure, clean, and obtains the world of the blessed, yea, he obtains the world of the blessed.'

•

Prachinashala Aupamanyava, Satyayajna Paulushi, Indradyumna Bhallaveya, Jana Sharkarakshya, and Budila Ashvatarashvi, these five great householders and great theologians came once together and held a discussion as to What is our Self, and what is Brahman.

They reflected and said: 'Sirs, there is that Uddalaka Aruni, who knows at present that Self, called Vaishvanara. Well, let us go to him,' They went to him.

But he reflected: 'Those great householders and great theologians will examine me, and I shall not be able to tell them all; therefore I shall recommend another teacher to them.'

He said to them: 'Sirs, Ashvapati Kaikeya knows at present that Self, caled Vaishvanara. Well, let us go to him.' They went to him.

When they arrived the king ordered proper presents to be made separately to each of them. And rising the next morning he said: 'In my kingdom there is no thief, no miser, no drunkard, no man without an altar in his house, no ignorant person, no adulterer, much less an adulteress. I am going to perform a sacrifice, Sirs, and as much wealth as I give each Ritvij priest, I shall give to you, Sirs. Please stay here.'

They replied: 'Every man ought to say for what purpose he comes. You know at present that Vaishvanara Self, tell us that.'

He said: 'Tomorrow I shall give you an answer.' Therefore on the next morning they approached him, carrying fuel in their hands like students, and he, without first demanding any preparatory rites, said to them :

•

'Aupamanyava, whom do you meditate on as the Self?' He replied: 'Heaven only, venerable king.' He said: 'The Self which you meditate on is the Vaishvanara Self, called Sutejas, having good light. Therefore every king of Soma libation is seen in your house.

'You eat food, and see your desire, a son, etc., and whoever thus meditates on that Vaishvanara Self, eats food, sees his desire, and has Vedic glory, arising from study and sacrifice in his house. That, however, is but the head of the Self, and thus your head would have fallen in a discussion, if you had not come to me.'

•

Then he said to Satyayajna Paulushi: 'O Prachinayogya, whom do you meditate on as the Self?' He replied: 'The sun only, venerable king.' He said: 'The Self which you meditate on is the Vaishvanara Self, called Vishvarupa multiform. Therefore much and manifold wealth is seen in your house.

'There is a car with mules, full of slaves and jewels. You eat food and see your desire, and whoever thus meditates on that Vaishvanara Self, eats food and sees his desire, and has Vedic glory in his house.

'That, however, is but the eye of the Self, and you would have become blind, if you had not come to me.'

•

Then he said to Indradyumna Bhallaveya: 'O Vaiyaghrapadya, whom do you meditate on as the Self?' He replied: 'Air only, venerable king.' He said: 'The Self which you meditate on is the Vaishvanara Self, called Prithagvartman, having various courses. Therefore offerings come to you in various ways, and rows of cars follow you in various ways.

'You eat food and see your desire, and whoever thus meditates on that Vaishvanara Self, eats food and sees his desire, and has Vedic glory in his house.

'That, however, is but the breath of the Self, and your breath would have left you, if you had not come to me.'

•

Then he said to Jana Sharkarakshya: 'Whom do you meditate on as the Self?' He replied: 'Ether only, venerable king.' He said: 'The Self which you meditate on is the Vaishvanara Self, called Bahula, full. Therefore you are full of offspring and wealth.

'You eat food and see your desire, and whoever thus meditates on that Vaishvanara Self, eats food and sees his desire, and has Vedic glory in his house.

'That, however, is but the trunk of the Self, and your trunk would have perished, if you had not come to me.'

•

Then he said to Budila Ashvatarashvi, 'O Vaiyaghrapadya, whom do you meditate on as the Self?' He replied: 'Water only, venerable king.' He said: 'The Self which you meditate on is the Vaishvanara Self, called Rayi, wealth. Therefore are you wealthy and flourishing.

'You eat food and see you desire, and whoever thus meditates on that Vaishvanara Self, eats food and sees his desire, and has Vedic glory in his house.

'That, however, is but the bladder of the Self, and your bladder would have burst, if you had not come to me.'

•

Then he said to Auddalaka Aruni: 'O Gautama, whom do you meditate on as the Self?' He replied: 'The earth only, venerable king.' He said: 'The Self which you meditate on is the Vaishvanara Self, called Pratishtha, firm rest. Therefore you stand firm with offspring and cattle.

'You eat food and see your desire, and whoever thus meditates on that Vaishvanara Self, eats food and sees his desire, and has Vedic glory in his house.

'That, however, are but the feet of the Self, and your feet would have given way, if you had not come to me.'

•

Then he said to them all: 'You eat your food, knowing that Vaishvanara Self as if it were many. But he who worships the Vaishvanara Self as a span long, and as identical with himself, he eats food in all worlds, in all beings, in all Selfs.

'Of that Vaishvanara Self the head is Sutejas, having good light, the eye Vishvarupa, multiform, the breath Prithagvartman, having various courses, the trunk Bahula, full, the bladder Rayi wealth, the feet the earth, the chest the altar, the hairs the grass on the altar, the heart the Garhapatya fire, the mind the Anvaharya fire, the mouth the Ahavaniya fire.

•

'Therefore the first food which a man may take, is in the place of Homa. And he who offers that first oblation, should offer it to Prana (upbreahthing), saying Svaha. Then Prana is satisfied.

'If Prana is satisfied, the eye is satisfied, if the eye is satisfied, the sun is satisfied, if the sun is satisfied, heaven is satisfied, if heaven is satisfied, whatever is under heaven and under the sun is satisfied. And through their satisfaction he the sacrificer or eater, himself is satisfied with offspring, cattle, health, brightness, and Vedic splendour.

•

'And he who offers the second oblation, should offer it to Vyana (backbreathing), saying Svaha. Then Vyana is satisfied.

'If Vyana is satisfied, the ear is satisfied, if the ear is satisfied, the moon is satisfied, if the moon is satisfied, the quarters are satisfied, if the quarters are satisfied, whatever is under the quarters and under the moon is satisfied. And through their satisfaction he, the sacrificer or eater, himself is satisfied with offspring, cattle, health, brightness, and Vedic splendour.

•

'And he who offers the third oblation, should offer it to Apana (downbreathing), saying Svaha. Then Apana is satisfied. If Apana is satisfied, the tongue is satisfied, if the tongue is satisfied, Agni (fire) is satisfied, if Agni is satisfied, the earth is satisfied, if the earth is satisfied, whatever is under the earth and under fire is satisfied.

'And through their satisfaction he, the sacrificer or eater, himself is satisfied with offspring, cattle, health, brightness, and Vedic splendour.

•

'And he who offers the fourth oblation, should offer it to Samana (onbreathing), saying Svaha. Then Samana is satisfied.

'If Samana is satisfied, the mind is satisfied, if the mind is satisfied, Parjanya, god of rain, is satisfied, if Parjanya is satisfied, lightning is satisfied, if lightning is satisfied, whatever is under Parjanya and under lightning is satisfied. And through their satisfaction he the sacrificer or eater himself is satisfied with offspring, cattle, health, brightness, and Vedic splendour.

•

'And he who offers the fifth oblation, should offer it to Udana (outbreathing), saying Svaha. Then Udana is satisfied.

'If Udana is satisfied, Vayu (air) is satisfied, if Vayu is satisfied, ether is satisfied, if ether is satisfied, whatever is under Vayu and under the ether is satisfied. And through their satisfaction he, the sacrificer or eater himself, is satisfied with offspring, cattle, health, brightness, and Vedic splendour.

•

'If, without knowing this, one offers an Agnihotra, it would be as if a man were to remove the live coals and pour his libation on dead ashes.

'But he who offers this Agnihotra with a full knowledge of its true purport, he offers it, i.e., he eats food in all worlds, in all beings, in all Selfs.

'As the soft fibres of the Ishika reed, when thrown into the fire, are burnt, thus all his sins are burnt whoever offers this Agnihotra with a full knowledge of its true purport.

'Even if he gives what is left his food to a Chandala, it would be offered in his (the Chandala's) Vaishvanara Self. And so it is said in this Shloka:

'As hungry children here on earth sit expectantly round their mother, so do all beings sit round the Agnihotra, yea, round the Agnihotra.'

6

Harih, Om. There lived once Shvetaketu Aruneya, the grandson of Aruna. To him his father, Uddalaka, the son of Aruna, said: 'Shvetaketu, go to school; for there is none belonging to our race, darling, who, not having studied the Veda, is, as it were, a Brahmin by birth only.'

Having begun his apprenticeship with a teacher when he was twelve years of age, Shvetaketu returned to his father, when he was twenty-four, having then studied all the Vedas, - conceited, considering himself well-read, and stern.

His father said to him: 'Shvetaketu, as you are so conceited, considering yourself so well-read, and so stern, my dear, have you ever asked for that instruction by which we hear what cannot be heard, by which we perceive what cannot be perceived, by which we know what cannot be known?'

'What is that instruction, Sir?' he asked.

The father replied: 'My dear, as by one clod of clay all that is made of clay is known, the difference being only a name, arising from speech, but the truth being that all is clay.

'And as, my dear, by one nugget of gold all that is made of gold is known, the difference being only a name, arising from speech, but the truth being that all is gold?

'And as, my dear, by one pair of nail-scissors all that is made of iron is known, the difference being only a name, arising from speech, but the truth being that all is iron,—thus, my dear, is that instruction.'

The son said: 'Surely those venerable men, my teachers did not know that. For if they had known it, why should they not have told it me? Do you, Sir, therefore tell me that.' 'Be it so,' said the father.

•

'In the beginning,' my dear, 'there was that only which is, one only, without a second. Others say, in the beginning there was that only which is not, one only, without a second; and from that which is not, that which is was born.

'But how could it be thus, my dear?' the father continued. 'How could that which is, be born of that which is not? No, my dear, only that which is, was in the beginning, one only, without a second.

'It thought, may I be many, may I grow forth. It sent forth fire.

'That fire thought, may I be many, may I grow forth. It sent forth water.

'And therefore whenever anybody anywhere is hot and perspires, water is produced on him from fire alone.

'Water thought, may I be many, may I grow forth. It sent forth food.

'Therefore whenever it rains anywhere, most food is then produced. From water alone is eatable food produced.

•

'Of all living things there are indeed three origins only, that which springs from an egg, that which springs from living being, and that which springs from a germ.

'That Being, i.e., that which had produced fire, water,

and earth, thought, let me now enter those three beings, fire, water, earth, with this living Self (Jivatma), and let me then develop names and forms.

'Then that Being having said, Let me make each of these three tripartite, so that fire, water, and earth should each have itself for its principal ingredient, besides an admixture of the other two, entered into those three beings (devata) with this living self only, and revealed names and forms.

'He made each of these tripartite; and how these three beings become each of them tripartite, that learn from me now, my friend!

•

'The red colour of burning fire (Agni) is the colour of fire, the white colour of fire is the colour of water, the black colour of fire is the colour of earth. Thus vanishes what we call fire, as a mere variety, being a name, arising from speech. What is true are the three colours or forms.

'The red colour of the sun (Aditya) is the colour of fire, the white of water, the black of earth. Thus vanishes what we call the sun, as a mere variety, being a name, arising from speech. What is true are the three colours.

'The red colour of the moon is the colour of fire, the white of water, the black of earth. Thus vanishes what we call the moon, as a mere variety, being a name, arising from speech. What is true are the three colours.

'The red colour of the lightning is the colour of fire, the white of water, the black of earth. Thus vanishes what we call the lightning, as a mere variety, being a name, arising from speech. What is true are the three colours.

'Great householders and great theologians of olden times who knew this, have declared the same, saying, "No one can henceforth mention to us anything which we have not heard, perceived, or known." Out of these three colours or forms they knew all.

'Whatever they thought looked red, they knew was the colour of fire. Whatever they thought looked white, they knew was the colour of water. whatever they thought looked black, they knew was the colour of earth.

'Whatever they thought was altogether unknown, they knew was some combination of those three beings (devata).

'Now learn from me, my friend, how those three beings, when they reach man, become each of them tripartite.

•

'The food when eaten becomes threefold; its grossest portion becomes faeces, its middle portion flesh, its subtilest portion mind.

'Water when drunk becomes threefold; its grossest portion becomes water, its middle portion blood, its subtlest portion breath.

'Fire, i.e., in oil, butter, etc., when eaten becomes threehold; its grossest portion becomes bone, its middle portion marrow, its subtlest portion speech.

'For truly, my child, mind comes of earth, breath of water, speech of fire.'

'Please, Sir, inform me still more,' said the son.

'Be it so, my child,' the father replied.

•

'That which is the subtle portion of curds, when churned, rises upwards, and becomes butter.

'In the same manner, my child, the subtile portion of food, when eaten, rises upwards, and becomes mind.

'That which is the subtle portion of water, when drunk, rises upwards, and becomes breath.

'That which is the subtle portion of fire, when consumed, rises upwards, and becomes speech.

'For mind, my child, comes of earth, breath of water, speech of fire.'

'Please, Sir, inform me still more,' said the son.

'Be it so, my child,' the father replied.

•

'Man (Purusha), my son, consists of sixteen parts. Abstain from food for fifteen days, but drink as much water as you like, for breath comes from water, and will not be cut off, if you drink water.'

Shvetaketu abstained from food for fifteen days. Then he came to his father and said: 'What shall I say?' The father said: 'Repeat the Rik, Yajus, and Saman verses,' He replied: 'They do not occur to me, Sir.'

The father said to him: 'As of a great lighted fire one coal only of the size of a firefly may be left, which would not burn much more than this, i.e., very little, thus, my dear son, one part only of the sixteen parts of you is left, and therefore with that one part you do not remember the Vedas. Go and eat!

'Then wilt thou understand me.' Then Shvetaketu ate, and afterwards approached his father. And whatever his father asked him, he knew it all by heart. Then his father said to him:

'As of a great lighted fire one coal of the size of firefly, if left, may be made to blaze up again by putting grass upon it, and will thus burn more than this.

'Thus, my dear son, there was one part of the sixteen parts left to you, and that, lighted up with food, burnt up, and by it you remember now the Vedas.' After that, he understood what his father meant when he said: 'Mind, my son, comes from food, breath from water, speech from fire.' He understood what he said, yea, he understood it.

•

Uddalaka Aruni said to his son Shvetaketu: 'Learn from me the true nature of sleep (Svapna). When a man sleeps here, then, my dear son, he becomes united with the True, he is gone to his own (Self). Therefore they say, Svapiti, he sleeps, because he is gone (*apita*) to his own (*sva*).

'As a bird when tied by a string flies first in every direction, and finding no rest anywhere, settles down at last on the very place where it is fastened, exactly in the same manner, my son, that mind the jiva, or living Self in mind, after flying in every direction, and finding no rest anywhere, settles down on breath for indeed, my son, mind is fastened to breath.

'Learn from me, my son, what are hunger and thirst. When a man is thus said to be hungry, water digests what has been eaten by him. Therefore as they speak of a cow-leader, a horse-leader, a man-leader, a horse-leader, a man-leader, so they call water, which digests food and causes hunger, food-leader. Thus by food digested, my son, know this offshoot, the body, to be brought forth, for this body could not be without a cause.

'And where could its root be except in food? And in the same manner, my son, as food too is an offshoot, seek after its root, water. And as water too is an offshoot, seek after its root, fire. And as fire too is an offshoot, seek after its root, the True. Yes, all these creatures, my son, have their root in the True, they dwell in the True, they rest in the True.

'When a man is thus said to be thirsty, fire carries away what has been drunk by him. Therefore as they speak of a cow-leader, of a horse-leader, of a man-leader, so they call fire, thirst, i.e. water-leader. Thus by water digested, my son, know this offshoot, the body, to be brought forth : this body could not be without a cause.

'And where could its root be except in water? As water is an offshoot, seek after its root, fire. As fire is an offshoot, seek after its root, the True. Yes, all these creatues, O son, have their root in the True, they dwell in the True, they rest in the True.

'And how these three beings (devata), fire, water, earth, O son, when they reach man, become each of them tripartite, has been said before. When a man departs from hence, his speech is merged in his mind, his mind in his breath, his breath in heat (fire), heat in the Highest Being.

'Now that which is that subtle essence, the root of all,

in it all that exists has its self. It is the True. It is the Self, and thou, O Shvetaketu, art it.'

'Please, Sir, inform me still more,' said the son.
'Be it so, my child,' the father replied.

•

'As the bees, my son, make honey by collecting the juices of distant trees, and reduce the juice into one form,

'And as these juices have no discrimination, so that they might say, I am the juice of this tree or that, in the same manner, my son, all these creatures, when they have become merged in the True, either in deep sleep or in death, know not that they are merged in the True.

'Whatever these creatures are here, whether a lion, or a wolf, or a boar, or a worm, or a midge, or a gnat, or a mosquito, that they become again and again.

'Now that which is that subtle essence, in it all that exists has its self. It is the True. It is the Self, and thou, O Svetaketu, art it.'

'Please, Sir, inform me still more,' said the son.
'Be it so, my child,' the father replied.

•

'These rivers, my son, run, the eastern like the Ganga toward the east, the western like the Sindhu toward the west. They go from sea to sea, i.e., the clouds lift up the water from the sea to the sky, and send it back as rain to the sea. They become indeed sea. And as those rivers, when they are in the sea, do not know, I am this or that river,

'In the same manner, my son, all these creatures, when they have come back from the True, know not that they have come back from the True. Whatever these creatures are here, whether a lion, or a wolf, or a boar, or a worm, or a midge, or a gnat, or a mosquito, that they become again and again.

'That which is that subtle essence, in it all that exists has its self. It is the True. It is the Self, and thou, O Shvetaketu, art it.'

'Please, Sir, inform me still more,' said the son.
'Be it so, my child,' father replied.

•

'If some one were to strike at the root of this large tree here, it would bleed, but live. If he were to strike at its stem, it would bleed, but live. If he were to strike at its top, it would bleed, but live. Pervaded by the living Self that tree stands firm, drinking in its nourishment and rejoicing:

'But if the life, the living Self, leaves one of its branches, that branch withers; if it leaves a second, that branch withers; if it leaves a third, that branch withers. If it leaves the whole tree, the whole tree withers. In exactly the same manner, my son, know this.' Thus he spoke:

'This body indeed withers and dies when the living Self has left it; the living Self dies not.

'That which is that subtle essence, in it all that exists has its self. It is the True. It is the Self, and thou, Shvetaketu, art it.'

'Please, Sir, inform me still more,' said the son.
'Be it so, my child,' father replied.

•

'Fetch me from thence a fruit of the Nyagrodha tree.'
'Here is one, Sir.'
'Break it.'
'It is broken, Sir.'
'What do you see there?'
'These seeds, almost infinitesimal.'
'Break one of them.'
'It is broken, Sir.'
'What do you see there?'
'Not anything, Sir.'

The father said: 'My son, that subtle essence which you do not perceive there, of that very essence this great Nyagrodha tree exists.

'Believe it, my son. That which is the subtie essence, in it all that exists has its self. It is the true. It is the Self, and thou, O Shvetaketu, art it.'

'Please Sir, inform me still more,' said the son.

'Be it so, my child,' the father replied.

●

'Place this salt in water, and then wait on me in the morning.;

The son did as he was commanded.

The father said to him: 'Bring me the salt, which you placed in the water last night.'

The son having looked for it, found it not, for of course, it was melted.

The father said: 'Taste it from the surface of the water. How is it?'

The son replied: 'It is salt.'

'Taste is from the middle. How is it?'

The son replied: 'It is salt.'

'Taste it from the bottom. How is it?'

The son replied: 'It is salt.'

The father said: 'Throw it away and then wait on me.'

He did so; but salt exists for ever.

Then the father said: 'Here also, in this body, forsooth, you do not perceive the True (Sat), my son; but there indeed it is.

'That which is the subtle essence, in it all that exists has its self. It is the True. It is the Self, and thou, O Shvetaketu, art it.'

'Please, Sir, inform me still more,' said the son.

'Be it so, my child,' the father replied.

●

'As one might lead a person with his eyes covered away from the Gandharas, and leave him then in a place where there are no human beings; and as that person would turn towards theeast, or the north, or the west, and shout. "I have been brought here with my eyes covered, I have been left here with my eyes covered."

'And as thereupon someone might loose his bandage and say to him, "Go in that direction, it is Gandhara, go in that direction;" and as thereupon, having been informed and being able judge for himself, he would by asking his way from village to village arrive at last at Gandhara, — in exactly the same manner does a man, who meets with a teacher to inform him, obtain the true knowledge. For him there is only delay so long as he is not delivered from the body; then he will be perfect.

'That which is the subtle essence, in it all that exists has its self. It is the True. It is the Self, and thou, O Shvetaketu, art it.'

'Please, Sir, inform me still more,' said the son.

'Be it so, my child,' the father replied.

•

'If a man is ill, his relatives assemble round him and ask: "Dost thou know me? Dost thou know me?" Now as long as his speech is not merged in his mind, his mind in breath, breath in heat (fire), heat in the Highest Being, he knows them.

'But when his speech is merged in his mind, his mind in breath, breath in heat (fire), heat in the Highest Being, then he knows them not.

'That which is the subtle essence, in it all that exists has its self. It is the True. It is the Self, and thou, O Shvetaketu, art it.'

'Please, Sir, inform me still more,' said the son.

'Be it so, my child,' the father replied.

•

'My child, they bring a man hither whom they have taken by the hand, and they say: "He has taken something, he has committed a theft." When he denies, they say, "Heat the hatchet for him." If he has committed the theft, then he makes himself to be what he is not. Then the falseminded, having covered his true Self by a falsehood, grasps the heated hatchet—he is burnt, and he is killed.

'But if he did not commit the theft, then he makes himself to be what he is. Then the trueminded, having covered his true Self by truth, grasps the heated hatchet—he is not burnt, and he is delivered.

'As that truthful man is not burnt, thus has all that exists its self in That. It is the True. It is the Self, and thou, O Shvetaketu, art it.' He understood what he said, yea, he understood it.

7

Narada approached Sanatkumara and said, 'Teach me, Sir!' Sanatkumara said to him: 'Please tell me what you know; afterward I shall tell you what is beyond.'

Narada said: 'I know the Rigveda, Sir, the Yajurveda, Samaveda, as the fourth the Atharvana, as the fifth the Itihasa-purana, the Bharata; the Veda of the Vedas, grammar; the Pitrya, the rules for the sacrifices for the ancestors; the Rasi, the science of numbers; the Daiva, the science of portents; the Nidhi, the science of time; the Vakovakya, logic; the Ekayana, ethics; the Devavidya, etymology; the Brahma-vidya, pronunciation, Siksha, ceremonial Kalpa, prosody, Chhandas; the Bhuta-vidya, the science of demons; the Kshatra-vidya, the science of weapons; the Nakshatra-vidya, astronomy; the Sarpa and Devajana-vidya, the science of serpents or poisons, and the sciences of the genii, such as the making of perfumes, dancing, singing, playing, and other fine arts. All this I know, Sir.

'But, Sir, with all this I know the Mantras only, the sacred books, I do not know the Self. I have heard from men like you, that he who knows the Self overcomes grief. I am in grief. Do, Sir, help me over this grief of mine.'

Sanatkumara said to him: 'Whatever you have read, is only a name.

'A name is Rigveda, Yajurveda, Samaveda, and as the fourth the Atharvana, as the fifth the Itihasa-purana, the Veda of the Vedas, the Pitrya, the Rasi, the Daiva, the Nidhi, the Vakovakya, the Ekayana, the Devavidya, the Brahmavidya, the Bhutavidya, the Kshatravidya, the Nakshatravidya, the Sarpa and Devajanavidya. All these are a name only. Meditate on the name.

'He who meditates on the name as Brahman, is, as it were, lord and master as far as the name reaches—he who meditates on the name as Brahman.'

'Sir, is there something better than a name?'

'Yes, there is something better than a name.'

'Sir, tell it me.'

•

'Speech is better than a name. Speech makes us understand the Rigveda, Yajurveda, Samaveda, and the fourth the Atharvana, as the fifth the Itihasa-purana, the Veda of the Vedas, the Pitrya, the Rasi, the Daiva, the Nidhi, the Vakovakya, the Ekayana, the Devavidya, the Brahmavidya, the Kshatravidya, the Nakshatravidya, the Sarpa and Devajanavidya; heaven, earth, air, ether, water, fire, gods, men, cattle, birds, herbs, trees, all beasts down to worms, midges, and ants; what is right and what is wrong; what is true and what is false; what is good and what is bad; what is pleasing and what is not pleasing. For if there were no speech, neither right nor wrong would be known, neither the true nor the false, neither the good nor the bad, neither the pleasant nor the unpleasant. Speech makes us understand all this. Meditate on speech.

'He who meditates on speech as Brahman, is, as it were, lord and master as far as speech reaches—he who meditates on speech as Brahman.'

'Sir, is there something better than speech?'

'Yes, there is something better than speech?'

'Sir, tell it me.'

•

'Mind (manas) is better than speech. For as the closed fist holds two Amalaka or two Kola or two Aksha fruits, thus does mind hold speech and name. For if a man is minded in his mind to read the sacred hymns, he reads them; if he is minded in his mind to perform any actions, he performs them; if he is minded to wish for sons and cattle, he wishes for them; if he is minded to wish for this world and the other, he wishes for them. For mind is indeed the self, mind is the world, mind is Brahman. Meditate on the mind.

'He who meditates on the mind as Brahman, is, as it were, lord and master as far as the mind reaches—he who meditates on the mind as Brahman.'

'Sir, is there something better than mind?'

'Yes, there is something better than mind?'

'Sir, tell it me.'

•

'Will (Sankalpa) is better than mind. For when a man wills, then he thinks in his mind, then he sends forth speech, and he sends it forth in a name. In a name the sacred hymns are contained, in the sacred hymns all sacrifices.

'All these therefore, beginning with mind and ending in sacrifice, centre in will, consist of will, abide in will. Heaven and earth willed, air and ether willed, water and fire willed. Through the will of heaven and earth rain wills; through the will of rain food wills; through the will of food the vital airs will; through the will of the vital airs the sacred hymns will; through the will of the sacred hymns the sacrifices will; through the will of the sacrifices the world as their reward wills; through the will of the world everything wills. This is will. Meditate on will.

'He who meditates on will as Brahman, he, being himself safe, firm, and undistressed, obtains the safe, firm, and undistressed worlds which he has willed; he is, as it were, lord and master as far as will reaches—he who meditates on will as Brahman.'

'Sir, is there something better than will?'

'Yes, there is something better than will?'

'Sir, tell it me.'

•

'Consideration (Chitta) is better than will. For when a man considers, then he wills, then he thinks in his mind, then he sends forth speech, and he sends it forth in a name. In a name the sacred hymns are contained, in the sacred hymns all sacrifices.

'All these, beginning with mind and ending in sacrifice, centre in consideration, consist of consideration, abide in consideration. Therefore if a man is inconsiderate, even if he possesses much learning, people say of him, he is nothing, whatever he may know; for, if he were learned, he would not be so inconsiderate. But if a man is considerate, even though he knows but little, to him indeed do people listen gladly. Consideration is the centre, consideration is the self, consideration is the support of all these. Meditate on consideration.

'He who meditates on consideration as Brahman, he, being himself safe, firm, and undistressed, obtains the safe, firm, and undistressed worlds which he has considered; he is, as it were, lord and master as far as consideration reaches —he who meditates on consideration as Brahman.'

'Sir, is there something better than consideration?'

'Yes, there is something better than consideration.?'

'Sir, tell it me.'

•

'Reflection (Dhyana) is better than consideration. The earth reflects, as it were, and thus does the sky, the heaven, the water, the mountains, gods and men. Therefore those who among men obtain greatness here on earth, seem to have obtained a part of the object of reflection because they show a certain repose of manner. Thus while small and vulgar people are always quarrelling, abusive, and slandering, great men seem to have obtained a part of the reward of reflection. Meditate on reflection.

'He who meditates on reflection as Brahman, is lord and master, as it were, as far as reflection reaches—he who meditates on reflection as Brahman.'

'Sir, is there something better than reflection?'

'Yes, there is something better than reflection.?'

'Sir, tell it me.'

●

'Understanding (Vijnana) is better than reflection. Through understanding we understand the Rigveda, the Yajurveda, the Samaveda, and as the fourth the Atharvana, as the fifth the Itihasa-purana, the Veda of the Vedas, the Pitrya, the Rasi, the Daiva, the Nidhi. The Vakovakya, the Ekayana, the Devavidya, the Brahmavidya, the Bhutavidya, the Kshatravidya, the Nakshatravidya. the Sarpa and Devajanavidya, the Nakshatravidya. The Sarpa and Devajanavidya, heaven, earth, air, ether, water, fire, gods, men, cattle, birds, herbs, trees, all beasts down to worms, midges, and ants; what is right and what is wrong; what is true and what is false; what is good and what is bad; what is pleasing and what is not pleasing; food and savour, this world and that, all this we understand through understanding. Meditate on understanding.

'He who meditates on understanding as Brahman, reaches the worlds where there is understanding and knowledge; he is, as it were, lord and master as far as understanding reaches—he who meditates on understanding as Brahman.'

'Sir, is there something better than understanding?'

'Yes, there is something better than understanding.?'

'Sir, tell it me.'

•

'Power (Bala) is better than understanding. One powerful man shakes a hundred men of understanding. If a man is powerful, he becomes a rising man. If he rises, he becomes a man who visits wise people. If he visits he becomes a follower of wise people. If he follows them, he becomes a seeing, a hearing, a perceiving, a knowing, a doing, an understanding man. By power the earth stands firm, and the sky, and the heaven, and the mountains, gods and men, cattle, birds, herbs, trees, all beasts down to worms, midges, and thus, by power the world stands firm. Meditate on power.

'He who meditates on power as Brahman, is, as it were, lord and master as far as power reaches—he who meditates on power as Brahman.'

'Sir, is there something better than power?'

'Yes, there is something better than power.?'

'Sir, tell it me.'

•

'Food (Anna) is better than power. Therefore if a man abstain from food for ten days, though he live, he would be unable to see, hear, perceive, think, act, and understand. But when he obtains food, he is able to see, hear, perceive, think, act, and understand. Meditate on food.

'He who meditates on food as Brahman, obtains the worlds rich in food and drink; he is, as it were, lord and master as far as food reaches—he who meditates on food as Brahman.'

'Sir, is there something better than food?'

'Yes, there is something better than food.?'

'Sir, tell it me.'

•

'Water (Ap) is better than food. Therefore if there is not sufficient rain, the vital spirits fall from fear that there will be less food. But if there is sufficient rain, the vital spirits rejoice, because there will be much food. This water, on assuming different forms, becomes this earth, this sky, this heaven, the mountains, gods and men, cattle, birds, herbs and trees, all beasts down to worms, midges, and arms. Water indeed assumes all these forms. Meditate on water.

'He who meditates on water as Brahman, obtains all wishes, he becomes satisfied; he is, as it were, lord and master as far as water reaches—he who meditates on water as Brahman.'

'Sir, is there something better than water?'

'Yes, there is something better than water.?'

'Sir, tell it me.'

•

'Fire (Tejas) is better than water. For fire united with air, warms the ether. Then people say, It is hot, it burns, it will rain. Thus does fire, after showing this sign itself first, create water. And thus again underclaps come with lightnings flashing upwards and across the sky. Then people say, There is lightning and thunder, it will rain. Then also does fire, after showing this sign first, create water. Meditate on fire.

'He who meditates on fire as Brahman, obtains, resplendent himself, resplendent worlds, full of light and free of darkness; he is, as it were, lord and master as far as fire reaches—he who meditates on fire as Brahman.'

'Sir, is there something better than fire?'

'Yes, there is something better than fire.?'

'Sir, tell it me.'

•

'Ether (Akasha) is better than fire. For in the ether exist both sun and moon, the lightning, stars, and fire. Through the ether we call, through the ether we hear, through the ether we answer. In the ether or space we rejoice when we are together, and rejoice not when we are separated. In the ether everything is born, and towards the ether everything tends when it is born. Meditate on ether.

'He who meditates on ether as Brahman, obtains the worlds of ether and of light, which are free from pressure and pain, wide and spacious; he is, as it were, lord and master as far as ether reaches—he who meditates on ether as Brahman.'

'Sir, is there something better than ether?'

'Yes, there is something better than ether?'

'Sir, tell it me.'

•

'Memory (Smara) is better than ether. Therefore where many are assembled together, if they have no memory, they would hear no one, they would not perceive, they would not understand. Through memory we know our sons, through memory our cattle. Meditate on memory.

'He who meditates on memory as Brahman, is, as it were, lord and master as far as memory reaches—he who meditates on memory as Brahman.'

'Sir, is there something better than memory?'

'Yes, there is something better than memory.?'

'Sir, tell it me.'

•

'Hope (Asha) is better than memory. Fired by hope does memory read the sacred hymns, perform sacrifices, desire sons and cattle, desire this world and the other. Meditate on hope.

'He who meditates on hope as Brahman, all his desires are fulfilled by hope, his prayers are not in vain; he is, as it were, lord and master as far as hope reaches—he who meditates on hope as Brahman'.

'Sir, is there something better than hope?'

'Yes, there is something better than hope.?'

'Sir, tell it me.'

•

'Spirit (Prana) is better than hope. As the spokes of a

wheel hold to the nave, so does all this, beginning with names and ending in hope, hold to spirit. That spirit moves by the spirit, it gives spirit to the spirit. Father means spirit, mother is spirit, brother is spirit, sister is spirit, tutor is spirit, Brahmin is spirit.

'For if one says anything unbecoming to a father, mother, brother, sister, tutor or Brahmin, then people say, Shame on thee! thou hast offended thy father, mother, brother, sister, tutor, or a Brahmin.

'But, if after the spirit has departed from them, one shoves them together with a poker, and burns them to pieces, no one would say, Thou offendest thy father, mother, brother, sister, tutor, or a Brahmin.

'Spirit then is all this. He who sees this, perceives this, and understands this, becomes an Ativadin, one who says great things. If people say to such a man, Thou art an Ativadin, he may say, I am an Ativadin; he need not deny it.'

•

'But in reality he is an Ativadin who declares the Highest Being to be the True (Satya).'

'Sir, may I become an Ativadin by the True?'

'But we must desire to know the True.'

'Sir, I desire to know the True.'

•

'When one understands the True, then one declares the True. One who does not understand it, does not declare the True. Only he who understands it, declares the True. This understanding, however, we must desire to understand.'

'Sir, I desire to understand it.'

•

'When one perceives, then one understands. One who does not perceive, does not understand. Only he who perceives, understands. This perception, however, we must desire to understand.'

'Sir, I desire to understand it.'

•

'When one believes, then one perceives. One who does not believe, does not perceive. Only he who believes, perceives. This belief, however, we must desire to understand.'

'Sir, I desire to understand it.'

•

'When one attends on a tutor, spiritual guide, then one believes. One who does not attend on a tutor, does not believe. Only he who attends, believes. This attention on a tutor, however, we must desire to understand.'

'Sir, I desire to understand it.'

•

'When one performs all sacred duties, then one attends really on a tutor. One who does not perform his duties, does not really attend on a tutor. Only he who performs his duties, attends on his tutor. This performance of duties, however, we must desire to understand.'

'Sir, I desire to understand it.'

•

'When one obtains bliss, in oneself, then one performs duties. One who does not obtain bliss, does not perform duties. Only he who obtains bliss, performs duties. This bliss, however, we must desire to understand.'

'Sir, I desire to understand it.'

•

'The Infinite (Bhuman) is bliss. There is no bliss in anything finite. Infinity only is bliss. This Infinity, however, we must desire to understand.'

'Sir, I desire to understand it.'

•

'Where one sees nothing else, hears nothing else, understands nothing else, that is the Infinite. Where one sees something else, hears something else, understands something else, that is the finite. The Infinite is immortal, the finite is mortal.'

'Sir, in what does the Infinite rest?'

'In its own greatness—or not even in greatness.

'In the world they call cows and horses, elephants and gold, slaves, wives, fields and houses greatness. I do not mean this,' thus he spoke; 'for in that case one being the possessor rests in something else, but the Infinite cannot rest in something different from itself.

•

'The Infinite indeed is below, above, behind, before, right and left—it is indeed, all this.

'Now follows the explanation of the Infinite as the I: I am below, I am above, I am behind, before, right and left —I am all this.

'Next follows the explanation of the Infinite as the Self: Self is below, above, behind, before, right and left—Self is all this.

'He who sees, perceives, and understands this, loves the Self, delights in the Self, revels in the Self, rejoices in the Self—he becomes a Svaraj, an autocrat or Self-ruler; he is lord and master in all the worlds.

'But those who think differently from this, live in perishable worlds, and have other beings for their rulers.

•

'To him who sees, perceives, and understands this, the spirit (Prana) springs from the Self, hope springs from the Self, memory springs from the Self; so do ether, fire, water, appearance and disappearance, food, power, understanding, reflection, consideration, will, mind, speech, names, sacred hymns, and sacrifices—aye, all this springs from the Self.

'There is this verse, "He who sees this, does not see death, nor illness, nor pain; he who sees this, sees everything, and obtains everything everywhere.

' "He is one before creation, he becomes three, fire, water, earth, he becomes five, he becomes seven, he becomes nine; then again he is called the eleventh, and hundred and ten and one thousand and twenty."

'When the intellectual aliment has been purified, the whole nature becomes purified. When the whole nature has been purified, the memory becomes firm. And when the memory of the Highest Self remains firm, then all the ties which bind us to a belief in anything but the Self are loosened.

'The venerable Sanatkumara showed to Narada, after his faults had been rubbed out, the other side of darkness. They call Sanatkumara Skanda, yea, Skanda they call him.'

8

Harih, Om. There is this city of Brahman, the body, and in it the palace, the small lotus of the heart, and in it that small ether. Now what exists within that small ether, that is to be sought for, that is to be understood.

And if they should say to him: 'Now with regard to that city of Brahman, and the palace in it, i.e., the small lotus of the heart, and the small ether within the heart, what is there within it that deserves to be sought for, or that is to be understood?'

Then he should say: 'As large as this ether (space) is, so large is that ether within the heart. Both heaven and earth are contained within it, both fire and air, both sun and moon, both lightning and stars; and whatever there is of him, the Self, here in the world, and whatever is not i.e., whatever has been or will be, all that is contained within it.'

And if they should say to him: 'If everything that exists is contained in that city of Brahman, all beings and all desires, whatever can be imagined or desired, then what is left of it, when old age reaches it and scatters it, or when it falls to pieces?'

Then he should say: 'By the old age of the body, the ether, or Brahman within it does not age; by the death of the body, the ether, or Brahman within it is not killed. That Brahman is the true Brahma-city, not the body. In it all desires are contained. It is the Self, free from sin, free from old age, from death and grief, from hunger and thirst, which desires nothing but what it ought to desire, and imagines nothing but what is ought to imagine. Now as here on earth people follow as they are commanded, and depend on the object which they are attached to, be it a country or a piece of land,

'And as here on earth, whatever has been acquired by exertion, perishes, so perishes whatever is qcquired for the next world by sacrifices and other good actions performed on earth. Those who depart from hence without having discovered the Self and those true desires, for them there is no freedom in all the worlds. But those who depart from hence, after having discovered the Self and those true desires. for them there is freedom in all the worlds.

•

'Thus he who desires the world of the fathers, by his mere will the fathers come to receive him, and having obtained the world of the fathers, he is happy.

'And he who desires the world of the mothers, by his mere will the mothers come to receive him, and having obtained the world of the mothers, he is happy.

'And he who desires the world of the brothers, by his mere will the brothers come to receive him, and having obtained the world of the brothers, he is happy.

'And he who desires the world of the sisters, by his mere will the sisters come to receive him, and having obtained the world of the sisters, he is happy.

'And he who desires the world of the friends, by his mere will the friends come to receive him, and having obtained the world of the friends, he is happy.

'And he who desires the world of perfumes and garlands, by his mere will perfumes and garlands come to him, and having obtained the world of perfumes and garlands, he is happy.

'And he who desires the world of food and drink, by his mere will food and drink come to him, and having obtained the world of food and drink, he is happy.

'And he who desires the world of song and music, by his mere will song and music come to him, and having obtained the world of song and music, he is happy.

'And he who desires the world of women, by his mere will women come to receive him, and having obtained the world of women, he is happy.

'Whatever object he is attached to, whatever object he desires, by his mere will it comes to him, and having obtained it, he is happy.'

•

'These true desires, however, are hidden by what is false; though the desires be true, they have a covering which is false. Thus, whoever belonging to us has departed this life, him we cannot gain back, so that we should see him with our eyes.

'Those who belong to us, whether living or departed, and whatever else there is which we wish for and do not obtain, all that we find there, if we descend into our heart, where Brahman dwells, in the ether of the heart. There are all our true desires, but hidden by what is false. As people who do not know the country, walk again and again over a gold treasure that has been hidden somewhere in the earth and do not discover it, thus do all these creatures day after day go into the Brahma-world (they are merged in Brahman, while asleep), and yet do not discover it, because they are carried away by untruth (they do not come to themselves, i.e., they do not discover the true Self in Brahman, dwelling in the heart).

'That Self abides in the heart. And this is the etymological explanation. The heart is called Hridayam, instead of Hridy-ayam, i.e., He who is in the heart. He who knows this, that He is in the heart, goes day by day, when in Sushupti, deep sleep, into heaven (Svarga), i.e., into the Brahman of the heart.

'Now that serene being which, after having risen from out of this earthly body, and having reached the highest light, appears in its true form, that is the Self,' thus he spoke when asked by his pupils. This is the immortal, the fearless, this is Brahman. And of that Brahman the name is the True, Sattyam.

This name Sattyam consists of three syllables, sat-ti-yam. *Sat* signifies the immortal, *ti*, the mortal, and with *yam* he binds both. Because he binds both, the immortal and the mortal, therefore it is *yam*. He who knows this goes day by day into heaven (Svarga).

•

That Self is a bank, a boundary, so that these worlds may not be confounded. Day and night do not pass that bank, nor old age, death, and grief; neither good nor evil deeds. All evil-doers turn back from it, for the world of Brahman is free from all evil.

'Therefore he who has crossed that bank, if blind, ceases to be blind; if wounded, ceases to be wounded; if afflicted, ceases to be afflicted. Therefore when that bank has been crossed, night becomes day indeed, for the world of Brahman is lighted up once for all.

And that world of Brahman belongs to those only who find it by abstinence—for them there is freedom in all the worlds.

•

What people call sacrifice (Yajna), that is really abstinence, Brahmacharya. For he who knows, obtains that world of Brahman, which others obtain by sacrifice, by means of abstinence.

What people call sacrifice (Ishta), that is really abstinence, for by abstinence, having searched (Ishtva), he obtains the Self.

What people call sacrifice (Sattrayana), that is really abstinence, for by abstinence he obtains from the *Sat* (the true), the safety (*trana*) of the Self.

What people call the vow of silence (Mauna), that is really abstinence, for he who by abstinence has found out the Self, meditates (*manute*).

What people call fasting (Anashakayana), that is really abstinence, for that Self does not perish (*na nasyati*), which we find out by abstinence.

What people call a hermit's life (Aranyayana), that is really abstinence. Ara and Nya are two lakes in the world of Brahman, in the third heaven from hence: and there is the lake Airammadiya, and the Ashvattha tree, showering down Soma, and the city of Brahman (Hiranyagarbha) Aparajita, and the golden Prabhuvimita, the hall built by Prabhu, Brahman.

Now that world of Brahman belongs to those who find the lakes Ara and Nya in the world of Brahman by means of abstinence; for them there is freedom in all the worlds.

•

Now those arteries of the heart consist of a brown substance, of a white, blue, yellow, and red substance, and so is the sun brown, white, blue, yellow and red.

As a very long highway goes to two places, to one at the beginning, and to another at the end, so do the rays of the sun go to both worlds, to this one and to the other. They start from the sun, and enter into those arteries; they start from those arteries, and enter into the sun.

And when a man is asleep, resposing, and at perfect rest, so that he sees no dream, then he has entered into those arteries. Then no evil touches him, for he has obtained the light of the sun.

And when a man falls ill, then those who sit round

him, say, 'Do you know me? Do you know me? As long as he has not departed from this body, he knows them.

'But when he departs from this body, then he departs upwards by those very rays towards the worlds which he has gained by merit, not by knowledge; or he goes out while meditating on Om and thus securing an entrance into the Brahmaloka. And while his mind is failing, he is going to the sun. For the sun is the door of the world of Brahman. Those who know, walk in; those who do not know, are shut out. There is this verse: 'There are a hundred and one arteries of the heart; one of them penetrates the crown of the head; moving upwards by it a man reaches the immortal; the others serve for departing in different directions, yea, in different directions.

•

Prajapati said: 'The Self which is free from sin, free from old age, from death and grief, from hunger and thirst, which desires nothing but what it ought to desire, and imagines nothing but what it ought to imagine, that it is which we must search out, that it is which we must try to understand. He who has searched out that Self and understands it, obtains all worlds and all desires.'

The Devas (gods) and Asuras (demons) both heard these words, and said: 'Well, let us search for that Self by which, if one has searched it out, all worlds and all desires are obtained.'

Thus saying Indra went from the Devas, Virochana from the Asuras, and both, without having communicated with each other, approached Prajapati, holding fuel in their hands, as is the custom for pupils approaching their master.

They dwelt there as pupils for thirty-two years. Then Prajapati asked them: 'For what purpose have you both dwelt here?"

They replied: 'A saying of yours is being repeated, "The Self which is free from sin, free from old age, from death and grief, from hunger and thirst, which desires nothing but what it ought to desire, and imagines nothing but what it ought to imagine, that it is which we must search out, that it is which we must try to understand. He who has searched out that Self and understands it, obtains all worlds and all desires." Now we both have dwelt here because we wish for that Self.'

Prajapati said to them: 'The person that is seen in the eye, that is the Self. This is what I have said. This is the immortal, the fearless, this is Brahman.'

They asked: 'Sir, he who is perceived in the water, and he who is perceived in a mirror, who is he?'

He replied: 'He himself indeed is seen in all these.'

•

'Look at your Self in a pan of water, and whatever you do not understand of your Self, come and tell me.'

They looked in the water-pan. Then Prajapati said to them: 'What do you see?'

They said: 'We both see the self altogether, a picture even to the very hairs and nails.'

Prajapati said to them: 'After you have adorned yourselves, have put on your best clothes and cleaned yourselves, look again into the waterpan.'

They, after having adorned themselves, having put on their best clothes and cleaned themselves, looked into the water-pan.

Prajapati said: 'What do you see?'

They said: 'Just as we are, well adorned, with our best clothes and clean, thus we are both there, Sir, well adorned, with our best clothes and clean.'

Prajapati said: 'That is the Self, this is the immortal, the fearless, this is Brahman.'

Then both went away satisfied in their hearts.

And Prajapati, looking after them, said: 'They both go away without having perceived and without having known the Self, and whoever of these two, whatever Devas or Asuras, will follow this doctrine (Upanishad), will perish.'

Now Virochana, satisfied in his heart, went to the Asuras and preached that doctrine to them, that the self, the body alone is to be worshipped, that the self, the body, alone is to be served, and that he who worships the self and serves the self, gains both worlds, this and the next.

Therefore they call even now a man who does not give alms here, who has no faith, and offers no sacrifices, an Asura, for this is the doctrine (Upanishad) of the Asuras. They deck out the body of the dead with perfumes, flowers, and fine raiment by way of ornament, and think they will thus conquer that world.

•

But Indra, before he had returned to the Devas, saw this difficulty. As this Self, the shadow in the water, is well adorned, when the body is well adorned, well dressed, when the body is well dressed, well cleaned, if the body is well cleaned, that self will also be blind, if the body is blind, lame, if the body is lame, crippled, if the body is crippled, and will perish in fact as soon as the body perishes. Therefore I see no good in this doctrine.

Taking fuel in his hand he came again as a pupil to Prajapati. Prajapati said to him: 'Maghavat (Indra), as you went away with Virochana, satisfied in your heart, for what purpose did you come back?'

He said: 'Sir, as this Self, the shadow, is well adorned, when the body is well adorned, well dressed, when the body is well dressed, well cleaned, if the body is well cleaned, that self will also be blind, if the body is blind, lame, if the body is lame, crippled, if the body is crippled, and will perish in fact as soon as the body perishes. Therefore I see no good in this doctrine.'

'So it is indeed, Maghavat,' replied Prajapati; 'but I shall explain him the true Self further to you. Live with me another thirty-two years.'

He lived with him another thirty-two years, and then Prajapati said:

•

'He who moves about happy in dreams, he is the Self, this is the immortal, the fearless, this is Brahman.'

Then Indra went away satisfied in his heart. But before he had returned to the Devas, he saw this difficulty. Although it is true that that self is not blind, even if the body is blind, nor lame, if the body is lame, though it is true that Self is not rendered faulty of it, the body.

Nor struck when the body is struck, nor lamed when it is lamed, yet it is as, if they struck him, the Self, in dreams as if they chased him. He becomes even conscious, as it were, of pain, and sheds tears. Therefore I see no good in this.

Taking fuel in his hands, he went again as a pupil to Prajapati. Prajapati said to him: 'Maghavat, as you went away satisfied in your heart, for what purpose did you come back?'

He said: 'Sir, although it is true that self is not blind even if the body is blind, nor lame, if the body is lame, though it is true that self is not rendered faulty by the faults of the body.

Nor struck when the body is struck, nor lamed when it is lamed, yet it is as if they struck him, the self, in dreams, as if they chased him. He becomes even conscious, as it were, of pain, and sheds tears. Therefore I see no good in this.'

'So it is indeed, Maghavat,' replied Prajapati; 'but I shall explain him the true Self further to you. Live with me another thirty-two years.'

He lived with him another thirty-two years. Then Prajapati said: 'When a man being asleep, reposing, and at perfect rest, sees no dreams, that is the Self, this is the immortal, the fearless, this is Brahman.'

Then Indra went away satisfied in his heart. But before he had returned to the Devas, he saw this difficulty. In truth he thus does not know himself that he is I, nor does he know anything that exists. He is gone to utter annihilation. I see no good in this.

Taking fuel in his hand he went again as a pupil to Prajapati. Prajapati said to him: 'Maghavat, as you went away satisfied in your heart, for what purpose did you come back?'

He said: 'Sir, in that way he does not know himself that he is I, nor does he know anything that exists. He is gone to utter annihilation. I see no good in this.'

'So it is indeed, Maghavat,' replied Prajapati, 'but I shall explain him the true Self further to you, and nothing more than this. Live here other five years.'

He lived there other five years. This made in all one hundred and one years, and therefore it is said that Indra Maghavat lived one hundred and one years as a pupil with Prajapati. Prajapati said to him:

•

'Maghavat, this body is mortal and always held by death. It is the abode of that Self which is immortal and without body. When in the body, by thinking this body is I and I am this body, the Self is held by pleasure and pain. So long as he is in the body, he cannot get free from pleasure and pain. But when he is free of the body, when he knows himself different from the body, then neither pleasure nor pain touches him.

'The wind is without body, the cloud, lightning, and thunder are without body (without hands, etc.) Now as these, arising from this heavenly ether (space), appear in their own form, as soon as they have approached the highest light.

'Thus does the serene being, arising from this body, appear in its own form, as soon as it has approached the highest light, the knowledge of Self. He in that state is the highest person. He moves about there laughing, playing, and rejoicing in his mind, be it with women, carriages, or relatives, never minding that body into which he was born.

'Like as a horse attached to a cart, so is the spirit, Prana, Prajnatman, attached to this body.

'Now where the sight has entered into the void, the open space, the black pupil of the eye, there is the person of the eye, the eye itself is the instrument of seeing. He who knows, let me smell this, he is the Self, the nose is the instrument of smelling. He who knows, let me say this, he is the Self, the tongue is the instrument of saying. He who knows, let me hear this, he is the Self, the ear is the instrument of hearing.

'He who knows, let me think this, he is the Self, the mind is his divine eye. He, the Self, seeing these pleasures, which to others are hidden like a buried treasure of gold, through his divine eye, i.e., the mind, rejoices.

'The Devas who are in the world of Brahman meditate on that Self, as taught by Prajapati to Indra, and by Indra to the Devas. Therefore all worlds belong to them, and all desires. He who knows that Self and understands it, obtains all worlds and all desires.' Thus said Prajapati, yea, thus said Prajapati.

•

From the dark, the Brahman of the heart, I come to the nebulous, the world of Brahman, from the nebulous to the dark, shaking off all evil, as a horse shakes his hairs, and as the moon frees herself from the mouth of Rahu. Having shaken off the body, I obtain, self-made and satisfied, the uncreated world of Brahman, yea, I obtain it.

•

He who is called ether (Akasha) is the revealer of all forms and names. That within which these forms and names are contained is the Brahman, the Immortal, the Self.

I come to the hall of Prajapati, to the house; I am the glorious among Brahmins, glorious among princes, glorious among men. I obtained that glory, I am glorious among the glorious. May I never go to the white, toothless yet devouring, white abode; may I never go to it.

•

Brahma (Hiranyagarbha or Parameshvara) told this to Prajapati (Kashyapa), Prajapati to Manu, his son, Manu to mankind. He who has learnt the Veda from a family of teachers, according to the sacred rule, in the leisure time left from the duties to be performed for the Guru, who, after receiving his discharge, has settled in his own house, keeping up the memory of what he has learnt by repeating it regularly in some sacred spot, who has begotten virtuous sons, and concentrated all his senses on the Self, never giving pain to any creature, except at the *tirthas*, sacrifices, etc., he who behaves thus all his life, reaches the world of Brahman, and does not return. Yea, he does not return.

10

Shvetasvatara Upanishad

At whose command we abide

Rishi Shvetashvatara—so named because he had a white mule—is believed to receive the Upanishad as a revelation through the power of Tapas, self mortification, not a teacher. It not only formulates the Yoga into a comprehensive theory, but contributes several new ideas to Vedanta, such as underlining the Self as the basic ground of certitude, the intellectual world-principle named as Brahman or Hiranyagarbha, the destruction of the world at the end of the Kalpa, etc. No wonder, it is a favourite of the intellectual thinkers.

1

The Brahma-students say: Is Brahman the cause? Whence are we born? Whereby do we live, and whither do we go? O ye who know Brahman, tell us at whose command we abide, whether in pain or in pleasure?

Should time, or nature, or necessity, or chance, or the elements be considered as the cause or he who is called the Person (Purusha, Vijnanatma)? It cannot be their union either, because that is not self dependent, and the self also is powerless, because there is, independent of him, a cause of good and evil.

The sages, devoted to meditation and concentration, have seen the power belonging to God himself, hidden in its own qualities (Guna). He, being one, superintends all those causes, time, self, and the rest.

We meditate on him who like a wheel has one felly with three tyres, sixteen ends, fifty spokes, with twenty counter-spokes, and six sets of eight; whose one rope is manifold, who proceeds on three different roads, and whose illusion arises from two causes.

We meditate on the river whose water consists of the five streams which is wild and winding with its five springs, whose waves are the five vital breaths, whose fountainhead is the mind, the course of the five kinds of perceptions. It has five whirlpools, its rapids are the five pains; it has fifty kinds of suffering, and five branches.

In that vast Brahma-wheel, in which all things live and rest, the bird flutters about, so long as he thinks that the self in him is different from the mover, the god, the lord. When he has been blessed by him, then he gains immortality.

But what is praised in the Upanishads is the Highest Brahman, and in it there is the triad. The Highest Brahman is the safe support, it is imperishable. The Brahma-students, when they have known what is within this world, are devoted and merged in the Brahman, free from birth.

The Lord (Isha) supports all this together, the perishable and the imperishable, the developed and the undeveloped. The living self, not being a lord, is bound, because he has to enjoy the fruits of works; but when he has known the god (Deva), he is freed from all fetters.

There are two, one knowing (Ishvara), the other not-knowing (Jiva), both unborn, one strong, the other weak; there is he, the unborn, through whom each man receives the recompense of his works; and there is the infinite Self appearing under all forms, but himself inactive. When a man finds out these three, that is Brahma.

That which is perishable is the Pradhana, the first, the immortal and imperishable is Hara. The one god rules the perishable, the Pradhana, and the living self. From meditating on him, from joining him, from becoming one with him there is further cessation of all illusion in the end.

When that god is known, all fetters fall off, sufferings

are destroyed, and birth and death cease. From meditating on him there arises, on the dissolution of the body, the third state, that of universal lordship; but he only who is alone, is satisfied.

This, which rests eternally within the self, should be known; and beyond this not anything has to be known. By knowing the enjoyer, the enjoyed, and the ruler, everything has been declared to be threefold, and this is Brahman.

As the form of fire, while it exists in the under-wood, is not seen, nor is its seed destroyed, but it has to be seized again and again by means of the stick and the under-wood, so it is in both cases, and the Self has to be seized in the body by means of the Pranava, Om.

By making his body the under-wood, and the syllable Om the upper-wood, man, after repeating the drill of meditation, will perceive the bright god, like the spark hidden in the wood.

As oil in seeds, as butter in cream, as water in dry river-beds, as fire in wood, so is the Self seized within the self, if man looks for him by truthfulness and penance;

If he looks for the Self that pervades everything, as butter is contained in milk, and the roots whereof are self-knowledge and penance. That is the Brahman taught by the Upanishad.

2

Savitri, the sun, having first collected his mind and expanded his thoughts, brought Agni (fire), when he had discovered his light, above the earth.

With collected minds we are at the command of the divine Savitri, that we may obtain blessedness.

May Savitri, after he has reached with his mind the gods as they rise up to the sky, and with his thoughts has reached heaven, grant these gods to make a great light to shine.

The wise sages of the great sage collect their mind and

collect their thoughts. He who alone knows the law (Savitri) has ordered the invocation; great is the praise of the divine Savitri.

Your old prayer has to be joined with praises. Let my song go forth like the path of the sun! May all the sons of the Immortal listen, they who have reached their heavenly homes.

Where the fire is rubbed, where the wind is checked, where the Soma flows over, there the mind is born.

Let us love the old Brahman by the grace of Savitri; if thou make thy dwelling there, the path will not hurt thee.

If a wise man hold his body with its three erect parts, chest, neck, and head, even, and turn his senses with the mind towards the heart, he will then in the boat of Brahman cross all the torrents which cause fear.

Compressing his breathings let him, who has subdued all motions, breathe forth through the nose with gentle breath. Let the wise man without fail restrain his mind, that chariot yoked with vicious horses.

Let him perform his exercises in a place level, pure, free from pebbles, fire, and dust, delightful by its sounds, its water, and bowers, not painful to the eye, and full of shelters and caves.

When Yoga is being performed, the forms which come first, producing apparitions in Brahman, are those of misty smoke, sun, fire, wind, fireflies, lightnings, and a crystal moon.

When, as earth, water, light, heat, and ether arise, the fivefold quality of Yoga takes place, then there is no longer illness, old age, or pain for him who has obtained a body, produced by the fire of Yoga.

The first results of Yoga they call lightness, healthiness, steadiness, a good complexion, an easy pronunciation, a sweet odour, and slight excretions.

As a metal disk (mirror), tarnished by dust, shines bright again after it has been cleaned, so is the one incarnate person satisfied and free from grief, after he has seen the real nature of the self.

And when by means of the real nature of his self he sees, as by a lamp, the real nature of Brahman, then having known the urborn, eternal god, who is beyond all natures, he is freed from all fetters.

He indeed is the god who pervades all regions: he is the first-born, as Hiranyagarbha, and he is in the womb. He has been born, and he will be born. He stands behind all persons, looking everywhere.

The god who is in the fire, the god who is in the water, the god who has entered into the whole world, the god who is in plants, the god who is in trees, adoration be to that god, adoration.

3

The snarer who rules alone by his powers, who rules all the worlds by his powers, who is one and the same, while things arise and exist,—they who know this are immortal.

For there is one Rudra only, they do not allow a second, who rules all the worlds by his powers. He stands behind all persons, and after having created all worlds he, the protector, rolls it up at the end of time.

That one god, having his eyes, his face, his arms, and his feet in every place, when producing heaven and earth, forges them together with his arms and his wings.

He the creator and supporter of the gods, Rudra, the great seer, the lord of all, he who formerly gave birth to Hiranyagarbha, may he endow us with good thoughts.

O Rudra, thou dweller in the mountains, look upon us with that most blessed form of thine which is auspicious, not terrible, and reveals no evil!

O lord of the mountains, make lucky that arrow which thou, a dweller in the mountains, holdest in thy hand to shoot. Do not hurt man or beast!

Those who know beyond this the High Brahman, the vast, hidden in the bodies of all creatures, and alone enveloping everything, as the Lord, they become immortal.

I know that great Person (Purusha) of sunlike lustre beyond the darkness. A man who knows him truly, passes over death; there is no other path to go.

This whole universe is filled by this Person (Purusha), to whom there is nothing superior, from whom there is nothing different, than whom there is nothing smaller or larger, who stands alone, fixed like a tree in the sky.

That which is beyond this world is without form and without suffering. They who know it, become immortal, but others suffer pain indeed.

That Bhagavat exists in the faces, the heads, the necks of all, he dwells in the cave of the heart of all beings, he is all-pervading, therefore he is the omnipresent Shiva.

That Person (Purusha) is the great lord; he is the mover of existence, he possesses that purest power of reaching everything, he is light, he is undecaying.

The Person (Purusha), not larger than a thumb, dwelling within, always dwelling in the heart of man, is perceived by the heart, the thought, the mind; they who know it become immortal.

The Person (Purusha) with a thousand heads, a thousand eyes, a thousand feet, having compassed the earth on every side, extends beyond it by ten fingers' breadth.

That Person alone (Purusha) is all this, what has been and what will be; he is also the lord of immortality; he is whatever grows by food.

Its hands and feet are everywhere, its eyes and head are everywhere, its ears are everywhere, it stands encompassing all in the world.

Separate from all the senses, yet reflecting the qualities of all the senses, it is the lord and ruler of all, it is the great refuge of all.

The embodied spirit within the town with nine gates, the bird flutters outwards, the ruler of the whole world, of all that rests and of all that moves.

Grasping without hands, hasting without feet, he sees without eyes, he hears without ears. He knows what can be known, but no one knows him; they call him the first, the great Person (Purusha).

The Self, smaller than small, greater than great, is hidden in the heart of the creature. A man who has left all grief behind, sees the majesty, the Lord, the passionless, by the grace of the creator, the Lord.

I know this undecaying, ancient one, the self of all things, being infinite and omnipresent. They declare that in him all birth is stopped, for the Brahma-students proclaim him to be eternal.

4

He, the sun, without any colour, who with set purpose by means of his power (Shakti) produces endless colours, in whom all this comes together in the beginning, and comes asunder in the end—may he, the god, endow us with good thoughts.

That Self indeed is Agni (fire), it is Aditya (sun), it is Vayu (wind), it is Chandramas (moon); the same also is the starry firmament, it is Brahman (Hiranyagarbha), it is water, it is Prajapati (Viraj).

Thou art woman, thou art man; thou art youth, thou art maiden; thou, as an old man, totterest along on thy staff; thou art born with thy face turned everywhere.

Thou art the dark-blue bee, thou art the green parrot with red eyes, thou art the thunder-cloud, the seasons, the seas. Thou art without beginning, because thou art infinite, thou from whom all worlds are born.

There is one unborn being, female, red, white, and black, uniform, but producing manifold offspring. There is one unborn being, male, who loves her and lies by her; there is another who leaves her, while she is eating what has to be eaten.

Two birds, inseparable friends, cling to the same tree. One of them eats the sweet fruit, the other looks on without eating.

On the same tree man sits grieving, immersed, bewildered, by his own impotence (An-isha). But when he sees the other lord (Isha) contented, and knows his glory, then his grief passes away.

He who does not know that indestructible being of the Rigveda, that highest etherlike Self wherein all the gods reside, of what use is the Rigveda to him? Those only who know it, rest contented.

That from which the maker (Mayin) sends forth all this—the sacred verses, the offerings, the sacrifices, the panaceas, the past, the future, and all that the Vedas declare—in that the other is bound up through that Maya.

Know then Prakriti (nature) is Maya (art), and the great Lord and Mayin (maker); the whole world is filled with what are his members.

If a man has discerned him, who being one only, rules over every germ (cause), in whom all this comes together and comes asunder again, who is the lord, the bestower of blessing, the adorable god, then he passes for ever into that peace.

He, the creator and supporter of the gods, Rudra, the great seer, the lord of all, who saw Hiranyagarbha being born, may he endow us with good thoughts.

He who is the sovereign of the gods, he in whom all the worlds rest, he who rules over all two-footed and four-footed beings, to that god let us sacrifice an oblation.

He who has known him who is more subtle than subtle, in the midst of chaos, creating all things, having many forms, alone enveloping everything, the happy one, *S*iva, passes into peace for ever.

He also was in time the guardian of this world, the lord of all, hidden in all beings. In him the Brahmarshis and the deities are united, and he who knows him cuts the fetters of death asunder.

He who knows *S*iva, the blessed, hidden in all beings, like the subtile film that rises out from the clarified butter, alone enveloping everything,—he who knows the god, is freed from all fetters.

That god, the maker of all things, the great Self, always dwelling in the heart of man, is perceived by the heart, the soul, the mind;—they who know it become immortal.

When the light has risen, there is no day, no night, neither existence nor non-existence; *S*iva, the blessed, alone is there. That is the eternal, the adorable light of Savitri,—and the ancient wisdon proceeded thence.

No one has grasped him above, or across, or in the middle. There is no image of him whose name is Great Glory.

His form cannot be seen, no one perceives him with the eye. Those who through heart and mind know him thus abiding in the heart, become immortal.

'Thou art unborn,' with these words some one comes near to thee, trembling. O Rudra, let thy gracious face protect me forever!

O Rudra! hurt us not in our offspring and descendants, hurt us not in our own lives, nor in our cows, nor in our horses! Do not slay our men in thy wrath, for, holding oblations, we call on thee always.

5

In the imperishable and infinite Highest Brahman, wherein the two, knowledge and ignorance, are hidden, the one, ignorance, perishes, the other, knowledge, is immortal; but he who controls both, knowledge and ignorance, is another.

It is he who, being one only, rules over every germ (cause), over all forms, and over all germs; it is he who, in the beginning, bears in his thoughts the wise son, the fiery, whom he wishes to look on while he is born.

In that field in which the god, after spreading out one net after another in various ways, draws it together again, the Lord, the great Self, having further created the lords, thus carries on his lordship over all.

As the car of the sun shines, lighting up all quarters,

above, below, and across, thus does that god, the holy, the adorable, being one, rule over all that has the nature of a germ.

He, being one, rules over all and everything, so that the universal germ ripens its nature, diversifies all natures that can be ripened, and determines all qualities.

Brahma (Hiranyagarbha) knows this, which is hidden in the Upanishads, which are hidden in the Vedas, as the Brahma-germ. The ancient gods and poets who knew it, they became it and were immortal.

But he who is endowed with qualities, and performs works that are to bear fruit, and enjoys the reward of whatever he has done, migrates through his own works, the lord of life, assuming all forms, led by the three Gunas, and following the three paths.

That lower one also, not larger than a thumb, but brilliant like the sun, who is endowed with personality and thoughts, with the quality of mind and the quality of body, is seen small even like the point of a goad.

That living soul is to be known as part of the hundredth part of the point of a hair, divided a hundred times, and yet it is to be infinite.

It is not woman, it is not man, nor is it neuter; whatever body it takes, with that it is joined.

By means of thoughts, touching, seeing, and passions the incarnate Self assumes successively in various places various forms, in accordance with his deeds, just as the body grows when food and drink are poured into it.

That incarnate Self, according to his own qualities, chooses (assumes) many shapes, coarse or subtle, and having himself caused his union with them, he is seen as another and another, through the qualities of his acts, and through the qualities of his body.

He who knows him who has no beginning and no end, in the midst of chaos, creating all things, having many forms, alone enveloping everything, is freed from all fetters.

Those who know him who is to be grasped by the mind,

who is not to be called the nest, the body, who makes existence and non-existence, the happy one, Siva, who also creates the elements, they have left the body.

6

Some wise men, deluded, speak of Nature, and others of Time as the cause of everything; but it is the greatness of God by which this Brahma-wheel is made to turn.

It is at the command of him who always covers this world, the knower, the time of time, who assumes qualities and all knowledge, it is at his command that this work, creation, unfolds itself, which is called earth, water, fire, air, and ether.

He who, after he has done that work and rested again, and after he has brought together one essence, the self, with the other, matter, with one, two, three, or eight, with time also and with the subtile qualities of the mind.

Who, after starting the works endowed with the three qualities, can order all things, yet when, in the absence of all these, he has caused the destruction of the work, goes on, being in truth different from all he has produced.

He is the beginning, producing the causes which unite the soul with the body, and, being above the three kinds of time, past, present, future, he is seen as without parts, after we have first worshipped that adorable god, who has many forms, and who is the true source of all things, as dwelling in our own mind.

He is beyond all the forms of the tree of the world and of time, he is the other, from whom this world moves round, when one has known him who brings good and removes evil, the lord of bliss, as dwelling within the self, the immortal, the support of all.

Let us know that highest great lord of lords, the highest deity of deities, the master of masters, the highest above, as god, the lord of the world, the adorable.

There is no effect and no cause known of him, no one is seen like unto him or better; his high power is revealed as manifold, as inherent, acting as force and knowledge.

There is no master of his in the world, no ruler of his, not even a sign of him. He is the cause, the lord of the lords of the organs, and there is of him neither parent nor lord.

That only god who spontaneously covered himself, like a spider, with threads drawn from the first cause, Pradhana, grant us entrance into Brahman.

He is the one God, hidden in all beings, all pervading, the self within all beings, watching over all works, dwelling in all beings, the witness, the perceiver, the only one, free from qualities.

He is the one ruler of many who seem to act, but really do not act; he makes the one seed manifold. The wise who perceive him within their self, to them belongs eternal happiness, not to others.

He is the eternal among eternals, the thinker among thinkers, who, though one, fulfils the desires of many. He who has known that cause which is to be apprehended by Sankhya philosophy and Yoga discipline, he is freed from all fetters.

The sun does not shine there, nor the moon and the stars, nor these lightnings, and much less this fire. When he shines, everything shines after him; by his light all this is lightened.

He is the one bird in the midst of the world; he is also like the fire of the sun that has set in the ocean. A man who knows him truly, passes over death; there is no other path to go.

He makes all, he knows all, the self-caused, the knower, the time of time, destroyer of time, who assumes qualities and knows everything, the master of nature and of man, the lord of the three qualities (guna), the cause of the bondage, the existance, and the liberation of the world.

He who has become that, he is the immortal, remaining the lord, the knower, the ever-present guardian of this world, who rules this world for ever, for no one else is able to rule it.

Seeking for freedom I go for refuge to that God who is the light of his own thoughts, he who first creates Brahman and delivers the Vedas to him;

Who is without parts, without actions, tranquil, without fault, without taint, the highest bridge to immortality—like a fire that has consumed its fuel.

Only when men shall roll up the sky like a hide, will there be an end of misery, unless God has first been known.

Through the power of his penance and through the grace of god has the wise Shvetashvatara truly proclaimed Brahman, the highest and holiest, to the best of ascetics, as approved by the company of Rishis.

This highest mystery in the Vedanta, delivered in a former age, should not be given to one whose passions have not been subdued, nor to one who is not a son, or who is not a pupil.

If these truths have been told to a high-minded man, who feels the highest devotion for God, and for his Guru as for God, then they will shine forth,—then they will shine forth indeed.

11

Brihadaranyaka Upanishad

The Brahman is unseen, but seeing

A large-sized Upanishad, it is also a conglomeration, like the Chhandogya Upanishad, of many independent works, divided into three parts. It presents the beautiful Madhu—or honey—nature of things, and the Atman-Brahman discussions carried out by Rishi Yajnavalkya with the famous king Janaka, and his two wives, Gargi and Maitreyi, as well as others. The dialogues are stimulating and throw interesting light on the social traditions of the times.

1

Verily the dawn is the head of the horse which is fit for sacrifice, the sun its eye, the wind its breath, the mouth the Vaishvanara fire, the ear the body of the sacrificial horse. Heaven is the back, the sky the belly, the earth the chest, the quarters the two sides, the intermediate quarters the ribs, the members the seasons, the joints the months and half-months, the feet days and nights, the bones the stars, the flesh and clouds. The half-digested food is the sand, the rivers the bowels, the liver and the lungs the mountains, the hairs the herbs and trees. As the sun rises, it is forepart, as it sets, the hindpart of the horse. When the horse shakes itself, then it lightens; when it kicks, it thunders; when it makes water, it rains; voice is its voice.

Verily Day arose after the horse as the golden vessel, called Mahiman (greatness), which, at the sacrifice, is placed before the horse. Its place is in the Eastern sea. The Night arose after the horse as the silver vessel, called Mahiman, which, at the sacrifice, is placed behind the horse. Its place is in the Western sea. Verily, these two vessels or greatnesses arose to be on each side of the horse.

As a racer he carried the Devas, as a stallion the Gandharvas, as a runner the Asuras, as a horse men. The sea is its kin, the sea is its birthplace.

•

In the beginning there was nothing to be perceived here whatsoever. By Death indeed all this was concealed,—by hunger; for death is hunger. Death the first being, thought, 'Let me have a body.' Then he moved about, worshipping. From him thus worshipping water was produced. And he said: 'Verily, there appeared to me, while I worshipped (*archate*), water (*ka*).' This is why water is called Ar-ka. Surely there is water, or pleasure, for him who thus knows the reason why water is called Arka.

Verily, water is Arka. And what was there as the froth of the water, that was hardened, and became the earth. On that earth Death rested, and from him, thus resting and heated, Agni (Viraj) proceeded, full of light.

That being divided itself threefold, Aditya (the sun) as the third, and Vayu (the air) as the third. That spirit (Prana) became threefold. The head was the Eastern quarter, and the arms this and that quarter (i.e. the N.E. and S.E., on the left and right sides). Then the tail was the Western quarter, and the two legs this and that quarter (i.e., the N.W. and S.W.). The sides were the Southern and Northern quarters, the back heaven, the belly the sky, the dust the earth. Thus he, Mrityu, as Arka, stands firm in the water, and he who knows this stands firm wherever he goes.

He desired, 'Let a second body be born of me,' and he, Death or Hunger, embraced Speech in his mind. Then the seed became the year. Before that time there was no year. Speech bore him so long as a year, and after that time sent him forth. Then when he was born, Death opened his mouth, as if to swallow him. He cried Bhan! and that became speech.

He thought, 'If I kill him, I shall have but little food.' He therefore brought forth by that speech and by that body (the year) all whatsoever exists, the Rik, the Yajus, the Saman, the metres, the sacrifices, men, and animals.

And whatever Death brought forth, that he resolved to eat (*ad*). Verily because he eats everything, therefore is Aditi (Death) called Aditi. He who thus knows why Aditi is called Aditi, becomes an eater of everything, and everything becomes his food.

He desired to sacrifice again with a greater sacrifice. He toiled and performed penance. And while he toiled and performed, penance, glorious power went out of him. Verily, glorious power means the senses (Prana). Then when the senses had gone out, the body took to swelling, and mind was in the body.

He desired that this body should be fit for sacrifice, and that he should be embodied by it. Then he become a horse (*ashva*), because it swelled (*asvat*), and was fit for sacrifice (*medhya*); and this is why the horse-sacrifice is called Ashvamedha.

Verily, he who knows him thus, knows the Ashvamedha. Then, letting the horse free, he thought, and at the end of a year he offered it up for himself, while he gave up the other animals to the deities. Therefore the sacrificers offered up the purified horse belonging to Prajapati, as dedicated to all the deities.

Verily, the shining sun is the Ashvemedha sacrifice, and his body is the year; Agni is the sacrificial fire, and these worlds are his bodies. These two are the sacrificial fire and the Ashvamedha sacrifice, and they are again one deity, Death. He who knows this overcomes another death, death does not reach him, death is his Self, he becomes one of those deities.

•

There were two kinds of descendants of Prajapati, the Devas and the Asuras. Now the Devas were indeed the younger, the Asuras the elder ones. The Devas, who were struggling in these worlds, said: 'Well, let us overcome the Asuras at the sacrifices (the Jyotishtoma) by means of the Udgitha.'

They said to speech (Vach): 'Do thou sing out for us the Udgitha.' 'Yes,' said speech, and sang the Udgitha. Whatever delight there is in speech, that she obtained for the Devas by singing the three Pavamanas; but that she pronounced well in the other nine Pavamanas, that was for herself. The Asuras knew: 'Verily, through this singer they will overcome us.' They therefore rushed as the singer and pierced her with evil. That evil which consists in saying what is bad, that is that evil.

Then the Devas said to breath (scent): 'Do thou sing out for us,' 'Yes,' said breath, and sang. Whatever delight there is in breath (smell), that he obtained for the Devas by singing; but that he smelled well, that was for himself. The Asuras knew: 'Verily, through this singer they will overcome us.' They therefore rushed at the singer, and pierced him with evil. That evil which consists in smelling what is bad, that is that evil.

Then they said to the eye: 'Do thou sing out for us.' 'Yes,' said the eye, and sang. Whatever delight there is in the eye, that he obtained for the Devas by singing; but that he saw well, that was for himself. The Asuras knew: 'Verily, through this singer they will overcome us.' They therefore rushed at the singer, and pierced him with evil. That evil which consists in seeing what is bad, that is that evil.

Then they said to the ear: 'Do thou sing out for us.' 'Yes,' said the ear, and sang. Whatever delight there is in the ear, that he obtained for the Devas by singing; but that he heard well, that was for himself. The Asuras knew: 'Verily, through this singer they will overcome us.' They therefore rushed at the singer, and pierced him with evil. That evil which consists in hearing what is bad, that is that evil.

Then they said to the mind: 'Do thou sing out for us.' 'Yes,' said the mind, and sang. Whatever delight there is in the mind, that he obtained for the Devas by singing; but that he thought well, that was for himself. The Asuras knew: 'Verily, through this singer they will overcome us.' They therefore rushed at the singer, and pierced him with evil. That evil which consists in thinking what is bad, that is that evil.

Thus they overwhelmed these deities with evils, thus they pierced them with evil.

Then they said to the breath in the mouth: 'Do thou sing for us.' 'Yes,' said the breath, and sang. The Asuras knew: 'Verily, through this singer they will overcome us.' They therefore rushed at him and pierced him with evil. Now as a ball of earth will be scattered when hitting a stone, thus they perished, scattered in all directions. Hence the Devas rose, the Asuras fell. He who knows this, rises by his self, and the enemy who hates him falls.

Then the Devas said: 'Where was he then who thus stuck to us?' It was the breath within the mouth and therefore called Ayasya; he was the sap (*rasa*) of the limbs (*anga*), and therefore called Angirasa.

That deity was called Dur, because Death was far (*duran*) from it. From him who knows this, Death is far off.

That deity, after having taken away the evil of those deities, death, sent it to where the end of the quarters of the earth is. There he deposited their sins. Therefore let no one go to a man, let no one go to the end of the quarters of the earth, that he may not meet there with evil, with death.

That deity, after having taken away the evil of those deities, death, carried them beyond death.

He carried speech across first. When speech had become freed from death, it became what is had been before, Agni (fire). That Agni, after having stepped beyond death, shines.

Then he carried breath (scent) across. When breath had become freed from death, it became Vayu (air). That Vayu, after having stepped beyond death, blows.

Then he carried the eye across. When the eye had become freed from death, it became Aditya (the sun). That Aditya, after having stepped beyond death, burns.

Then he carried the ear across. When the ear had become freed from death, it became the quarters, space. These are our quarters, space, which have stepped beyond death.

Then he carried the mind across. When the mind had become freed from death, it became the moon. That moon, after having stepped beyond death, shines. Thus does that deity carry him, who know this, across death.

Then vital breath by singing, obtained for himself eatable food. For whatever food is eaten, is eaten by breath alone, and in it breath rests.

The Devas said: 'Verily, thus far, whatever food there is, thou hath by singing acquired it for thyself. Now therefore give us a share in that food.' He said: 'You there, enter into me.' They said 'Yes,' and entered all into him. Therefore whatever food is eaten by breath, by it the other senses are satisfied.

If a man knows this, then his own relations come to him in the same manner; he becomes their supporter, their chief leader, their strong ruler. An if ever any one tries to oppose one who is possessed of such knowledge among his own relatives, then he will not be able to support his own belongings. But he who follows the man who is possessed of such knowledge, and who with his permission wishes to support those whom he has to support, he indeed will be able to support his own belongings.

He was called Ayasya Angirasa, for he is the sap (*rasa*) of the limbs (*anga*). Verily, breath is the sap of the limbs. Yes, breath is the sap of the limbs. Therefore from whatever limb breath goes away, that limb withers, for breath verily is the sap of the limbs.

He (breath) is also Brihaspati, for speech is Brihati (Rigveda), and he is her lord; therefore he is Brihaspati.

He (breath) is also Brahminspati, for speech is Brahman (Yajurveda), and he is her lord; therefore he is Brahminspati.

He (breath) is also Saman, the Udgitha, for speech is Saman (Samaveda), and that is both speech (*sa*) and breath (*ama*). This is why Saman is called Saman.

Or because he is equal (*sama*) to a grub, equal to a gnat, equal to an elephant, equal to these three worlds, nay, equal to his universe, therefore he is Saman. He who thus knows this Saman, obtains union and oneness with Saman.

He (breath) is Udgitha. Breath verily is *ut*, for by breath this universe is upheld (*uttabdha*); and speech is *githa*, song. And because he is *ut* and *githa*, therefore he (breath) is Udgitha.

And thus Brahmadatta Chaikitaneya, the grandson of Chikitana, while taking Soma, said: 'May this Soma strike my head off, if Ayasya Angirasa sang another Udgitha than this. He sang it indeed as speech and breath.'

He who knows what is the property of this Saman, obtains property. Now verily, its property is one only. Therefore let a priest, who is going to perform the sacrificial work of a Sama-singer, desire that his voice may have a good tone, and let him perform the sacrifice with a voice that is in good tone. Therefore people who want a priest for a sacrifice, look out for one who possesses a good voice, as for one who possesses property. He who thus knows what is the property of that Saman, obtains property.

He who knows what is the gold of that Saman, obtains gold. Now verily, its gold is tone only. He who thus knows what is the gold of that Saman, obtain gold.

He who knows what is the support of that Saman, he is supported. Now verily its support is speech only. For, as supported in speech, that breath is sung as that Saman. Some say the support is in food.

Next follows the Abhyaroha (the ascension) of the Pavamana verses. Verily the Prastotri begins to sing the Saman, and when he begins, then let the sacrificer recite these three Yajus verses:

'Lead me from the unreal to the real! Lead me from darkness to light! Lead me from death to immortality!'

Now when he says, 'Lead me from the unreal to the real' the unreal is verily death, the real immortality. He therefore say 'Lead me from death to immortality, make me immortal.'

When he says, 'Lead me from darknes to light,' darkness is verily death, light immortality. He therefore says, 'Lead me from death to immortality, make me immortal.'

When he says, 'Lead me from death to immortality,' there is nothing there, as it were, hidden, obscure, requiring explanation.

Next come the other Stotras with which the priest may obtain food for himself by singing them. Therefore let the sacrificer, while these Stotras are being sung, ask for a boon, whatever desire he may desire. An Udgatri priest who knows this obtains by his singing whatever desire he may desire either for himself or for the sacrificer. This knowledge indeed is called the conqueror of the worlds. He who thus knows this Saman, for him there is no fear of his not being admitted to the worlds.

•

In the beginning this was Self alone, in the shape of a Person (Purusha). He looking round saw nothing but his Self. He first said, 'This is I;' therefore he became I by name. Therefore even now, if a man is asked, he first says, 'This is I,' and then pronounces the other name which he may have. And because before (*purva*) all this, the Self burnt down (*ush*) all evils, therefore he was a person (*pur-usha*). Verily, he who knows this, burns down every one who tries to be before him.

He feared, and therefore any one who is lonely, fears.

He thought, 'As there is nothing but myself, why should I fear?' Thence his fear passed away. For what should he have feared? Verily, fear arises from a second only.

But he felt no delight. Therefore a man who is lonely feels no delight. He wished for a second. He was so large as man and wife together. He then made this his Self to fall in two (*pat*), and thence arose husband (*pati*) and wife (*patni*). Therefore Yajnavalkya said: 'We two are thus, each of us, like half a shell.' Therefore the void which was there, is filled by the wife. He embraced her, and men were born.

She thought, 'How can he embrace me, after having produced me from himself? I shall hide myself.'

She then became a cow, the other became a bull and embraced her, and hence cows were born. The one became a mare, the other a stallion; the one a male ass, the other a female ass. He embraced her, and hence one-hoofed animals were born. The one became a she-goat, the other a he-goat; then one became an ewe, the other a ram. He embraced her, and hence goats and sheep were born. And thus he created everything that exists in pairs, down to the ants.

He knew, 'I indeed am this creation, for I created all this.' Hence he became the creation, and he who knows this lives in this his creation.

Next he thus produced fire by rubbing. From the mouth, as from the fire-hole, and from the hands he created fire. Therefore both the mouth and the hands are inside without hair, for the fire-hole is inside without hair.

And when they say, 'Sacrifice to this or sacrifice to that god,' each god is but his manifestation, for he is all gods.

Now, whatever there is moist, that he created from seed; this is Soma. So far verily is this universe either food or eater. Soma indeed is food, Agni eater. This is the highest creation of Brahman, when he created the gods from his better part, and when he, who was then mortal, created the immortals. Therefore it was the highest creation. And he who knows this, lives in this his highest creation.

Now all this was then undeveloped. It became developed by form and name, so that one could say, 'He, called so and so, is such a one.' Therefore at present also all this is developed by name and form, so that one can say, 'He, called so and so, is such a one.'

He, Brahman or the Self, entered thither, to the very tips of the finger-nails, as a razor might be fitted in a razor-case, or as fire in a fire-place.

He cannot be seen, for, in part only, when breathing, he is breath by name; when speaking, speech by name; when seeing, eye by name; when hearing, ear by name; when thinking, mind by name. All these are but the names of his acts. And he who worships him as the one or the other, does not know him, for he is apart from this (when qualified) by the one or the other (predicate). Let men worship him as Self, for in the Self all these are one. This Self is the footstep of everything, for through it one knows everything. And as one can find again by footsteps what was lost, thus he who knows this finds glory and praise.

This, which is nearer to us than anything, this Self, is dearer than a son, dearer than wealth, dearer than all else.

And if one were to say to one who declares another than the Self dear, that he will lose what is dear to him, very likely it would be so. Let him worship the Self alone as dear. He who worships the Self alone as dear, the object of his love will never perish.

Here they say: 'If men think that by knowledge of Brahman they will become everything, what then did that Brahman know, from whence all this sprang?'

Verily, in the beginning this was Brahman, that Brahman knew its Self only, saying, 'I am Brahman.' From it all this sprang. Thus, whatever Deva was awakened so as to know Brahman, he indeed became Brahman; and the same with Rishis and men. The Rishi Vamadeva saw and understood it, singing, 'I was Manu (moon), I was the sun.' Therefore now also he who thus knows that he is Brahman, becomes all this, and even the Devas cannot prevent it, for he himself is their Self.

Nof if a man worships another deity, thinking the deity is one and he another, he does not know. He is like a beast for the Devas. For verily, as many beasts nourish a man, thus does every man nourish the Devas. If only one beast is taken away, it is not pleasant; how much more when many are taken! Therefore it is not pleasant to the Devas that men should know this.

Verily, in the beginning this was Brahman, one only. That being one, was not strong enough. it created still further the most excellent Kshatra (power), viz., those Kshatras among the Devas,—Indra, Varuna, Soma, Rudra, Parjanya, Yama, Mrityu, Ishana. Therefore there is nothing beyond the Kshatra, and therefore at the Rajasuya sacrifice the Brahmin sits down below the Kshatriya. He confers that glory on the Kshatra alone. But Brahman is nevertheless the birth-place of the Kshatra. Therefore though a king is exalted, he sits down at the end of the sacrifice below the Brahman, as his birthplace. He who injures him, injures his own birthplace. He becomes worse, because he has injured one better than himself.

He was not strong enough. He created the Vish (people), the classes of Devas which in their different orders are called Vasus, Rudras Adityas, Vishvedevas, Maruts.

He was not strong enough. He created the Shudra, as Pushan as nourisher. This earth verily is Pushan, the nourisher; for the earth nourishes all this whatsoever.

He was not strong enough. He created still further the most excellent Law (Dharma). Law is the Kshatra (power) of the Kshatriya, therefore there is nothing higher than the Law. Thenceforth even a weak man rules a stronger with the help of the Law, as with the help of a king. Thus the Law is what is called the true. And if a man declares what is true, they say he declares the Law; and if he declares the Law, they say he declares what is true. Thus both are the same.

There are then this Brahman, Kshatra, Vish, and Shudra. Among the Devas that Brahman existed as Agni (fire) only, among men as Brahmin, as Kshatriya through the (divine) Kshatriya, as Vaishya through the divine Vaishya, as Shudra through the divine Shudra. Therefore people wish for their furture state among the Devas through Agni, the sacrificial fire, only; and among men through the Brahmin, for in these two forms did Brahman exist.

Now if a man departs this life without having seen his true future life in the Self, then that Self, not being known, does not receive and bless him, as if the Veda had not been read, or as if a good work had not been done. Nay, even if one who does not know the Self, should perform here on earth some great holy work, it will perish for him in the end. Let a man worship the Self only as his true state. If a man worships the Self only as his true state, his work does not perish, for whatever he desires that he gets from that Self.

Now verily, this Self of the ignorant man is the world of all creatures. In so far as man sacrifices and pours out libations, he is the world of the Devas; in so far as he repeats the hymns, etc., he is the world of the Rishis; in so far as he offers cakes to the Fathers and tries to obtain offspring, he is the world of the Fathers; in so far as he gives shelter and food to men, he is the world of men; in so far as he finds fodder and water for the animals he is the world of the animals; in so far as quadrupeds, birds, and even ants live in his houses, he is their world. And as every one wishes his own world not be injured, thus all beings wish that he who knows this should not be injured. Verily, this is known and has been well reasoned.

In the beginning this was Self alone, one only. He desired, 'Let there be a wife for me that I may have offspring, and let there be wealth for me that I may offer sacrifices.' Verily, this is the whole desire, and, even if wishing for more, he would not find it. Therefore now also a lonely person desires, 'Let there be a wife for me that I may have offspring, and let there be wealth for me that I may have offspring, and let there be wealth for me that I may offer sacrifices.' And so long as he does not obtain either of these things, he thinks he is incomplete. Now his completeness is made up as follows: mind is his self (husband) ; speech the wife; breath the child; the eye all wordly wealth, for he finds it with the eye; the ear his divine wealth, for he hears it with the ear. The body (Atman) is his work, for with the body he works. This is the fivefold sacrifice, for fivefold is the animal, fivefold man, fivefold all this whatsoever. He who knows this, obtains all this.

•

'When the father of creation had produced by knowledge and penance the seven kinds of food, one of his foods was common to all beings, two he assigned to the Devas,

'Three he made for himself, one he gave to the animals. In it all rests, whatsoever breathes and breathes not.

'Why then do these not perish, though they are always eaten? He who knows this imperishable one, he eats food with his face.

'He goes even to the Devas, he lives on strength.'

When it is said, that 'the father produced by knowledge and penance the seven kinds of food,' it is clear that it was he who did so. When it is said, that 'one of his foods was common,' then that is that common food of his which is eaten. He who eats that common food, is not removed from evil, for verily, that food is mixed property. When it is said, that 'two he assigned to the Devas,' that is the Huta, which is sacrificed in fire, and the Prahuta, which is given away at a sacrifice. But they also say, the new-moon and full-mon sacrifices are here intended, and therefore one should not offer them as *ishti* or with a wish.

When it is said, that 'one he gave to animals,' that is milk. For in their infancy both men and animals live on milk.

And therefore they either make a new-born child lick *ghrita* (butter), or they make it take the breast. And they call a new-born creature 'atrinada,' i.e., not eating herbs. When it is said, that 'in it all rests, whatsoever breathes and breathes not,' we see that all this, rests and depends on milk.

And when it is said that a man who sacrifices with milk a whole year, overcomes death again, let him not think so. No, on the very day on which he sacrifices, on that day he overcomes death again; for he who knows this, offers to the gods the entire milk.

When it is said, 'why do these not perish, though they are always eaten,' we answer, verily, the Person is the imperishable, and he produces that food again and again.

When it is said, 'he who knows this imperishable one,' then, verily, the Person is the imperishable one, for he produces this food by repeated thought, and whatever he does not work by his works, that perishes.

When it is said, that 'he eats food with his face,' then face means the mouth, he eats it with his mouth.

When it is said, that 'he goes even to the Devas, he lives on strength,' that is meant as praise.

When it is said, that 'he made three for himself,' that means that he made mind, speech, and breath for himself.' As people say, 'My mind was elsewhere, I did not see; my mind was elsewhere, I did not hear,' it is clear that a man sees with his mind and hears with his mind. Desire, representation, doubt, faith, want of faith, all this is mind. Therefore even if a man is touched on the back, he knows it through the mind.

Whatever sound there is, that is speech. Speech indeed in intended for an end or object, it is nothing by itself.

The upbreathing, the downbreathing, the backbreathing, the outbreathing, the onbreathing, all that is breathing is Prana only. Verily that Self consists of it; that Self consists of speech, mind, and breath.

These are the three worlds: earth is speech, sky mind,

heaven breath.

These are the three Vedas: the Rigveda is speech, the Yajurveda mind, the Samaveda breath.

These are the Devas, Fathers, and men: the Devas the speech, the Fathers mind, men breath.

These are father, mother, and child: the father is mind, the mother speech, the child breath.

These are what is known, what is to be known, and what is unknown.

What is known, has the form of speech, for speech is known. Speech, having become this, protects man.

What is to be known, has the form of mind, for mind is what is to be known. Mind, having become this, protects man.

What is unknown, has the form of breath, for breath is unknown. Breath, having become this, protects man.

Of that speech, which is the food of Prajapati, earth is the body, light the form, this fire. And so far as speech extends, so far extends the earth, so far extends fire.

Next, of this mind heaven is the body, light the form, this sun. And so far as this mind extends, so far extends heaven, so far extends the sun. If they, fire and sun, embrace each other, then wind is born, and that is Indra, and he is without a rival. Verily, a second is a rival, and he who knows this, has no rival.

Next, of this breath water is the body, light the form, this moon. And so far as this breath extends, so far extends water, so far extends the moon.

These are all alike, all endless. And he who worships them as finite, obtains a finite world, but he who worships them as infinite, obtains as infinite world.

That Prajapati is the year, and he consists of sixteen digits. The nights indeed are his fifteen digits, the fixed point his sixteenth digit. He is increased and decreased by the nights. Having on the new-moon night entered with the sixteenth part into everything that has life, he is thence born again in the morning. Therefore let no one cut off the life of any living thing on that night, not even of a lizard, in honour of that deity.

Now verily, that Prajapati, consisting of sixteen digits, who is the year, is the same as a man who knows this. His wealth constitutes the fifteen digits, his Self the sixteenth digit. He is increased and decreased by that wealth. His Self is the nave, his wealth the felly. Therefore even if he loses everything, if he lives but with his Self, people say, he lost the felly (which can be restored again).

Next, there are verily three worlds, the world of men, the world of the Fathers, the world of th Devas. The world of men can be gained by a son only, not by any other work. By sacrifice the world of the Fathers, by knowledge the world of the Devas is gained. The world of the Devas is the best of worlds, therefore they praise knowledge.

Next, follows the handling over. When a man thinks he is going to depart, he says to his son: 'Thou art Brahman, the Veda, so far as acquired by the father; thou art the sacrifice, so far as performd by the father; thou art the world.' The son answers: 'I am Brahman, I am the sacrifice, I am the world.' Whatever has been learnt by the father that, taken as one, is Brahman. Whatever sacrifices there are, they, taken as one, are the sacrifice. Whatever worlds there are, they, taken as one, are the world. Verily, here ends this, what has to be done by a father, study, sacrifice, etc. 'He, the son, being all this, preserved me from this world, thus he thinks. therefore they call a son who is instructed to do all this, a world-son, and therefore they instruct him.

When a father who knows this, departs this world, then he enters into his son together with his own spirits, with speech, mind, and breath. If there is anything done amiss by the father, of all that the son delivers him, and therefore he is called Putra, son. By help of his son the father stands firm in this world. Then these divine immortal spirits, speech, mind, and death enter into him.

From the earth and from fire, divine speech enters into him. And verily, that is divine speech whereby, whatever he says, come to be.

From heaven and the sun, divine mind enters into him. And verily, that is divine mind whereby he becomes joyful, and grieves no more.

From water and the moon, divine breath (spirit) enters into him. And verily, that is divine breath which, whether moving or not moving, does not tire, and therefore does not perish. He who knows this, becomes the Self of all beings. As that deity Hiranyagarbha is, so does he become. And as all beings honour that deity with sacrifice, etc., so do all beings honour him who knows this.

Whatever grief these creatures suffer, that is all one and therefore disappears. Only what is good approaches him; verily, evil does not approach the Devas.

Next follows the consideration of the observances. Prajapati created the active senses. When they had been created, they strove among themselves. Voice held, I shall speak; the eye held, I shall see; the ear held, I shall hear; and thus the other actions too, each according to its own act. Death, having become weariness, took them and seized them. Having seized them, death held them back from their work. Therefore speech grows weary, the eye grows weary, the ear grows weary. But death did not seize the central breath. Then the others tried to know him, and said: 'Verily, he is the best of us, he who, whether moving or not, does not tire and does not perish. Well, let all of us assume his form.' Thereupon they all assumed his form, and therefore they are called after him 'breathes' (spirits).

In whatever family there is a man who knows this, they call that family after his name. And he who strives with one who knows this, withers away and finally dies. So far with regard to the body.

Now with regard to the deities.

Agni held, I shall burn; Aditya (the sun) held, I shall warm; Chandramas (the moon) held, I shall shine; and thus also the other deities, each according to the deity. And as it was with the central breath among the breaths, so it was with Vayu, the wind among those deities. The other deities fade, not Vayu. Vayu is the deity that never sets.

And here there is this Shloka:

'He from whom the sun rises, and into whom it sets '(he verily rises from the breath, and sets in the breath)

'Him the Devas made the law, the only is today, and he tomorrow also', whatever these Devas determined then, that they perform today also.

Therefore let a man perform one observance only, let him breathe up and let him breathe down, that the evil death may not reach him. And when he performs it, let him try to finish it. Then he obtains through it union and oneness with that deity, Prana.

•

Verily, this is a triad, name, form, and work. Of these names, that which is called Speech is the Uktha (hymn, supposed to mean also origin), for from it all names arise. It is their Saman (song, supposed to mean also sameness), for it is the same as all names.

Next, of the forms, that which is called Eye is the Uktha (hymn), for whom it all forms arise. It is their Saman (song), for it is the same as all forms. It is their Brahman (prayer), for it supports all forms.

Next, of the works, that which is called Body is the Uktha (hymn), for from it all works arise. It is their Saman (song), for it is the same as all works. It is their Brahman (prayer), for it supports all works.

That being a triad is one, this Self; and the Self, being one, is that triad. This is the immortal, covered by the true. Verily, breath is the immortal, name and form are the true, and by them the immortal is covered.

2

There was formerly the proud Gargya Balaki, a man of great reading. He said to Ajatasatru of Kashi, 'Shall I tell you Brahman?' Ajatasatru said: 'We give a thousand cows for that speech of yours, for verily all people run away, saying, Janaka, the king of Mithila, is our patron.'

Gargya said: 'The person that is in the sun, that I adore as Brahman.' Ajatasatru said to him: 'No, no! Do not speak to me on this. I adore him verily as the supreme, the head of all beings, the king. Whoso adores him thus, becomes supreme, the head of all beings, a king.'

Gargya said: 'The person that is in the moon (and in the mind), that I adore as Brahman.' Ajatasatru said to him: 'No, no! Do no speak to me on this. I adore him verily as the great, clad in white raiment, as Soma, the king.' Whoso adores him thus, Soma is poured out and poured forth for him day by day, and his food does not fail.

Gargya said: 'The person that is in the lightning (and in the heart), that I adore as Brahman.' Ajatasatru said to him: 'No, no! Do not speak to me on this. I adore him verily as the luminous.' Whoso adores him thus, becomes lumonous, and his offspring becomes luminous.

Gargya said: 'The person that is in the ether (and in the ether of the heart), that I adore as Brahman.' Ajatasatru said to him: 'No no! Do not speak to me on this. I adore him as what is full, and quiescent.' Whoso adores him thus, becomes filled with offspring and cattle, and his offspring does not cease from this world.

Gargya said: 'The person that is in the wind (and in the breath), that I adore as Brahman.' Ajatasatru said to him: 'No no! Do not speak to me on this. I adore him as Indra Vaikuntha, as the unconquerable army of the Maruts.' Whoso adores him thus, becomes victorious, unconquerable, conquering his enemies.

Gargya said: 'The person that is in the fire (and in the heart), that I adore as Brahman.' Ajatasatru said to him:

'No, no! Do not speak to me on this. I adore him as powerful.' Whoso adores him thus, becomes powerful, and his offspring becomes powerful.

Gargya said: 'The person that is in the water (in seed, and in the heart), that I adore as Brahman.' Ajatasatru said to him: 'No, no! Do not speak to me on this. I adore him as likeness.' Whoso adores him thus, to him comes what is proper, not what is improper; what is born from him, is like unto him.

Gargya said: 'The person that is in the mirror, that I adore as Brahman.' Ajatasatru said to him: 'No, no! Do not speak to me on this. I adore him verily as the brilliant.' Whoso adores him thus, he becomes brilliant, his offspring becomes brilliant, and with whomsoever he comes together, he outshines them.

Gargya said: 'The sound that follows a man while he moves, that I adore as Brahman.' Ajatasatru said to him; 'No, no! Do not speak to me on this. I adore him verily as life.' Whoso adores him thus, he reaches his full age in this world, breath does not leave him before the time.

Gargya said: 'The person that is in space, that I adore as Brahman.' Ajatasatru said to him: 'No, no! Do not speak to me on this. I adore him verily as the second who never leaves us.' Whoso adores him thus, becomes possessed of a second, his party is not cut off from him.

Gargya said: 'The person that consists of the shadow, that I adore as Brahman.' Ajatasatru said to him: 'No, no! Do not speak to me on this. I adore him verily as death.' Whoso adores him thus, he reaches his whole age in this world, death does not approach him before the time.

Gargya said: 'The person that is in the body, that I adore as Brahman.' Ajatasatru said to him: 'No, no! Do not speak to me on this. I adore him verily as embodied.' Whoso adores him thus, becomes embodied, and his offspring becomes embodied.

Then Gargya became silent.

Ajatasatru said: 'Thus far only?' 'Thus far only,' he replied. Ajatasatru said: 'This does not suffice to know the true Brahman.' Gargya replied: 'Then let me come to you as a pupil.'

Ajatasatru said: 'Verily, it is unnatural that a Brahmin should come to a Kshatriya, hoping that he should tell him the Brahman. However, I shall make you know him clearly,' thus saying he took him by the hand and rose.

And the two together came to a person who was asleep. He called him by these names, 'Thou, great one, clad in white raiment, Soma, King.' He did not rise. Then rubbing him with his hand, he woke him, and he arose.

Ajatasatru said: 'When this man was thus asleep, where was then the Person (Purusha), the intelligent? and from whence did he thus come back?' Gargya did not know this?

Ajatasatru said: 'When this man was thus asleep, then the intelligent Person (Purusha), having through the intelligence of the senses (Pranas) absorbed within himself all intelligence, lies in the ether, which is in the heart. When he takes in these different kinds of intelligence, then it is said that the man sleeps. Then the breath is kept in, speech is kept in, the ear is kept in, the eye is kept in, the mind is kept in.

'But when he moves about in sleep and dream, then these are his worlds. He is, as it were, a great king; he is, as it were, a great Brahmin; he rises, as it were, and he falls. And as a great king might keep in his own subjects, and move about, according to his pleasure, within his own domain, thus does that person who is endowed with intelligence keep in the various senses (Pranas) and move about, according to his pleasure, within his own body while dreaming.

'Next, when he is in profound sleep, and knows nothing, there are the seventy-two thousand arteries called Hita, which from the heart spread through the body. Through them he moves forth and rests in the surrounding body. And as a young man, or a great king, or a great Brahmin, having reached the summit of happiness, might rest, so does he then rest.

'As the spider comes out with its thread, or as small sparks come forth from fire, thus do all senses, all worlds, all Devas, all beings come forth from that Self. The Upanishad (the true name and doctrine) of that Self is "the True of the True." Verily, the senses are the true, and he is the true of the true.'

•

Verily, he who knows the babe with his place, his chamber, his post, and his rope, he keeps off the seven relatives who hate him. Verily, by the young is meant the inner life, by his place this body, by his chamber this head, by his post the vital breath, by his rope the food.

Then the seven imperishable ones approach him. There are the red lines in the eye, and by them Rudra clings to him. There is the water in the eye, and by it Parjanya clings to him. There is the pupil and by it Aditya (sun) clings to him. There is the dark iris, and by it Agni clings to him. There is the white eye-ball, and by it Indra clings to him. With the lower eye-lash the earth, with the upper eye-lash the heaven clings to him. He who knows this, his food does never perish.

On this there is this Shloka:

'There is a cup having its mouth below and its bottom above. Manifold glory has been placed into it. On its lip sit the seven Rishis, the tongue as the eighth communicates with Brahman.' What is called the cup having its mouth below and its bottom above is this head, for its mouth (the mouth) is below, its bottom (the skull) is above. When it is said that manifold glory has been placed into it, the senses verily are manifold glory, and he therefore means the senses. When he says that the seven Rishis sit on its lip, the Rishis are verily the active senses, and he means the senses. And when he says that the tongue as the eighth communicates with Brahman, it is because the tongue, as the eighth, does communicate with Brahman.

These two, the two ears are the Rishis Gautama and Bharadvaja; the right Gautama, the left Bharadvaja. These two, the eyes, are the Rishis Vishvamitra and Jamadagni; the right Vishvamitra, the left Jamadagni. These two (the nostrils, are the Rishis Vasishtha and Kasyapa; the right Vasishtha, the left Kasyapa. The tongue is Atri, for with the tongue food is eaten, and Atri is meant for Atti, eating. He who knows this, becomes an eater of everything, and everything becomes his food.

•

There are two forms of Brahman, the material and the immaterial, the mortal and the immortal, the solid and the fluid, *sat* (being) and *tya* (that), (i.e. *sat-tya,* true).

Everything except air and sky is material, is mortal, is solid, is definite. The essence of that which is material, which is mortal, which is solid, which is definite is the sun that shines, for he is the essence of *sat,* the definite.

But air and sky are immaterial, the immortal, and fluid, are indefinite. The essence of that which is immaterial, which is immortal, which is fluid, which is indefinite, is the person in the disk of the sun, for he is the essence of *tyad,* the indefinite. So far with regard to the Devas.

Now with regard to the body. Everything except the breath and the ether within the body is material, is mortal, is solid, is definite. The essence of that which is material, which is mortal, which is solid, which is definite is the eye, for it is the essence of *sat,* the definite.

But breath and the ether within the body are immaterial, are immortal, are fluid, are indefinite. The essence of that which is immaterial, which is immortal, which is fluid, which is indefinite is the person in the right eye, for he is the essence of *tyad,* the indefinite.

And what is the appearance of that person? Like a saffron-coloured raiment, like white wool, the cochineal, like the flame of fire, like the white lotus, like sudden lightning.

He who knows this, his glory is like unto sudden lightning.

Next follows the teaching of Brahman by No, no! for there is nothing else higher than this, if one says: 'It is not so.' Then comes the name 'the True of the True,' the senses being the True, and he the Brahman the True of them.

•

Now when Yajnavalkya was going to enter upon another state, he said: 'Maitreyi, verily I am going away from this my house into the forest. Forsooth, let me make a settlement between thee and that Katyayani, my other wife.'

Maitreyi said: 'My Lord, if this whole earth, full of wealth, belonged to me, tell me, should I be immortal by it?' 'No,' replied Yajnavalkya; 'like the life of rich people will be thy life. But there is no hope of immortality by wealth.'

And Maitreyi said: 'What should I do with that by which I do not become immortal? What my Lord knoweth of immortality, tell that to me.'

Yajnavalkya replied: 'Thou who art truly dear to me, thou speakest dear words. Come, sit down, I will explain it to thee, and mark well what I say.'

And he said: 'Verily, a husband is not clear, that you may love the husband; but that you may love the Self, therefore a husband is dear.

'Verily, sons are not dear, that you may love the sons; but that you may love the Self, therefore sons are dear.

'Verily, wealth is not dear, that you may love wealth; but that you may love the Self, therefore wealth is dear.

'Verily, the Brahmin-class is not dear, that you may love the Brahman-class; but that you may love the Self, therefore the Brahmin-class is dear.

'Verily, the Kshatra-class is not dear, that you may love the Kshatra-class; but that you may love the Self, therefore the Kshatra-class is dear.

'Verily, the worlds are not dear, that you may love the

worlds; but that you may love the Self, therefore the worlds are dear.

'Verily, the Devas are not dear, that you may love the Devas; but that you may love the Self, therefore the Devas are dear.

'Verily, creatures are not dear, that you may love the creatures; but that you may love the Self, therefore are creatures dear.

'Verily, everything is not dear that you may love everything; but that you may love the Self, therefore everything is dear.

'Verily, the Self is to be seen, to be heard, to be perceived, to be marked, O Maitreyi! When we see, hear, perceive, and know the Self, then all this is known.

'Whosoever looks for the Brahmin-class elsewhere than in the Self, was abandoned by the Brahmin-class. Whosoever looks for the Kshatra class elsewhere than in the Self, was abandoned by the Kshatra-class. Whosoever looks for the worlds elsewhere than in the Self, was abandoned by the Devas. Whosoever looks for creatures elsewhere than in the Self, was abandoned by the creatures. Whosoever looks for anything elsewhere than in the Self, was abandoned by everything. This Brahmin-class, this Kshatra-class, these worlds, these Devas, these creatures, this everything, all is that Self.

'Now as the sounds of a drum, when beaten, cannot be seized externally by themselves, but the sound is seized, when the drum is seized or the beater of the drum;

'And as the sounds of a conch-shell, when blown, cannot be seized externally by themselves, but the sound is seized, when the shell is seized or the blower of the shell;

'And as the sounds of a lute, when played, cannot be seized externally by themselves, but the sound is seized, when the lute is seized or the player of the lute;

'As clouds of smoke proceed by themselves out of a lighted fire kindled with damp fuel, thus, verily, O Maitreyi, has been breathed forth from this great Being what we have as Rigveda, Yajurveda, Samaveda, Atharvangirasas, Itihasa (legends), Purana (cosmogonis), Vidya (knowledge), the Upanishads, Shlokas (verses), Sutras (prose rules), Anuvyakhyanas (glosses), Vyakhyanas (commentaries). From him alone all these were breathed forth.

'As all waters find their centre in the sea, all touches in the skin, all tastes in the tongue, all smells in the nose, all colours in the eye, all sounds in the ear, all percepts in the mind, all knowledge in the heart, all actions in the hands, all movements in the feet, and all the Vedas in speech,—

'As a lump of salt, when thrown into water, becomes dissolved into water, and could not be taken out again, but wherever we taste the water it is salt,—thus verily, O Maitreyi, does this great Being, endless, unlimited, consisting of nothing but knowledge, rise from out of these elements and vanish again in them. When he has departed, there is no more knowledge, I say, O Maitreyi.' Thus spoke Yajnavalkya.

Then Maitreyi said: 'Here thou hast bewildered me, Sir, when thou sayest that having departed, there is no more knowledge.'

But Yajnavalkya replied: 'O Maitreyi, I say nothing that is bewildering. This is enough, O beloved, for wisdom.

'For when there is as it were duality, then one sees the other, one smells the other, one hears the other, one salutes the other, one perceives the other, one knows the other; but when the Self only is all this, how should he smell another, how should he see another, how should he hear another, how should he salute another, how should he perceive another, how should he know another? How should he know Him by whom he knows all this? How, O beloved, should he know himself, the Knower?'

•

This earth is the honey, Madhu, the effect of all beings and all beings are the honey, Madhu, the effect of this earth.

Likewise this bright, immortal person in this earth, and that bright immortal person incorporated in the body, both are Madhu. He indeed is the same as that Self, that Immortal, that Brahman, that All.

This water is the honey of all beings, and all beings are the honey of this water. Likewise this bright, immortal person in this water, and that bright, immortal person existing as seed in the body both are Madhu. He indeed is the same as that Self, that Immortal, that Brahman, that All.

This fire is the honey of all beings, and all beings are the honey of this fire. Likewise this bright, immortal person in this fire, and that bright, immortal person, existing as speech in the body, both are Madhu. He indeed is the same as that Self, that Immortal, that Brahman, that All.

This air is the honey of all beings, and all beings are the honey of this air. Likewise this bright, immortal person in this air, and that bright, immortal person existing as breath in the body, both are Madhu. He indeed is the same as that Self, that Immortal, that Brahman, that All.

This sum is the honey of all beings, and all beings are the honey of this sun. Likewise this bright, immortal person in this sun, and that bright, immortal person existing as the eye in the body, both are Madhu. He indeed is the same as that Self, that Immortal, that Brahman, that All.

This space is the honey of all beings, and all beings are the honey of this space. Likewise this bright, immortal person in this space, and that bright, immortal person existing as the ear in the body, both are Madhu. He indeed is the same as that Self, that Immortal, that Brahman, that All.

This moon is the honey of all beings, and all beings are the honey of this moon. Likewise this bright, immortal person in this moon, and that bright, immortal person existing as mind in the body, both are Madhu. He indeed is the same as that Self, that Immortal, that Brahman, that All.

This lightning is the honey of all beings, and all beings are the honey of this lightning. Likewise this bright, immortal person in this lightning, and that bright, immortal person existing as light in the body, both are Madhu. He indeed is the same as that Self, that Immortal, that Brahman, that All.

This thunder is the honey of all beings, and all beings are the honey of this thunder. Likewise this bright, immortal person in this thunder, and that bright, immortal person existing as sound and voice in the body, both are Madhu. He indeed is the same as that Self, that Immortal, that Brahman, that All.

This ether is the honey of all beings, and all beings are the honey of this ether. Likewise this bright, immortal person in this ether, and that bright, immortal person existing as heart—ether in the body, both are Madhu. He indeed is the same as that Self, that Immortal, that Brahman, that All.

This law (Dharma) is honey of all beings, and all beings are the honey of this law. Likewise this bright, immortal person in this law, and that bright, immortal person in this law, and that bright, immortal person existing as law in the body, both are Madhu. He indeed is the same as that Self, that Immortal, that Brahman, that All.

This true (Satyam) is the honey of all beings, and all beings are the honey of this true. Likewise this bright, immortal person in what is true, and that bright, immortal person existing as the true in the body, both are Madhu. He indeed is the same as that Self, that Immortal, that Brahman, that All.

This mankind is the honey of all beings, and all beings are the honey of this mankind. Likewise this bright, immortal person in mankind, and that bright, immortal person existing as man in the body, both are Madhu. He indeed is the same as that Self, that Immortal, that Brahman, that All.

This Self is the honey of all beings, and all beings are the honey of this Self. Likewise this bright, immortal person in this Self, and that bright, immortal person, the Self, both are Madhu. He indeed is the same as that Self, that Immortal, that Brahman, that All.

And verily this Self is the lord of all beings, the king of all beings. And as all spokes are contained in the axle and in the felly of a wheel, all beings, and all those selfs, of the earth, water, etc., are contained in that Self.

Verily, Dadhyach Atharvana proclaimed this honey to the two Ashvins, and a Rishi, seeing this, said:

'O Ashvins, you fixed a horse's head on Atharvana Dadhyach, and he, wishing to be true to his promise, proclaimed to you the honey; both that of Tvashtri and that which is to be your secret, O ye strong ones.'

Verily, Dadhyach Atharvana proclaimed this honey to the two Ashvins, and a Rishi, seeing this, said:

'He the Lord made bodies with two feet, he made bodies with four feet. Having first become a bird, he entered the bodies as Purusha, as the Person.' This very Purusha is in all bodies the Purisaya, i.e., he who in the body and is therefore called Purusha. There is nothing that is not covered by him, nothing that is not filled by him.

Verily, Dadhyach Atharvana proclaimed this honey to the two Ashvins, and a Rishi, seeing this, said:

He the Lord became like unto every form, and this is meant to reveal the true form of the Atman. Indra the Lord appears multiform through the Mayas appearances, for his horses (senses) are yolked, hundreds and ten.

This Atman is the horses, this Atman is the ten, the thousands, many and endless. This is the Brahman, without cause and without effect, without anything inside or outside; this Self is Brahman, ominpresent and omniscient. This is the teaching of the Upanishads.

3

Adoration to Paramatman! the Highest Self!

Janaka Vaideha, the king of the Videhas, sacrificed with a sacrifice at which many presents were offered to the priests of the Ashvamedha. Brahmins of the Kurus and the Panchalas had come thither, and Janaka Vaideha wished to know, which of those Brahmins was the best read. So he enclosed a thousand cows, and ten padas of gold were fastened to each pair of horns.

And Janaka spoke to them: 'Ye venerable Brahmins, he who among you is the wisest, let him drive away these cows.'

Then those Brahmins dared not, but Yajnavalkya said to his pupil: 'Drive them away, my dear.'

He replied: 'O glory of the Saman,' and drove them away.

The Brahmins became angry and said: 'How could he call himself the wisest among us?'

Now there was Ashvala, the Hotri priest of Janaka Vaideha. He asked him: Are you indeed the wisest among us, O Yajnavalkya?' He replied: 'I bow before the wises' the best knower of Brahman, but I wish indeed to have these cows.'

Then Ashvala, the Hotri priest, undertook to question him.

'Yajnavalkya,' he said, 'everything here connected with the sacrifice is reached by death, everything is overcome by death. By what means then is the sacrificer freed beyond the reach of death?'

Yajnavalkya said: 'By the Hotri priest, who is Agni (fire), who is speech. For speech is the Hotri of the sacrifice or the sacrificer, and speech is Agni, and he is the Hotri. This constitutes freedom, and perfect freedom from death.'

'Yajnavalkya,' he said, 'everything here is reached by day and night, everything is overcome by day and night. By what means then is the sacrificer freed beyond the reach of day and night?

Yajnavalkya said: 'By the Adhvaryu priest, who is the eye, who is Aditya (the sun). For the eye is the Adhvaryu of the sacrifice, and the eye is the sun, and he is the Adhvaryu. This constitutes freedom, and perfect freedom.'

'Yajnavalkya,' he said, 'everything here is reached by

the waxing and waning of the moon, everything is overcome by the waxing and waning of the moon. By what means then is the sacrificer freed beyond the reach of the waxing and waning of the moon?'

Yajnavalkya said: 'By the Udgatri priest, who is Vayu (the wind), who is the breath. for the breath is the Udgatri of the sacrifice, and the breath is the wind, and he is the Udgatri. This constitutes freedom, and perfect freedom.'

'Yajnavalkya,' he said, 'this sky is, as it were, without an staircase. By what approach does the sacrificer approach the Svarga world?'

Yajnavalkya said: 'By the Brahman priest, who is the mind, who is the moon. For the mind is the Brahman of the sacrifice, and the mind is the moon, and he is the Brahman. This constitutes freedom, and perfect freedom. These are the complete deliverances from death.'

Next follow the achievements.

'Yajnavalkya,' he said, 'how many Rik verses will the Hotri priest employ today at this sacrifice?'

'Three,' replied Yajnavalkya.

'And what are these three?'

'Those which are called Puronuvakya, Yajya, and, thirdly, Shasya.'

'What doest he gain by them?'

'All whatsoever has breath.'

'Yajnavalkya,' he said, 'how many oblations will the Adhvaryu priest employ today at this sacrifice?'

'Three,' replied Yajnavalkya.

'And what are these three?'

'Those which, when offered, flame up; those which, when offered, make an excessive noise; and those which, when offered, sink down.

'What does he gain by them?'

'By those which, when offered, flame up, he gains the Deva (god) world, for the Deva world flames up, as it were. By those which, when offered, make an excessive noise, he gains the Pitri (father) world, for the Pitri world is excessively noisy. By those which, when offered, sink down, he gains the Manushya (man) world, for the Manushya world, is, as it were, down below.'

'Yajnavalkya,' he said, 'with how many deities does the Brahmin priest on the right protect today this sacrifice?'

'The mind alone; for the mind is endless, and the Vishvedevas are endless, and he thereby gains the endless world.'

'Yajnavalkya,' he said, 'how many Stotriya hymns will the Udgatri priest employ today at this sacrifice?'

'Three,' replied Yajnavalkya.

'And what are these three?'

'Those which are called Puronuvakya, Yajya, and, thirdly, Shasya.'

'And what are these with regard to the body (adhyatmam)?'

'The Puronuvakya is Prana (upbreathing), the Yajya the Apana (downbreathing), the Shasya the Vyana (backbreathing).'

'What does he gain by them?'

'He gains the earth by the Puronuvakya, the sky by the Yajya, heaven by the Shasya.'

After that Ashvala held his peace.

•

Then Jaratkarava Artabhaga asked. 'Yajnavalkya,' he said, 'how many Grahas are there, and how many Atigrahas?'

'Eight Grahas,' he replied, 'and eight Atigrahas.'

'And what are these eight Grahas and eight Atigrahas?'

'Prana (breath) is one Graha, and that is seized by Apana (downbreathing) as the Atigraha, for one smells with the Apana.'

'Speech (Vak) is one Graha, and that is seized by name (naman) as the Atigraha, for with speech one pronounces names.'

'The tongue is one Graha, and that is seized by taste

as the Atigraha, for with the tongue one perceives tastes.'

'The eye is one Graha, and that is seized by form as the Atigraha, for with the eye one sees forms.'

'The ear is one Graha, and that is seized by sound as the Atigraha, for with the ear one hears sounds.'

'The mind is one Graha, and that is seized by desires as the Atigraha for with the mind one desires desires..'

'The arms are one Graha, and these are seized by work as the Atigraha, for with the arms one works work.'

'The skin is one Graha, and that is seized by touch as the Atigraha, for with the skin one perceives touch. These are the eight Grahas and the eight Atigrahas.'

'Yajnavalkya,' he said, 'everything is the food of death. What then is the deity to whom death is food?'

'Fire (Agni) is death, and that is the food for water. Death is conquered again.'

Yajnavalkya,' he said, 'when such a person (a sage) dies, do the vital breaths (Pranas) move out of him or not?'

'No,' replied Yajnavalkya; 'they are gathered up in him, he swells, he is inflated, and thus inflated the dead lies at rest.'

'Yajnavalkya,' he said, 'when such a man dies, what does not leave him?"

'The name,' he replied, 'for the name is endless, the Vishvedevas are endless, and by it he gains the endless world.'

'Yajnavalkya,' he said, 'when the speech of this dead person enters into the fire, breath into the air, the eye into the sun, the mind into the moon, the hearing into space, into the earth the body, into the ether the self, into the shrubs the hairs of the body, into the trees the hairs of the head, when the blood and the seed are deposited in the water, where is then that person?'

Yajnavalkya said: 'Take my hand, my friend. We two along shall know of this; let this question of ours not be discussed in public.'

Then these two went out and argued, and what they

said was Karman (work) what they praised was Karman, that a man becomes good by good work, and bad by bad work. After that Jaratkarava Artabhaga held his peace.

•

Then Bhujyu Lahyayani asked. 'Yajnavalkya,' he said, 'we wandered about as students, and came to the house of Patanchala Kapya. He had a daughter who was possessed by a Gandharva. We asked him, "Who art thou?" and he replied: "I am Sudhanva, the Angirasa." And when we asked him about the ends of the world, we said to him. "Where were the Parikshitas?" Where then were the Parikshitas? I ask thee, Yajnavalkya, where were the Parikshitas?'

Yajnavalkya said: 'He said to thee, I suppose, that they went where those go who have performed a horse-sacrifice?'

He said: 'And where do they go who have performed a horse-sacrifice?'

Yajnavalkya replied: 'Thirty-two journeys of the car of the sun is this world. The earth surrounds it on every side, twice as large, and the ocean surrounds this earth on every side, twice as large. Now there is between them a space as large as the edge of a razor or the wing of a mosquito. Indra, having become a bird, handed them through the space to Vayu (the air), and Vayu, holding them within himself, conveyed them to where they dwell who have performed a horse-sacrifice. Somewhat in this way did he praise Vayu indeed. Therefore Vayu is everything by itself, and Vayu is all things together. He who knows this, conquers death.'

After that Bhujyu Lahayayani held his peace.

•

Then Ushasta Chakrayana asked. 'Yajnavalkya,' he said, 'tell me the Brahman which is visible, not invisible, the Self (atman), who is within all.'

Yajnavalkya replied: 'This, thy Self, who is within all.'

'Which Self, O Yajnavalkya, is within all?'

Yajnavalkya replied: ' He who breathes in the

upbreathing, he is thy Self, and within all. He who breathes in the downbreathing, he is thy Self, and within all. He who breathes in the onbreathing, he is thy Self, and within all. He who breathes in the outbreathing, he is thy Self, and within all. This is thy Self, who is within all.'

Ushasta Chakrayana said: 'As one might say, this is a cow, this is a horse, thus has this been explained by thee. Tell me the Brahman which is visible, not invisible, the Self, who is wthin all.'

Yajnavalkya replied: ' This, thy Self, who is within all.'

'Which Self, O Yajnavalkya, is within all?'

Yajnavalkya replied: 'Thou couldst not see the true seer of sight, thou couldst not hear the true hearer of hearing, nor perceive the perceiver of perception, nor know the knower of knowledge. This is thy Self, who is within all. Everything else is of evil.'

After that Ushasta Chakrayana held his peace.

Then Kahola Kaushitakeya asked. 'Yajnavalkya,' he said, 'Tell me the Brahman which is visible, not invisible, the Self (Atman), who is wthin all.'

Yajnavalkya repied: 'This, thy Self, who is within all.'

'Which Self, O Yajnavalkya, is within all?'

Yajnavalkya repied: 'He who overcomes hunger and thirst, sorrow, passion, old age, and death. When Brahmins know that Self, and have risen above the desire for sons, wealth, and new worlds, they wander about as mendicants. For a desire for sons is desire for wealth, a desire for wealth is desire for worlds. Both these are indeed desires.Therefore let a Brahmin, after he has done with learning, wish to stand by real strength; after he has done with that strength and learning, he becomes a Muni (a Yogin); and after he has done with what is the knowledge of a Muni, he is a Brahmin. By whatever means he has become a Brahmin, he is such indeed. Everything else is of evil.'

After that Kahola Kaushitakeya held his peace.

•

Then Gargi Vachakhavi asked. 'Yajnavalkya,' she said, 'everything here is woven, like warp and woof, in water. What then is that in which water is woven, like warp and woof?'

'In air, O Gargi,' he replied.

'In what then is air woven, like warp and woof?'

'In the worlds of the sky, O Gargi,' he replied.

'In what then are the worlds of the sky woven, like warp and woof?'

'In the worlds of the Gandharvas, O Gargi,' he replied.

'In what then are the worlds of the Gandharvas woven, like warp and woof?'

'In the worlds of Aditya (sun), O Gargi,' he replied.

'In what then are the worlds of Aditya woven, like warp and woof?'

'In the worlds of Chandra (moon), O Gargi.' he replied.

'In what then are the worlds of Chandra woven, like warp and woof?'

'In the worlds of the Nakshatras (stars), O Gargi.' he replied.

'In what then are the worlds of the Devas (gods) woven, like warp and woof?'

'In the worlds of Indra, O Gargi,' he replied.

'In what then are the worlds of Indra woven, like warp and woof?'

'In the worlds of Prajapati, O Gargi,' he replied.

'In what then are the worlds of Prajapati woven, like warp and woof?'

'In the worlds of Brahman, O Gargi,' he replied.

'In what then are the worlds of Brahman woven, like warp and woof?'

Yajnavalkya said: 'O Gargi, do not ask too much, lest thy head should fall off. Thou askest too much about a deity about which we are not to ask too much. Do not askest too much about a deity about which we are not to ask too much. Do not ask too much, O Gargi.'

After that Gargi Vachaknavi held her peace.

•

Then Uddalaka Aruni asked. 'Yajnavalkya,' he said, 'we dwelt among the Madras in the houses of Patanchala Kapya, studying the sacrifice. His wife was possessed of a Gandharva, and we asked him: "Who art thou?" He answered: "I am Kabandha Atharvana." And he said to Patanchala Kapya and to us students: "Dost thou know, Kapya, that thread by which this world and the other world, and all beings are strung together?' And Patanchala Kapya replied: "I do not know it, Sir." He said again to Patanachala Kapya and to us students: "Dost thou know, Kapya, that puller (ruler) within (Antaryamin), who within pulls (rules) this world and the other world and all beings?" And Patanchala Kapya replied: "I do not know it, Sir." He said again to Patanchala Kapya and to us students: "He, O Kapya, who knows that thread and him who pulls it within, he knows Brahman, he knows the worlds, he knows the Devas, he knows the Vedas, he knows the Bhutas (creatures), he knows the Self, he knows everything." Thus did he, the Gandharva, say to them, and I know it. If thou, O Yajnavalkya, without knowing that string and the puller within, drivest away those Brahma-cows (the cows offered as a prize to him who best knows Brahman), thy head will fall of.'

Yajnavalkya said: "Gautama, I believe I know that thread and the puller within.'

The other said: 'Anybody may say, I know. Tell what thou knowest.'

Yajnavalkya said: 'Vayu (Air) is that thread, O Gautama. By air, as by a thread, O Gautama, this world and the other worlds, and all creatures are strung together. Therefore, O Gautama, people say of a dead person that his limbs have become unstrung; for by air, as by a thread, O Gautama, they were strung together.'

The other said: ' So it is, O Yajnvalkya. Tell now who is the puller within.'

Yajnavalkya said: 'He who dwells in the earth, and within the earth, whom the earth does not know, whose body the earth is, and who pulls (rules) within, the immortal.

'He who dwells in the water, and within the water, whom the water does not know, whose body the water is, and who rules the water within, he is thy Self, the ruler within, the immortal.

'He who dwells in the fire, and within the fire, whom the fire does not know, whose body the fire is, and who rules the fire within, he is thy Self, the ruler within, the immortal.

'He who dwells in the sky, and within the air (Vayu), whom the air does not know, whose body the air is, and who rules the air within, is thy Self, the ruler within, the immortal.

'He who dwells in the heaven (Dyu), and within the heaven, whom the heaven does not know, whose body the heaven is, and who rules the heaven within, he is thy Self, the ruler within, the immortal.

'He who dwells in the sun (Aditya), and within the sun, whom the sun does not know, whose body the sun is, and who rules the sun within, he is thy Self, the ruler within, the immortal.

'He who dwells in the space (Disah), and within the space, whom the space does not know, whose body the space is, and who rules the space within, he is thy Self, the ruler within, the immortal.

'He who dwells in the moon and starts (Chandra-tarakam), and within the moon and stars, whom the moon and stars do not know, whose body the moon and stars are, and who rules the moon and stars within, he is thy Self, the ruler, within, the immortal.

'He who dwells in the darkness (Tamas), and within the darkness, whom the darkness does not know, whose body the darkness is, and who rules the darkness within, he is thy Self, the ruler within, the immortal.

'He who dwells in the light (Tejas), and within the light,

whom the light does not know, whose body the light is, and who rules the light within, he is thy Self, the ruler within, the immortal.

So far with respect to the gods (Adhidaivatam); now with respect to beings (Adhibhutam).

Yajnavalkya said: 'He who dwells in all beings, and within all beings, whom all beings do not know, whose body all beings are, and who rules all beings within, he is thy Self, the ruler within, the immortal.

'He who dwells in the breath (Prana), and within the breath, whom the breath does not know, whose body the breath is, and who rules the breath within, he is thy Self, the ruler within, the immortal.

'He who dwells in the tongue (Vach), and within the tongue, whom the tongue does not know, whose body the tongue is, and who rules the tongue within, he is thy Self, the ruler within, the immortal.

'He who dwells in the eye, and within the eye, whom the eye does not know, and whose body the eye is, and who rules the eye within, he is thy Self, the ruler within, the immortal.

'He who dwells in the ear, and within the ear, whom the ear does not know, whose body the ear is, and who rules the ear within, he is thy Self, the ruler within, the immortal.

'He who dwells in the mind, and within the mind, whom the mind does not know, whose body the mind is, and who rules the mind within, he is thy Self, the ruler within, the immortal.

'He who dwells in the skin, and within the skin, who the skin does not know, whose body the skin is, and who rules the skin within, he is thy Self, the ruler within, the immortal.

'He who dwells in knowledge, and within knowledge, whom knowledge does not know, whose body knowledge is, and who rules knowledge within, he is thy Self, the ruler within, the immortal.

'He who dwells in the seed, and within the seed, whom the seed does not know, whose body the seeed is, and who rules the seed within, he is thy Self, the ruler within, the immortal; unseen, but seeing; unheard, but hearing; unperceived, but perceiving; unknown, but knowing. There is no other seer but he, there is no other hearer but he, there is no other perceiver but he, there is no other knower but he. Everything else is of evil.'

After that Uddalaka Aruni held his peace.

•

Then Vachaknavi said: 'Venerable Brahmin, I shall ask him two questions. If he will answer them, none of you, I think, will defeat him in any argument concerning Brahman.'

Yajnavalkya said: 'Ask, O Gargi.'

She said: 'O Yajnavalkya, as the son of a warrior from the Kashis or Videhas might string his lossened bow, take two pointed foe-piercing arrows in his hand and rise to do battle, I have risen to fight thee with two questions. Answer me these questions.'

Yajnavalkya said: 'Ask, O Gargi.'

She said: 'O Yajnavalkya, that of which they say that it is above the heavens, beneath the earth, embracing heaven and earth, past, present, and future, tell me in what is it woven, ike warp and woof?'

Yajnavalkya said: 'That of which they say that it is above the heavens, beneath the earth, embracing heaven and earth, past, present, and future, that is woven, like warp and woof, in the ether (Akasa).'

She said: 'I bow to thee, O Yajnavalkya, who hast solved me that question. Get thee ready for the second.'

Yajnavalkya said: 'Ask, O, Gargi! She said, 'O Yajnavalkya, that of which they say that it is above the heavens, beneath the earth, embracing heaven and earth, past, present, and future, tell me in what is it woven, like warp and woof?'

Yajnavalkya said: 'That of which they say that it is above the heavens, beneath the earth, embracing heaven and earth, past, present, and future, that is woven, like warp and woof, in the ether.'

Gargi said: 'In what then is the ether woven, like warp and woof?'

He said: 'O Gargi, the Brahmins call this the Akshara the imperishable. It is neither coarse nor fine, neither short nor long, neither red like fire nor fluid like water; it is without shadow, without darkness, without air, without ether, without attachment, without taste, without smell, without eyes, without ears, without speech, without mind, without light (vigour), without breath, without a mouth (or door), without measure, having no within and no without, it devours nothing, and no one devours it.

'By the command of that Akshara, the imperishable, O Gargi, sun and moon stand apart. By the command of that Akshara, O Gargi, heaven and earth stand apart. By the command of that Akshara, O Gargi, what are called moments (*nimesha*), hours (*muhurta*), days and nights, half-months, months, seasons, years, all stand apart. By the command of that Akshara, O Gargi, some rivers flow to the East from the white mountains, others to the West, or to any other quarter. By the command of that Akshara, O Gargi, men praise those who give, the gods follow the sacrificer, the fathers, the Darvi-offering.

'Whosover, O Gargi, without knowing that Akshara, the imperishable, offers oblations in this world, sacrifices, and performs penance for a thousand years, his work will have an end. Whosoever, O Gargi, without knowing this Akshara, departs this world, he is miserable like a slave. But he, O Gargi, who departs this world, knowing this Akshara, he is a Brahmin.

'That Brahman,' O Gargi, 'is unseen, but seeing; unheard, but hearing; unperceived, but perceiving; unknown, but knowing. There is nothing that sees but it, nothing that hears but it, nothing that perceives but it, nothing that knows but it. In that Akshara then, O Gargi, the ether is woven, like warp and woof.'

Then said Gargi: 'Venerable Brahmin, you may consider it a great thing, if you get off by bowing before him. No one, I believe, will defeat him in any argument concerning Brahman.'

After that Vachaknavi held her peace.

•

Then Vidagdha Shakalya asked him: 'How many gods are there, O Yajnavalkya?'

He repied with this very Nivid: 'As many as are mentioned in the Nivid of the hymn of praise addressed to the Vishvedevas, three and three hundred, three and three thousand.'

'Yes,' he said, and asked again: 'How many gods are there really, O Yajnavalkya?'

'Thirty-three,' he said.

'Yes,' he said, and asked again: 'How many gods are there really, O Yajnavalkya?'

'Six,' he said.

'Yes,' he said, and asked again: 'How many gods are there really, O Yajnavalkya?'

'Two,' he said. 'yes' he said, and asked again: 'How many gods are there really, O Yajnavalkya?'

'One and a half,' he said.

'Yes,' he said, and asked again: 'How many gods are there really, O Yajnavalkya?'

'One,' he said.

'Yes,' he said, and asked: 'Who are these three and three hundred, three and three thousand?'

Yajnavalkya replied: 'They are only the various powers of them, in reality there are only thirty-three gods.'

He aksed: 'Who are those thirty-three?'

Yajnavalkya repied: 'The eight Vasus, the eleven Rudras, the twelve Adityas. They make thirty-one, and Indra and Prajapati make the thirty-three.'

He asked: 'Who are the Vasus.'

Yajnavalkya replied: 'Agni (fire), Prithivi (earth), Vayu (air, Antariksha (sky), Aditya (sun), Dyu (heaven), Chandramas (moon), the Nakshatras (stars), these are the Vasus, for in them all that dwells, this world rests; and therefore they are called Vasus.'

He asked: 'Who are the Rudras?'

Yajnavalkya replied: 'These ten vital breaths (Pranas, the senses, i.e., the five Jnanendriyas, and the five Karmendriyas), and Atman', as the eleventh. When they depart from this mortal body, they make us cry (*rodayanti*), and because they make us cry, they are called Rudras.'

He asked: 'Who are the Adityas?'

Yajnavalkya replied: 'The twelve months of the year, and they are Adityas, because they move along (*yanti*), taking up everything (*adadanah*). Because they move along, taking up everything, therefore they are caled Adityas.'

He asked: 'And who is Indra, and who is Prajapati?'

Yajnavalkya replied: 'Indra is thunder, Prajapati is the sacrifice.'

He asked: 'And what is the thunder?'

Yajnavalkya replied: 'The thunderbolt.'

He asked: 'And what is the sacrifice?'

Yajnavalkya replied, 'The animals.'

He asked, 'Who are the six?'

Yanjnavalkya replied: 'Agni (fire), Prithivi (earth), Vayu (air), Antariksha (sky), Aditya (sun), Dyu (heaven), they are the six, for they are all this, the six.'

He asked: 'Who are the three gods?'

Yajnavalkya replied: 'These three worlds, for in them all these gods exist.'

He asked: 'Who are the two gods?'

Yajnavalkya replied: 'Food and breath.'

He asked: 'Who is the one god and a half?'

Yjanavalkya replied: 'He that blows.'

Here they say: 'How is it that he who blows like one only, should be called one and a half (Adhyardhya)?' And the answer is: 'Because, when the wind was blowing, everything grew (Adhyardhnot).'

He asked: 'Who is the one god?'

Yajnavalkya replied: 'Breath (Prana), and he is Brahman (the Sutratman), and they call him That (*tyad*).'

Shakalya said: 'Whosoever knows that person or god whose dwelling is the earth, whose sight (world) is fire, whose mind is light,—the principle of every living self, he indeed is a teacher, O Yajnavalkya.'

Yajnavalkya said: 'I know that person, the principle of every self, of whom thou speakest. This material person, "he is he." But tell me, Shakalya, who is his deity?'

Shakalya repied: The Immortal.'

Shakalya said: 'Whosoever knows that person whose dwelling is a body capable of sensual love, whose sight is the heart, whose mind is light,— the principle of every self, he indeed is a teacher, O Yajnavalkya. Yajnavalkya replied: 'I know that person, the principe of every self, of whom thou speakest. This love-made (loving) person, "he is he." But tell me, Shakalya, who is his devata?'

Shakaly replied: 'The women.'

Shakalya said: 'Whosoever knows that person whose dwelling are the colours, whose sight is the eye, whose mind is light,—the principle of every self, he indeed is a teacher, O Yajnavalkya.'

Yajnavalkya replied: 'I know that person, the principle of every self, of whom thou speakest. That person is the sun, "he is he." But tell me, Sakalya, who is his devata?'

Shakalya replied: 'The True.'

Shakalya said: 'Whosoever knows that person whose dwelling is ether, whose sight is the ear, whose mind is light,— the principle of every self, he indeed is a teacher, O Yajnavalkya.'

Yajnavalkya replied: 'I know that person, the principle of every self, of whom thou speakest. The person who hears and answers, "he is he." But tell me, Sakalya, who is his devata?'

Shakalya said: 'Whosoever knows that person whose dwelling is darkness, whose sight is the heart, whose mind is light,—the principle of every self, he indeed is a teacher, O Yajnavalkya.'

Yajnavalkya replied: 'I know that person, the principle of every self, of whom thou speakest. The shadowy person, "he is he." But tell me, Shakalya, who is his devata?'

Shakalya replied: 'Death.'

Shakalya said: 'Whosoever knows that person whose dwelling are bright colours, whose sight is the eye, whose mind is light,—the principle of every self, he indeed is a teacher, O Yajnavalkya.'

Yajnavalkya replied: 'I know that person, the principle of every self, of whom thou speakest. The person in the looking-glass, 'he is he'. But tell me, Shakalya, who is his devata?'

Shakalya repied: 'Vital Breath' (*Asu*).

Shakalya said: 'Whosoever knows that person whose dwelling is water, whose sight is the heart, whose mind is light,— the principle of every self, he indeed is a teacher, O Yajnavalkya.'

Yajnavalkya replied: ' I know that person, the principle of every self, of whom thou speakest. The person is the water, "he is he." But tell me, Shakalya, who is his devata?'

Shakalya replied: 'Varuna.'

Shakalya said: 'Whoosoever knows that person whose dwelling is seed, whose sight is the heart, whose mind is light,—the principle of every self, he indeed is a teacher, O Yjanavalkya.'

Yajnavalkya replied: 'I know that person, the principle of every self, of whom thou speakest. The filial person, "he is he." But tell me, Shakalya, who is his devata?'

Shakalya replied: 'Prajapati.'

Yajnavalkya said: 'Shakalya, did those Brahmins, who themselves shrank from the contest, make thee the victim?'

Shakalya said: 'Yajnavalkya, because thou hast decried the Brahmins of the Kuru-Panchalas, what Brahman dost thou know?'

Yajnavalkya said: 'I know the quarters with their deities and their abodes.'

Shakalya said: 'If thou knowest the quarters with their deities and their abodes, which is thy deity in the Eastern quarter?' Yajnavalkya said: 'Aditya (the sun).'

Shakalya said: 'In what does that Aditya abide?'

Yajnavalkya said: 'In the eye.'

Shakalya said: 'In what does the eye abide?'

Yajnavalkya said: 'In the colours, for with the eye he sees the colours.'

Shakalya said: 'And in what then do the colours abide?'

Yajnavalkya said: 'In the heart, for we know colours by the heart, for colours abide in the heart.'

Shakalya said: 'So it is indeed, O Yajnavalkya.'

Shakalya said: 'Which is thy deity in the Southern quarter?'

Yajnavalkya said: 'Yama.'

Yajnavalkya said: 'In the sacrifice.'

Shakalya said: 'In what does the sacrifice abide?'

Yajnavalkya said: 'In the Dakshina (the gifts to be given to the priests).'

Shakalya said: 'In what does the Dakshina abide?'

Yajnavalkya said: 'In Shraddha (faith), for if a man believes, then he gives Dakshina, and Dakshina truly abides in faith.'

Shakalya said: 'And in what then does faith abide?'

Yajnavalkya said: 'In the heart, for by the heart faith knows, and therefore faith abides in the heart.'

Shakalya said: 'So it is indeed, O Yajnavalkya.'

Shakalya said: 'Which is thy deity in the Western quarter?'

Yajnavalkya said: 'In the water.'

Shakalya said: 'In what does the water abide?'

Yajnavalkya said,' In the seed.'

Shakalya said,' And in what does the seed abide?'

Yajnavalkya said: 'In the heart. And therefore also they

say of a son who is like his father, that he seems as if slipt from his heart or made from his heart; for the seed abides in the heart.'

Shakalya said: 'So it is indeed, O Yajnavalkya.'

Shakalya said: 'Which is thy deity in the Northern quarter?'

Yajnavalkya said: 'Soma.'

Shakalya said: 'In what does that Soma abide?'

Yajnavalkya said: 'In the Diksha.'

Shakalya said: 'In what does the Diksha abide?'

Yajnavalkya said: 'In the True; and therefore they say to one who has performed the Diksha. Speak what is true, for in the True indeed the Diksha abides.'

Shakalya said: 'And in what does the True abide?'

Yajnavalkya said: 'In the heart, for with the heart do we know what is true, and in the heart indeed the True abides.'

Shakalya said: 'So it is indeed, O Yajnavalkya.'

Shakalya said: 'Which is thy deity in the zenith?'

Yajnavalkya said: 'Agni.'

Shakalya said: 'In what does that Agni abide?'

Yajnavalkya said: 'In speech.'

Shakalya said: 'And in what does speech abide?'

Yajnavalkya said: 'In the heart.'

Shakalya said: 'And in what does the heart abide?'

Yajnavalkya said: 'O Ahallika (idiot), when you think the heart could be anywhere else away from us, if it were away from us, the dogs might eat it, or the birds tear it.'

Shakalya said: 'And in what dost thou (thy body) and the Self (thy heart) abide?'

Yajnavalkya said: 'In the Prana (breath).'

Shakalya said: 'In what does the Prana abide?'

Yajnavalkya said: 'In the Apana (downbreathing).'

Shakalya said: 'In what does the Apana abide?'

Yajnavalkya said: 'In the Vyana (backbreathing).'

Shakalya said: 'In what does the Vyana abide?'

Yajnavalkya said : 'In the Udana (the outbreathing).'

Shakalya said: 'In what does the Udana abide?'

Yajnavalkya said: 'In the Samana. That Self (Atman) is to be described by No, no! He is incomprehensible, for he cannot be (is not) comprehended; he is imperishable, for he cannot perish; he is unattached, for he does not attach himself; unfettered, he does not suffer, he does not fail.

'These are the eight abodes (the earth, etc.), the eight worlds (fire, etc.), the eight gods (the immortal food, etc.), the eight persons (the corporeal, etc.). He who after dividing and uniting these persons. went beyond the Samana, that person, taught in the Upanishads, I now ask thee to teach me. If thou shalt not explain him to me, thy head will fall.'

Shakalya did not know him, and his head fell, nay, thieves took away his bones, mistaking them for something else's.

Then Yajnavalkya said: 'Reverend Brahmins, whosoever among you desires to do so, may now question me. Or question me, all of you. Or whosoever among you desires it, I shall question him, or I shall question all of you.'

But those Brahmins didst not say anything.

Then Yajnavalkya questioned them with these Shlokas:

'As a mighty tree in the forest, so in truth is man, his hairs are the leaves, his outer skin is the bark.

'From his skin flows forth blood, sap from the skin of the tree; and thus from the wounded man comes forth blood, as from a tree that is struck.

'The lumps of his flesh are in the tree the layers of wood, the fibre is strong like the tendons. The bones are the hard wood within, the marrow is made like the marrow of the tree.

'But, while the tree, when felled, grows up again more young from the root, from what root, tell me, does a mortal grow up, after he has been felled by death?

'Do not say, "from seed," for seed is produced from the living; but a tree, springing from a grain, clearly rises again after death.

'If a tree is pulled up with the root, it will not grow again; from what root then, tell me, does a mortal grow up, after he has been felled by death?

'Once born, he is not born again; for who should create him again?

'Brahman, who is knowledge and bliss, he is the principle, both to him who gives gifts, and also to him who stands firm, and knows.'

4

When Janaka Vaideha was sitting to give audience, Yajnavalkya approached, and Janaka Vaideha said: 'Yajnavalkya, for what object did you come, wishing for cattle, or for subtle questions?'

Yajnavalkya replied: 'For both, Your Majesty; 'Let us hear what anybody may have told you.'

Janaka Vaideha replied: 'Jitvan Shailina told me that speech (Vach) is Brahman.'

Yajnavalkya said: 'As one who had the benefit of a good father, mother, and teacher might tell, so did Shailina tell you, that speech is Brahman; for what is the use of a dumb person? But did he tell you the body and the resting-place of that Brahman?'

Janaka Vaideha said: 'He did not tell me.'

Yajnavalkya said: 'Your Majesty, this Brahman stands on one leg only.'

Janaka Vaideha said: 'Then tell me, Yajnavalkya.'

Yajnavalkya said: 'The tongue is its body, ether its place, and one should worhsip it as knowledge.'

Janaka Vaideha said: 'What is the nature of that knowledge?'

Yajnavalkya replied : 'Your Majesty, speech itself is knowledge. For through speech, Your Majesty, friend is known to be a friend, and likewise the Rigveda, Yajurveda, Samaveda, the Atharvangirasas, the Itihasa (tradition), Purana-vidya (Knowledge of the past), the Upanishads, Shlokas (verses), Sutra (rules), Anuvyakhyanas and Vyakhyanas (commentaries, etc.); what is sacrificed, what is poured out, what is to be eaten and drunk, this world and the other world and all creatures. By speech alone, Your Majesty, Brahman is known, speech indeed, O king, is the Highest Brahman. Speech does not desert him who worships that Brahman with such knowledge, all creatures approach him, and having become a god, he goes to the gods.'

Janaka Vaideha said: 'I shall give you for this a thousand cows with a bull as big as an elephant.'

Yajnavalkya said: 'My father was of opinion that one should not accept a reward without having fully instructed a pupil.'

Yajnavalkya said: 'Let us hear what anybody may have told you.'

Janaka Vaideha replied: 'Udanka Shaulbayan told me that life (Prana) is Brahman.'

Yajnavalkya said: 'As one who had the benefit of a good father, mother, and teacher might tell, so did Udanka Shaulbayana tell you that life is Brahman; for what is the use of a person without life? But did he tell you the body and the resting-place of that Brahman?'

Janaka Vaideha said: 'He did not tell me.'

Yajnavalkya said: 'Your Majesty, this Brahman stands on one leg only.'

Janaka Vaideha said: 'Then tell me, Yajnavalkya.'

Yajnavalkya said: 'Breath is its body, ether its place, and one should worship it as what is dear.'

Janaka Vaideha said: 'What is the nature of that which is dear?'

Yajnavalkya replied: 'Your Majesty, life itself is that which is dear;' because for the sake of life, Your Majesty, a man sacrifices even for him who is unworthy of sacrifice, he accepts presents from him who is not worthy to bestow presents, nay, he goes to a country, even when there is fear of being hurt, for the sake of life. Life, O King, is the Highest Brahman. Life does not desert him who worhsips that Brahman with such knowledge, all creatures approach him, and having become a god, hegoes to the gods.'

Janaka Vaideha said: 'I shall give you for this a thousand cows with a bull as big as an elephant.'

Yajnavalkya said: 'My father was of opinion that one should not accept a reward without having fully instructed a pupil.'

Yajnavalkya said: 'Let us hear what anybody may have told you.'

Janaka Videha replied: Barku Varshna told me that sight (Chakshus) is Brahman.'

Yajnavalkya said: 'As one who had the benefit of a good father, mother, and teacher might tell, so did Barku Varshna tell you that sight is Brahman; for what is the use of a person who cannot see? But did he tell you the body and the resting-place of that Brahman?'

Janaka Vaideha said: 'He did not tell me.'

Yajnavalkya said: 'Your Majesty, this Brahman stands on one leg only.'

Janaka Vaideha said: 'Then tell me, Yajnavalkya.'

Yajnavalkya said: 'The eye is its body, ether its place, and one should worship it as what is true.'

Janaka Vaideha said: 'What is the nature of that which is true?'

Yajnavalkya replied: 'Your Majesty, sight itself is that which is true; for if they say to a man who sees with his eye, "Didst thou see?" and he says, "I saw," then it is true. Sight, O King, is the Highest Brahman. Sight does not desert him who worships that Brahman with such knowledge, all creatures approach him, and having become a god, he goes to the gods.'

Janaka Vaideha said: 'I shall give you for this a thousand cows with a bull as big as an elephant.'

Yajnavalkya said: 'My father was of opinion that one should not accept a reward without having fully instructed a pupil.'

Yajnavalkya said: 'Let us hear what anybody may have told you.'

Janaka Vaideha replied; 'Gardabhivibhit Bharadvaja told me that hearing (Srotra) is Brahman.'

Yajanavalkya said: 'As one who had the benefit of a good father, mother, and teacher might tell, so did Gardabhivibhita Bharadvaja tell you that hearing is Brahman; for what is the use of a person who cannot hear? But did he tell you the body and the resting-place of that Brahman?

Janaka Vaideha said: 'He did not tell me.'

Yajnavalkya said: 'Your Majesty, this Brahman stands on the one leg only.'

Janaka Vaideha said: 'Then tell me, Yajnavalkya.'

Yajanavalkya said: 'The ear is its body, ether its place, and we should worship it as what is endless.'

Janaka Vaideha said: 'What is the nature of that which is endless?'

Yajnavalkya replied: 'Your Majesty, space (Disah) itself is that which is endless, and therefore to whatever space (quarter) he goes, he never comes to the end of it. For space is endless. Space indeed, O King, is hearing, and hearing indeed, O King, is the Highest Brahman. Hearing does not desert him who worships that Brahman with such knowledge, all creatures approach him, and having become a god, he goes to the gods.'

Janak Vaideha said: 'I shall give you for this a thousand cows with a bull as big as an elephant.'

Yajnavalkya said: 'My father was of opinion that one should not accept a reward without having fully instructed a pupil.'

Yajanavalkya said: 'Let us hear what anybody may have told you.'

Janaka Vaideha replied: 'Satyakama Jabala told me that mind (manas) is Brahman.'

Yajnavalkya said: 'As one who had the benefit of a good

father, mother, and teacher might tell, so did Satyakama Jabala tell you that mind is Brahman; for what is the use of a person without mind? But did he tell you the body and the resting-place of that Brahman?'

Janaka Vaideha said: 'He did not tell me.'

Yajnavalkya said: 'Your Majesty, this Brahman stands on one leg only.

Janaka Vaideha said: 'Then tell me, Yajnavalkya.'

Yajnavalkya said: 'Mind itself is its body, ether its place, and we should worship it as bliss.'

Janak Vaideha said: 'What is the nature of bliss?'

Yajnavalkya replied: 'Your Majesty, mind itself; for with the mind does a man desire a woman, and a like son is born of her, and he is bliss. Mind indeed, O King, is the Highest Brahman. Mind does not desert him who worships that Brahman with such knowledge, all creatures approach him, and having become a god, he goes to the gods.'

Janaka Vaideha said: 'I shall give you for this a thousand cows with a bull as big as an elephant.'

Yajnavalkya said : My father was of opinion that one should not accept a reward without having fuly instructed a pupil.'

Yajnavalkya said: 'Let us hear what anybody may have told you.'

Janaka Vaideha replied: 'Vidagdha Shakalya told me that the heart (Hridaya) is Brahman.'

Yajnavalkya said : 'As one who had the benefit of a good father, mother, and teacher might tell, so did Vidagdha Shakalya tell you that the heart is Brahman; for what is the use of a person without a heart? But did he tell you the body and the resting-place of that Brahman?'

Janaka Vaideha said: 'He did not tell me.'

Yajnavalkya said: 'Your Majesty, this Brahman stands on one leg only.'

Janaka Vaideha said: 'Then tell me, Yajnavalkya.'

Yajnavalkya said : 'The heart itself is its body, ether its

place, and we should worship it as certainty (Sthiti).'

Janaka Vaideha said: 'What is the nature of certainty?'

Yajna valkya replied: 'Your Majesty, the heart itself; for the heart indeed, O King, is the body of all things, the heart is the resting-place of all things, for in the heart, O King, all things rest. The heart indeed, O King, is the Highest Brahamn. The heart does not desert him who worships that Brahman with such knowledge, all creatures approach him, and having become a god, he goes to the gods.'

Janaka Vaideha said : 'I shall give you for this a thousand cows with a bull as big as an elephant.'

Yajnavalkya said: 'My father was of opinion that one should not accept a reward without having fully instructed a pupil.'

•

Janaka Vaideha, descending from his throne, said: 'I bow to you, O Yajnavalkya, teach me.'

Yajnavalkya said: 'Your Majesty, as a man who wishes to make a long journey, would furnish himself with a chariot or a ship, thus is your mind well furnished by these Upanishads. Your are honourable, and wealthy, you have learnt the Vedas and been told the Upanishads. Whither then will you go when departing hence?'

Janaka Vaideha said: 'Sir, I do not know whither I shall go.'

Yajnavalkya said: 'Then I shall tell you this, whither you will go.'

Janaka Vaideha said: 'Tell it, Sir.'

Yajnavalkya said: 'That person who is in the right eye, he is called Indha, and him who is Indha they call indeed Indra mysteriously, for the gods love what is mysterious, and dislike what is evident.

'Now that which in the shape of a person is in the right eye, is his wife, Viraj. Their meeting-place is the ether within the heart, and their food the red lump within the heart. Again, their covering is that which is like network within the heart, and the road on which they move, from sleep to waking, is the artery that rises upwards from the heart. Like a hair divided into a thousand parts,, so are the veins of it, which are called Hita, placed firmly within the heart. Through these indeed that food flows on flowing, and he the Taijasa receives as it were purer food than the corporeal Self, the Vaishvanara.

'The Taijasa's Eastern quarter are the Pranas which go to the East;

'His Southern quarter are the Pranas which go to the South;

'His Western quarter are the Pranas which go to the West;

'His Northern quarter are the Pranas which go to the North;

'His Upper (Zenith) quarter are the Pranas which go upward;

'His Lower (Nadir) quarter are the Pranas which go downward;

'All the quarters are all the Pranas. And he, the Atman in that state, can only be described by No, no! He is incomprehensible, for he cannot be comprehended; he is undecaying, for he cannot be comprehended; he is undecaying, for he cannot decay; he is not attached, for he does not attach himself; he is unbound, he does not suffer, he does not perish. O Janaka, you have indeed reached fearlessness,'— thus said Yajnavalkya.

Then Janaka said: 'May that fearlessness come to you also who teachest us fearlessness. I bow to you. Here are the Videhas, and here am I thy slave.'

•

Yajnavalkya came to Janaka Vaideha, and he did not mean to speak with him. But when formerly Janaka Vaideha and Yajnavalkya had a disputation on the Agnihotra, Yajnavalkya had granted him a boon, and he chose that he might be free to ask him any question he liked. Yajnavalkya granted it, and thus the King was the first to ask him a question.

'Yajnavalkya, he said, 'what is the light of man?'

Yajnavalkya replied: 'The sun, O King; for, having the sun alone for his light, man sits, moves about, does his work, and returns.'

Janaka Vaideha said: So indeed it is, O Yajnavalkya.'

Janaka Vaideha said: When the sun has set, O Yajnavalkya, what is then the light of man?'

Yajnavalkya replied: 'The moon indeed is his light; for, having the moon alone for his light, man sits, moves about, does his work, and returns.'

Janaka Vaideha said: 'So indeed it is, O Yajnavalkya.'

Janaka Vaideha said: 'When the sun has set, O Yajnavalkya, and the moon has set, what is the light of man?'

Yajnavalkya replied: 'Fire indeed is his light; for, having fire alone for his light, man sits, moves about, does his work, and returns.'

Janaka Vaideha said: 'When the sun has set O Yajnavalkya, and the moon has set, and the fire is gone out, what is then the light of man?'

Yajnavalkya replied: 'Sound indeed is his light; for, having sound alone for his light, man sits, moves about, does his work, and returns. Therefore, O King, when one cannot see even one's own hand, yet when a sound is raised, one goes towards it.'

Janaka Vaideha said: 'So indeed it is, O Yajnavalkya.'

Janaka Vaideha said: 'When the sun has set, O Yajnavalkya, and the moon has set, and the fire is gone out, and the sound hushed, what is then the light of man?'

Yajnavalkya said: 'He who is that Self?'

Yajnavalkya replied: 'He who is within the heart, surrounded by the Pranas (senses), the person of light, consisting of knowledge. He, remaining the same, wanders along the two worlds, as if thinking, as if moving. During sleep in dream, he transcends this world and all the forms of death, all that falls under the sway of death, all that is perishable.

'On being born that person, assuming his body, becomes united with all evils; when he departs and dies, he leaves all evils behind.

'And there are two states for that person, the one here in this world, the other in the other world, and as a third an intermediate state, the state of sleep. When in that intermediate state, he sees both those states together, the one here in this world, and the other in the other world. Now whatever his admission to the other world may be, having gained that admission, he sees both the evils and the blessings.

'And when he falls asleep, then after having taken away with him the material from the whole world, destroying and building it up again, he sleeps, dreams, by his own light. In that state the person is self-illuminated.

'There are no real chariots in that state, no horses, no roads, but he himself sends forth, creates, chariots, horses, and roads. There are no blessings there, no happiness, no joys, but he himself sends forth blessings, happiness, and joys. There are no tanks there, no lakes, no rivers, but he himself sends for the tanks, lakes, and rivers.

'On this there are these verses:

'After having subdued by sleep all that belongs to the body, he not asleep himself, looks down upon the sleeping senses. Having assumed light he goes again to his place, the golden person, the lonely bird.

'Guarding with the breath (Prana, life) the lower nest, the immortal moves away from the nest; that immortal one goes wherever he likes, the golden person, the lonely bird.

Going up and down in his dream, the god makes manifold shapes for himself, either rejoicing together with women, or laughing with his friends or seeing terrible sights.

'People may see his playground, but himself no one ever sees. Therefore they say, "Let no one wake a man suddenly, for it is not easy to remedy, if he does not get back rightly to his body."

'Here some people object and say: "No, this sleep is the same as the place of waking, for what he sees while awake, that only he sees when asleep." No, here in sleep the person is self-illuminated as we explained before.'

Janaka Vaideha said: 'I give you, Sir, a thousand. Speak on for the sake of my emancipation.'

Yajnavalkya said: 'That person having enjoyed himself in that state of bliss (*samprasada*, deep sleep), having moved about and seen both good and evil, hastens back again as he came, to the place from which he started, the place of sleep, to dream. And whatever he may have seen there, he is not followed, affected, by it, for that person is not attached to anything.'

Janaka Vaideha said: So it is indeed, Yajnavalkya. I give you, Sir, a thousand. Speak on for the sake of my emancipation.'

Yajnavalkya said: 'That person having enjoyed himself in that sleep, dream, having moved about and seen both good and evil, hastens back again as he came, to the place from which he started, to be awake And whatever he may have seen there, he is not affected by it, for that person is not attached to anything.'

Janaka Vaideha said: 'So it is indeed, Yajnavalkya. I give you, Sir, a thousand. Speak on for the sake of my emancipation.'

Yajanavalkya said: 'That person having enjoyed himself in that state of waking, having moved about and seen both good and evil, hastens back again as he came, to the place from which he started, to the state of dream.

'In fact, as a large fish moves along the two banks of a river, the right and the left, so does that person move along these two states, the state of sleeping and the state of waking.

'And as a falcon, or any other swift bird, after he has

roamed about here in the air, becomes tired, and folding his wings is carried to his nest, so does that person hasten to that state where, when asleep, he desires no more desires, and dreams no more dreams.

'There are in his body the veins called Hita, which are as small as a hair divided a thousandfold, full of white, blue, yellow, green, and red. Now when, as it were, they kill him, when, as it were, they overcome him, when, as it were, an elephant chases him, when, as it were, he falls into a well, he fancies, through ignorance, that danger which he commonly sees in waking. But when he fancies that he is, as it were, a god, or that he is, as it were, a king, or "I am this altogether," that is his highest world.

'This inded is his true form, free from desires, free from evil, free from fear. Now as a man, when embraced by a beloved wife, knows nothing that is without, nothing that is within, thus this person, who embraced by the intelligent (Prajna) Self, knows nothing that is without, nothing that is within. This indeed is his true form, in which his wishes are fulfilled, in which the Self only is his wish, in which no wish is left,—free from any sorrow.

'Then a father is not a father, a mother not a mother, the worlds not worlds, the gods not gods, the Vedas not Vedas. Then a thief is not a thief, murderer not a murderer, a Chandala not a Chandala, a Paulkasa not a Paulkasa, a Shramana not a Shramana, a Tapasa not a Tapasa. He is not followed by good, not followed by evil, for he has then overcome all the sorrows of the heart.

'And when it is said that there in the Sushupti he does not see, yet he is seeing, though he does not see. For sight is inseparable from the seer, because it cannot perish. But there is then no second, nothing else different from him that he could see.

'And when it is said that there in the Sushupti he does not smell, yet he is smelling, though he does not smell. For smelling is inseparable from the smeller, because it cannot perish. But there is then no second, nothing else different from him that he could smell.

'And when it is said that there in the Sushupti he does not taste, yet he is tasting, though he does not taste. For tasting is inseparable from the taster, because it cannot perish. But there is then no second, nothing else different from him that he could taste.

'And when it is said that there in the Sushupti he does not speak, yet he is speaking, though he does not speak. For speaking is inseparable from the speaker, because it cannot perish. But there is then no second, nothing else different from him that he could speak.

'And when it is said that there in the Sushupti he does not hear, yet he is hearing, though he does not hear. For hearing is inseparable from the hearer, because it cannot perish. But there is then no second, nothing else different from him that he could hear.

'And when it is said that there in the Sushupti he does not think, yet he is thinking, though he does not think. For thinking is inseparable from the thinker, because it cannot perish But there is then no second, nothing else different from him that he could think.

'And when it is said that there in the Sushupti he does not touch, yet he is touching, though he does not touch, for touching is inseparable from the toucher, because it cannot perish. But there is then no second, nothing else different from him that he could think.

'And when it is said that there in the Sushupti he does not know, yet he is knowing, though he does not know. For knowing is inseparable from the knower, because it cannot perish. But there is then no second, nothing else different from him that he could know.

'When in waking and dreaming there is, as it were, another, then can one see the other, then can one smell the other, then can one speak to the other, then can one hear the other, then can one think the other, then can one touch the other, then can one know the other.

'An ocean is that one seer, without any duality; this

is the Brahma-world, O King.' Thus did Yajnavalkya teach him.' This is his highest goal, this is his highest success, this is his highest world, this is his highest bliss. All other creatures live on a small portion of that bliss.'

'If a man is healthy, wealthy, and lord of others, surrounded by all human enjoyments, that is the highest blessing of men. Now a hundred of these human blessings make one blessing of the fathers who have conquered the world of the fathers. A hundred blessings of the fathers who have conquered this world make one blessing in the Gandharva world. A hundred blessings in the Gandharva world make one blessing of the Devas by merit, work, sacrifice, who obtain their godhead by merit. A hundred blessings of the Devas by merit make one blessing of the Devas by birth, also of Shrotriya who is without sin, and not overcome by desire. A hundred blessings of the Devas by birth make one blessing in the world of Prajapati, also of a Shrotriya who is without sin, and not overcome by desire. A hundred blessings in the world of Prajapati make one blessing in the world of Brahman, also of a Shrotriya who is without sin, and not overcome by desire. And this is the highest blessing.

'This is the Brahma-world, O King,' thus spake Yajnavalkya.

Janak Vaideha said: I give you, Sir, a thousand. Speak on for the sake of my emancipation.'

Then Yajnavalkya was afraid lest the King, having become full of understanding, should drive him from all his positions.

And Yajnavalkya said: 'That person, having enjoyed himself in that state of dream, having moved about and seen both good and bad, hastens back again as he came, to the place from which he started, to the state of waking.

'Now as a heavy-laden carriage moves along groaning, thus does this corporeal Self, mounted by the intelligent Self, move along groaning, when a man is thus going to expire.

'And when the body grows weak through old age, or

becomes weak through illness, at that time that person, after separating himself from his members, as mango, or fig. or Pippala-fruit is separated from the stalk, hastens back, with food and drink, saying, "He comes back, he approaches, thus do all the elements wait on him who knows this, saying, "That Brahman comes, that Brahman approaches."

'And as policemen, magistrates, equerries, and governors gather round a king who is departing, thus do all the senses (Pranas) gather round the Self at the time of death, when a man is thus going to expire.'

•

Yajnavalkya continued: 'Now when that Self, having sunk into weakness, sinks as it were, into unconsciousness, then gather those senses (Pranas) around him, and he, taking with him those elements of light, descends into the heart. When that person in the eye trurns away, then he ceases to know any forms.

'"He has become one," they say, "he does not see." "He has become one," the say, "he does not smell." "He has become one," they say, "he does not taste." "He has become one, they say, "he does not speak." He has become one," they say, "he does not hear." "He has become one," they say, "he does not touch." "He has become one," they say, "he does not know." The point of his heart becomes lighted up, and by that light the self departs, either through the eye, or through the skull, or through other places of the body. And when he thus departs, life (the chief Prana) departs after him, and when life thus departs, all the other vital spirits (Pranas) depart after it. He is conscious, and being conscious he follows and departs.

'Then both his knowledge and his work take hold of him, and his acquaintance with former things.

'And as a caterpiller, after having reached the end of a blade of grass, and after having made another approach to another blade, draws itself together towards it, thus does this Self, after having thrown off this body and dispelled all ignorance, and after making another approach to another body, draw himself together towards it.

'And as a goldsmith, taking a piece of gold, turns it into another, newer and more beautiful shape, so does this Self, after having thrown off this body and dispelled all ignorance, make unto himself another, newer and more beautiful shape, whether it be like the Fathers, or like the Gandharvas, or like the Devas, or like Prajapati, or like Brahman, or like other beings.

'That Self is indeed Brahman, consisting of knowledge, mind, life, sight, hearing, earth, water, wind, ether, light and no light, desire and no desire, anger and no anger, right or wrong, and all things. Now as a man is like this or like that, according as he acts and according as he behaves, so will he be:— a man of good acts will become good, a man of bad acts, bad. He becomes pure by pure deeds, bad by bad deeds.

'And here they say that a person consists of desires. And as is his desire, so is his will; and as is his will, so is his deed; and whatever deed he does, that he will reap.

'And here there is this verse: "To whatever object a man's own mind is attached, to that he goes strenuously together with his deed; and having obtained the last results of whatever deed he does here on earth, he returns again from that world which is the temporary reward of his deed to this world of action."

'So much for the man who desires. But as to the man who does not desire, who, not desiring, freed from desires, is satisfied in his desires, or desires the Self only, his vital spirits do not depart elsewhere,—being Brahman, he goes to Brahamn.

'On this there is this verse: "When all desires which once entered his heart are undone, then does man."

'And as the slough of a snake lies on an ant-hill, dead and cast away, thus lies this body; but that disembodied immortal spirit (Prana, life) is Brahman only, is only light.'

Janaka Vaideha said: 'Sir, I give you a thousand.'

'On this there are these verses:

'The small, old path stretching far away has been found by me. On it sages who know Brahman move on to the Svarga-loka (heaven), and thence higher on, as entirely free.

'On that path they say that there is white, or blue, or yellow, or green, or red; that path was found by Brahman, and on it goes whoever knows Brahman, and who has done good, and obtained splendour.

'All who worship what is not knowledge (Avidya) enter into blind darkness,' those who delight in knowledge, enter, as it were, into greater darkness.

'There are indeed those unblessed worlds, covered with blind darkness. Men who are ignorant and not enlightened go after death to those worlds.

'If a man understands the Self, saying, "I am He," what could he wish or desire that he should pine after the body.

'Whoever has found and understood the Self that has entered into this patched-together hiding place, he indeed is the creator, for he is the maker of everything, his is the world, and he is the world itself.

'While we are here, we may know this; if not, I am ignorant, and there is great destruction. Those who know it, become immortal, but others suffer pain indeed.

'If a man clearly beholds this Self as God, and as the lord of all that is and will be, then he is no more afraid.

'He behind whom the year revolves with the days, him the gods worship as the light of lights, as immortal time.

'He in whom the five beings and the other rest, him alone I believe to be the Self,—I who know, believe him to be Brahman; I who am immortal, believe him to be immortal.

'They who know the life of life, the eye of eye, the ear of the ear, the mind of the mind, they have comprehended the ancient, primeval Brahman.

'By the mind alone it is to be perceived, there is in it no diversity. He who perceives there in any diversity, goes from death to death.

'This eternal being that can never be proved, is to be perceived in one way only; it is spotless, beyond the ether, the unborn Self, great and eternal.

'Let a wise Brahmin, after he has discovered him, practise wisdom. Let him not seek after many worlds, for that is mere weariness of the tongue.

'And he is that great unborn Self, who consists of knowledge, is surrounded by the Pranas, the ether within the heart. In it there reposes the ruler of all, the lord of all, the king of all things, the protector of all things. He is a bank and a boundary, so that these worlds may not be confounded. Brahmin seek to know him by the study of the Veda, by sacrifice, by gifts, by penance, by fasting, and he who knows him, becomes a Muni. Wishing for that world, for Brahman, only, mendicants leave their homes.

'Knowing this, the people of old did not wish for offspring. What shall we do with offspring, they said, we who have this Self and this world of Brahman? And they, having risen above the desire for sons, wealth, and new worlds, wander about as mendicants. For desire for sons is desire for wealth, and desire for wealth is desire for worlds. Both these are indeed desires only. He, the Self, is to be described by No, no! He is incomprehensible, for he cannot be comprehended; he is imperishable, for he cannot perish; he is unattached, for he does not attach himself; unfettered, he does not suffer, he does not fail. Him who knows, these two do not overcome, whether he says that for some reason he has done evil, or for some reason he has done good—he overcomes both, and neither what he has done, nor what he has omitted to do affects him.

'This has been told by a verse: "This eternal greatness of the Brahmin does not grow larger by work, nor does it grow smaller. Let man try to find, know, its trace, for having found, known, it, he is not sullied by any evil deed.

'He therefore that knows it, after having become quiet, subdued, satisfied, patient, and collected, sees self in Self, sees all as Self. Evil does not overcome him, he overcomes all evil. Evil does not burn him, he burns all evil. Free from evil, from from spots, free from doubt, he becomes a true Brahmin; this is the Brahma-world, O King,'—thus spoke Yajnavalkya.

Janaka Vaideha said: Sir, I give you the Videhas, and also myself, to be together your slaves.'

This indeed is the great, the unborn Self, the strong, the giver of wealth. He who knows this obtains wealth.

This great, unborn Self, undecaying, undying, immortal, fearless, is indeed Brahman. Fearless is Brahman, and he who knows this becomes verily, the fearless Brahman.

•

Yajnavalkya had two wives, Maitreyi and Katyayani. Of these Maitreyi was conversant with Brahman, but Katyayani possessed such knowledge only as women possess. And Yajnavalkya, when he wished to get ready for another state of life, when he wished to give up the state of a householder, and retire into the forest,

Said, 'Maitreyi, verily I am going away from this my house into the forest. Forsooth, let me make a settlement between thee and that Katyayani.'

Maitreyi said: 'My Lord, if this whole earth, full of wealth, belonged to me, tell me, should I be immortal by it, or no?'

'No,' replied Yajnavalkya, 'like the life of rich people will be thy life. But there is no hope of immortality by wealth.'

And Maitreyi said: 'What should I do with that by which I do not become immortal? What my Lord knoweth of immortality, tell that clearly to me.'

Yajnavalkya replied: 'Thou who art truly dear to me, thou hast increased what is dear to me in thee. Therefore, if you like, Lady, I will explain it to thee, and mark well what I say.'

And he said: 'Verily, a husband is not dear, that you may love the husband; but that you may love the Self, therefore a husband is dear.

'Verily, a wife is not dear, that you may love the wife; but that you may love the Self, theefore a wife is dear.

'Verily, sons are not dear, that you may love the sons; but that you may love the Self, thefrefore sons are dear.

'Verily, wealth is not dear, that you may love wealth; but that you may love the Self, therefore wealth is dear.

'Verly, the Brahmin-class is not dear, that you may love the Brahmin-class; but that you may love the Self, therefore the Brahmin-class is dear.

'Verily, the Kshatra-class is not dear, that you may love the Kshatra-class; but that you may love the Self, therefore the Kshatra-class is dear.

'Verily, the worlds are not dear, that you may love the worlds, but that you may love the self, therefore the worlds are dear.

'Verily, the Devas are not dear, that you may love the Devas; but that you may love the Self, therefore the Devas are dear.

'Verily, the Vedas are not dear, that you may love the Vedas; but that you may love the Self, therefore the Vedas are dear.

'Verily, creatures are not dear, that you may love the creatures; but that you may love the Self, therefore are creatures dear.

'Verily, everything is not dear, that you may love everything; but that you may love the Self, therefore everything is dear.

'Verily, the Self is to be seen, to be heard, to be perceived, to be marked, O Maitreyi! When the Self has been seen, heard, perceived, and known, then all this is known.

Whosoever looks for the Brahmin-class elsewhere than in the Self, was abandoned by Brahmin-class. Whosoever looks for the Kshatra-class elsewhere than in the Self, was abandoned by the Kshatra-class. Whosoever looks for the worlds elsewhere than in the Self, was abandoned by the worlds. Whosoever looks for the Devas elsewhere than in the Self, was abandoned by the Devas. Whosoever looks for the Vedas elsewhere than in the Self, was abandoned by the Vedas. Whosoever looks for the creatures elsewhere than in the Self, was abandoned by the creatures. Whosoever looks for anything elsewhere than in the Self, was abandoned by anything.

'This Brahmin-class, this Kshatra-class, these worlds, these Devas, these Vedas, all these beings, this everything, all is that Self.

'Now as the sounds of a drum, when beaten, cannot be seized externally by themselves, but the sound is seized, when the drum is seized, or the beater of the drum;

'And as the sounds of a conch-shell, when blown, cannot be seized externally by themselves, but the sound is seized, when the shell is seized, or the blower of the shell;

'And as the sounds of a lute, when played, cannot be seized externally by themselves, but the sound is seized, when the lute is seized, or the player of the lute;

'As clouds of smoke proceed by themselves out of lighted fire kindled with damp fuel, thus verily, O Maitreyi, has been breathed forth from this great Being what we have as Rigveda, Yajurveda, Samaveda, Atharvangirasas, Itihasa, Purana, Vidya, Upanishads, Shlokas, Sutras, Anuvyakhyanas, Vyakhyanas, what is sacrificed, what is poured out, food, drink, this world and the other world, and all creatures. From him alone all these were breathed forth.

'As all waters find their centre in the sea, all touches in the skin, all tastes in the tongue, all smells in the nose, all colours in the eye, all sounds in the ear, all percepts in the mind, all knowledge in the heart, all actions in the hands, all movements in the feet, and all the Vedas in speech,—

'As a mass of salt has neither inside nor outside, but is altogether a mass of taste, thus indeed has that Self neither inside nor outside, but is altogether a mass of knowledge; and having risen from out of these elements, vanishes again in them. When he has departed, there is no more knowledge, I say, O Maitreyi,'—thus spoke Yajnavalkya.

Then Maitreyi said: 'Here, Sir, thou hast landed me in utter bewilderment. Indeed, I do not understand him.'

But he replied: 'O Maitreyi, I say nothing that is bewildering. Verily, beloved, that Self is imperishable, and of an indestructible nature.

'For when there is, as it were, duality, then one sees the other, one smells the other, one tastes the other, one salutes the other, one hears the other, one perceives the other, one touches the other, one knows the other; but when the Self only is all this, how should he see another, how should he smell another, how should he taste another, how should he salute another, how should he hear another, how should he touch another, how should he know another? How should he know Him by whom he knows all this? That Self is to be described by No. no! He is incomprehensible, for he cannot be comprehended; he is imperishable, for he cannot perish; he is unattached, for he does not attach himself; unfettered, he does not suffer, he does not fail. How, O beloved, should he know the Knower? Thus, O Maitreyi, thou hast been instructed. Thus far goes immortality.

Having said so, Yajnavalkya went away into the forest.

5

That, the invisible Brahman, is full, this the visible Brahman, is full. This full visible Brahman proceeds from that full invisible Brahman. On grasping the fulness of this full visible Brahman there is left that full invisible Brahman.

Om is ether, is Brahman. 'There is the old ether the invisible, and the visible ether of the atmosphere,' thus said Kauravyayaniputra. This Om is the Veda, the means of knowledge, thus the Brahmins know. One knows through it all that has to be known.

•

The threefold descendants of Prajapati, gods, men, and Asuras, evil spirits, dwelt as Brahmancharins (students) with their father Prajapati. Having finished their studentship the gods said: 'Tell us something, Sir.' He told them the syllable Da. Then he said: 'Did you understand?' They said: 'We did understand. You told us "Damyata," Be subdued.' Yes, he said, 'you have understood.'

Then the men said to him: 'Tell us something, Sir.' He told them the same syllable Da. Then he said: 'Did you understand?' They said: 'We did understand. You told us, "Datta," Give.' 'Yes,' he said, 'you have understood.'

Then the Asuras said to him: 'Tell us something, Sir.' He told them the same syllable Da. Then he said, 'Did you understand?' They said: 'We did understand. You told us, "Dayadham," Be merciful.' Yes,' he said, 'you have understood.'

The divine voice of thunder repeats the same, Da Da Da, that is, Be subdued, Give, Be merciful. Therefore let that triad be taught, Subduing, Giving, and Mercy.

•

Prajapati is the heart, is this Brahman, is all this. The heart, Hridaya, consists of three syllables. One syllable is *hri*, and to him who knows this, his own people and others bring offerings. One syllable is *da*, and to him who knows this, his own people and others bring gifts. One syllable is *yam*, and he who knows this, goes to heaven as his world.

•

This heart indeed is even that, it was indeed the true Brahman. And whosoever knows this great glorious first-born as the true Brahman, he conquers these worlds, and conquered likewise may that enemy be! yes, whosoever knows this great glorious first-born as the true Brahman; for Brahman is the true.

•

In the beginning this world was water. Water produced the true, and the true is Brahman. Brahman produced

Prajapati, Prajapati the Devas (gods). The Devas adore the true (Satyam) alone. This Satyam consists of three syllables. One syllable is *sa*, another *t(i)*, the third *yam*. The first and last syllables are true, in the middle there is the untrue. This untrue is on both sides enclosed by the true, and thus the true preponderates. The untrue does not hurt him who knows this.

Now what is the true, that is the Aditya (the sun), the person that dwells in yonder orb, and the person in the right eye. These two rest on each other, the former resting with his rays in the latter, the latter with his Pranas (senses) in the former. When the latter is on the point of departing this life, he sees that orb as white only, and those rays of the sun do not return to him.

Now of the person in that solar orb Bhuh is the head, for the head is one, and that syllable is one; Bhuvah the two arms, for the arms are two, and these syllables are two; Svah the foot, for the feet are two, and these syllables are two. Its secret name is Ahar (day), and he who knows this, destroys (*hanti*) evil and leaves (*jahati*) it.

Of the person in the right eye Bhuh is the head, for the head is one, and that syllable is one; Bhuvah the two arms, for the arms are two, and these syllables are two; Svar the foot, for the feet are two, and these syllables are two. Its secret name is Aham (ego), and he who knows this, destroys (*hanti*) evil and leaves (*jahati*) it.

•

That person, under the form of mind (Manas), being light indeed, is within the heart, small like a grain of rice or barley. He is the ruler of all, the lord of all—he rules all this, whatsoever exists.

•

They say that lightning is Brahman, because lightning (Vidyut) is called so from cutting off (*vidanat*). Whosoever knows this, that lightning is Brahman, him, that Brahman, cuts off from evil, for lightning indeed is Brahman.

•

Let him meditate on speech as a cow. Her four udders are the words Svaha, Vashat, Hanta, and Svadha. The gods live on two of her udders, the Svaha and the Vashat, men on the Hanta, the fathers on the Svadha. The bull of that cow is breath (Prana), the calf the mind.

•

Agni Vaishvanara is the fire within man by which the food that is eaten is cooked, i.e., digested. Its noise is that which one hears, if one covers one's ear. When he is on the point of departing this life, he does not hear that noise.

•

When the person goes away from this world, he comes to the wind. Then the wind makes room for him, like the hole of a carriage wheel, and through it he mounts higher, he comes to the sun. Then the sun makes room for him, like the hole of a Lambara, musical instrument, and through it he mounts higher. He comes to the moon. Then the moon makes room for him, like the hole of a drum, and through it he mounts higher, and arrives at the world where there is no sorrow, no snow. There he dwells eternal years.

•

This is indeed the highest penance, if a man, laid up with sickness, suffers pain. He who knows this, conquers the highest world.

This is indeed the highest penance, if they carry a dead person into the forest. He who knows this, conquers the highest world.

This is indeed the highest penance, if they place a dead person on the fire. He who know this, conquers the highest world.

•

Some say that food is Brahman, but this is not so, for

food decays without life (Prana). Others say that life (Prana) is Brahman, but this is not so, for life dries up without food. Then these two deities, food and life, when they have become one, reach that highest state, are Brahman. Thereupon Pratrida said to his father: 'Shall I be able to do any good to one who knows this, or shall I be able to do him any harm?' The father said to him, beckoning with his hand: 'Not so, O Pratrida; for who could reach the highest state, if he has only got to the oneness of these two?' He then said to him: Vi; verily, food is Vi, for all these beings rest (*vishtani*) on food.' He then said: 'Ram; verily, life is Ram, for all these beings delight (*ramante*) in life. All beings rest on him, all beings delight in him who knows this.'

•

Next follows the Uktha. Verily, breath (Prana) is Uktha, for breath raises up (*utthapayati*) all this. From him who knows this, there is raised a wise son, knowing the Uktha; he obtains union and oneness with the Uktha.

Next follows the Yajus. Verily, breath is Yajus, for all these beings are joined in breath. For him who knows this, all beings are joined to procure his excellence; he obtains union and oneness with the Yajus.

Next follows the Saman. Verily, breath is the Saman, for all these beings meet in breath. For him who knows this, all beings meet to procure his excellence; he obtains union and onencess with the Saman.

Next follows the Kshatra. Verily, breath is the Kshatra, for breath is Kshatra, i.e., breath protects (*trayate*) him from being hurt (*kshanitoh*). He who knows this, obtains Kshatra (power), which requires no protection; he obtains union and oneness with Kshatra.

•

The words Bhumi (earth), Antariksha (sky), and Dyu (heaven) form eight syllables. One foot of the Gayatri consists of eight syllables. This one foot of it is that, i.e., the three worlds. And he who thus knows that foot of it, conquers as far as the three worlds extend.

The Rikas, the Yajumshi, and the Samani form eight syllables. One foot, the second, of the Gayatri consists of eight syllables. This, one foot of it is that, i.e., the three Vedas, the Rigveda, Yajuriveda, and Sama-veda. And he who thus knows that foot of it, conquers as far as that threefold knowledge extends.

The Prana (the upbreathing), the Apana (the down-breathing), and the Vyana (the backbreathing) form eight syllables. One foot, the third, of the Gayatri consists of eight syllables. This one foot of it is that, i.e., the three vital breaths. And he who thus knows that foot of it, conquers as far as there is anything that breathes. And of that, Gayatri, or speech, this indeed is the fourth (*turiya*), the bright (*darsata*) foot, shining high above the skies. What is here called turiya, the fourth, is meant for chaturtha, the fourth; what is called Darshatam Padam, the bright foot, is meant for him who is, as it were, seen, the person in the sun; and what is called Parorajas, the one who shines high above the skies, is meant for him who shiness higher and higher above every sky. And he who thus knows that foot of the Gayatri, shines thus himself also with hapiness and glory.

That Gayatri, as described before with its three feet, rests on that fourth foot, the bright one, high above the sky. And that again rests on the True (Satyam), and the True is the eye, for the eye is known to be true. And therefore even now, if two persons come disputing, the one saying, I saw, the other, I heard, then we should trust the one who says, I saw. And the True again rests on force (*balam*), and force is life (Prana), and that True rests on life. Therefore they say, force is stronger than the True. Thus does that Gayatri rest with respect to the self as life. That Gayatri protects (*tatre*) the vital breaths (*gayas*); the *gayas* are the Pranas (vital breaths), and it protects them. And because it protects (*tatre*) the vital breaths (*gayas*), therefore it is called Gayatri. And that Savitri verse which the teacher teaches, that is it, the life, the Prana, and indirectly the Gayatri; and whomsoever he teaches, he protects his vital breaths.

Some teach that Savitri as an Anushtubh verse, saying that speech is Anushtubh, and that we teach that speech. Let no one do this, but let him teach the Gayatri as Savitri. And even if one who knows this receives what seems to be much as his reward as a teacher, yet this is not equal to one foot of the Gayatri.

If a teacher were to receive as his fee these three worlds full of all things, he would obtain that first foot of the Gayatri. And if a man were to receive as his fee everything as far as this threefold knowledge extends, he would obtain that second foot of the Gayatri. And if a man were to receive as his fee everything whatsoever breathes, he would obtain that third foot of the Gayatri. But 'that fourth bright foot, shining high above the skies', cannot be obtained by anybody—whence then could one receive such a fee?

The adoration of Gayatri:

'O Gayatri, thou hast one foot, two feet, three feet, four feet. Thou art footless, for thou art not known. orship to thy fourth bright foot above the skies. If one who knows this hates some one and says, "May he not obtain this," or "May this wish not be accomplished to him," then that wish is not accomplished to him against whom he thus prays, or if he says, "May I obtain this."

And thus Janaka Vaideha spoke on this point to Budila Ashvatarashvi: How is it that thou who spokest thus as knowing the Gayatri, hast become an elephant and carriest me?' He answered: 'Your Majesty, I did not know this mouth. Agni, fire, is indeed its mouth; and if people pile even what seems much wood on the fire, it consumes it all. And thus a man who knows this, even if he commits what seems much evil, consumes it all and becomes pure, clean, and free from decay and death.'

•

The face of the True, the Brahman, is covered with a golden disk. Open that, O Pushan, that we may see the nature of the True.

O Pushan, only seer, Yama (judge), Surya (sun), son of Prajapati, spread thy rays and gather them! The light which is thy fairest form, I see it. I am what he is, the person in the sun.

Breath to air and to the immortal! Then this my body ends in ashes. Om! Mind, remember! Remember thy deeds! Mind, remember! Remember thy deeds!

Agni, lead us on to wealth, beatitude, by a good path, thou, O God, who knowest all things! Keep far from us crooked evil, and we shall offer thee the fullest praise!

6

Harih, Om. He who knows the first and the best, becomes himself the first and the best among his people. Breath is indeed the first and the best. He who knows this, becomes the first and the best. He who knows this, becomes the first and the best among his people, and among whomsoever he wishes to be so.

He who knows the richest, becomes himself the richest among his people. Speech is the richest. He who knows this, becomes the richest among his people, and among whomsoever he wishest to be so.

He who knows the firm rest, becomes himself firm on even and uneven ground. He who knows this, stands firm on even and uneven ground.

He who knows success, whatever desire he desires, it succeeds to him. The ear indeed is success. For in the ear are all these Vedas successful. He who knows this, whatever desire he desires, it succeeds to him.

He who knows the home, becomes a home of his own people, a home of all men. The mind indeed is the home.

He who knows this, becomes a home of his own people and a home of all men.

He who knows generation, becomes rich in offspring and cattle. Seed indeed is generation. He who knows this, becomes rich in offspring and cattle.

These Pranas (senses), when quarrelling together as to who was the best, went to Brahman and said: 'Who is the richest of us?' He replied: 'He by whose departure this body seems worst, he is the richest.'

The tongue (speech) departed, and having been absent for a year, it came back and said: 'How have you been able to live without me?' They replied: 'Like unto people, not speaking with the tongue, but breathing with breath, seeing with the eye, hearing with the ear, knowing with the mind, generating with seed. Thus we have lived.' Then speech entered in.

The eye (sight) departed, and having been absent for a year, it came back and said: 'How have you been able to live without me?' They replied: 'Like blind people, not seeing with eye, but breathing with the breath, speaking with the tongue, hearing with the ear, knowing with the mind, generating with seed. Thus we have lived'. Then the eye entered in.

The ear (hearing) departed, and having been absent for a year, it came back and said: 'How have you been able to live without me?' They replied: 'Like deaf people, not hearing with the ear, but breathing with the breath, speaking with the tongue, seeing with the eye, knowing with the mind, generating with seed. Thus we have lived.' Then the ear entered in.

The mind departed, and having been absent for a year, it came back and said: 'How have you been able to live without me?' They replied: 'Like fools, not knowing with their mind, but breathing with the breath, seeing with the eye, hearing with the ear, generating with seed. Thus we have lived.' Then the mind entered in.

The seed departed, and having being absent for a year, it came back and said: 'How have you been able to live without me?' They replied: 'Like impotent people, not generating with seed, but breathing with the breath, seeing with the eye, hearing with the ear, knowing with the mind. Thus we have lived.' Then the seed entered in.

The vital breath, when on the point of departing, tore up these senses, as a great, excellent horse of the Sindhu country might tear up the pegs to which he is tethered. They said to him: 'Sir, do not depart. We shall not be able to live without thee.' He said: 'Then make me an offering.' They said: 'Let it be so.'

Then the tongue said: 'If I am the richest, then thou art the richest by it.' The eye said: 'If I am the firm rest, then thou art possessed of firm rest by it.' The ear said, 'If I am success, then thou art possessed of success by it.' The mind said, 'If I am the home, thou art the home by it.' The seed said, 'If I am the generation, thou art possessed of generation by it.' He said: 'What shall be food, what shall be dress for me?'

They replied: 'Whatever there is, even unto dogs, worms, insects, and birds, that is thy food, and water thy dress. He who thus knows the food of Ana (the breath), by him nothing is eaten that is not proper food, nothing is received that is not proper food. Shrotriyas who know this, rinse the mouth with water when they are going to eat, and rinse the mouth with water after they have eaten, thinking that thereby they make the breath dressed with water.'

•

Shvetaketu Aruneya went to the settlement of the Panchalas. He came near to Pravahana Jaivali, who was walking about surrounded by his men. As soon as the king saw him, he said:

My boy!' Shvetaketu replied: 'Sir!'

Then the king said: 'Have you been taught by your father?' 'Yes,' he replied.

The king said: 'Do you know how men, when they depart from here, separate from each other?' 'No,' he replied.

'Do you know how they come back to this world?' 'No,' he replied.

'Do you know how that world does never become full with the many who again and again depart thither?' 'No, he replied.

'Do you know at the offering of which libation the waters become endowed with a human voice and rise and speak?' 'No,' he replied.

'Do you know the access to the path leading to the Devas and to the path leading to the Fathers, i.e., by what deeds men gain access to the path leading to the Devas or to that leading to the Fathers? For we have heard even the saying of a Rishi: I heard of two paths for men, one leading to the Fathers, the other leading to the Devas. On those paths all that lives moves on, whatever there is between father (sky) and mother (earth).'

Shvetaketu said: 'I do not know even one of all these questions.

Then the king invited him to stay and accept his hospitality. But the boy, not caring for hospitality, ran away, went back to his father, and said: 'Thus then you called me formerly well-instructed!' The father said: 'What then, you sage?' The son replied: 'That fellow of a Rajanya asked me five questions, and I did not know one of them.'

'What were they?' said the father.

'These were they,' the son replied, mentioning the different heads.

The father said: 'You know me, child, that whatever I know, I told you. But come, we shall go thither, and dwell there as students.'

'You may go, Sir,' the son replied.

Then Gautama went where Pravahana Jaivali was, and the king offered him a seat, ordered water for him, and gave him the proper offerings. Then he said to him: 'Sir, we offer a boon to Gautama.'

Gautama said: 'That boon is promised to me; tell me the same speech which you made in the presence of my boy.'

He said: 'That belongs to divine boons, name one of the human boons.'

He said: 'You know well that I have plenty of gold, plenty of cows, horses, slaves, attendants, and apparel; do not heap on me what I have already in plenty, in abundance, and superabundance.'

The king said: 'Gautama, do you wish for instruction from me in the proper way?'

Gautama replied: 'I come to you as a pupil.'

In word only have former sages though Brahmins come as pupils to people of lower rank, but Gautama actually dwelt as a pupil of Pravahana, who was a Rajanya in order to obtain the fame of having respectfully served his master.

The king said: 'Do not be offended with us, neither you nor your forefathers, because this knowledge has before now never dwelt with any Brahmin. But I shall tell it to you, for who could refuse you when you speak thus?

'The altar (fire), O Gautama, is that world (heaven); the fuel is the sun itself, the smoke his rays, the light the day, the coals the quarters, the sparks the intermediate quarters. On that altar the Devas offer the Shraddha libation consisting of water. From that oblation rises Soma, the king (the moon).

'The altar, O Gautama, is Parjanya, the god of rain; the fuel is the year itself, the smoke the clouds, the light the lightning, the coals the thunderbolt, the sparks the thunderings. On that altar the Devas offer Soma, the king (the moon). From that oblation rises rain.

'The altar, O Gautama, is this world; the fuel is the earth itself, the smoke the fire, the light the night, the coals the moon, the sparks the stars. On that altar the Devas offer rain. From that oblation rises food.

'The altar, O Gautama, is man; the fuel the opened mouth, the smoke the breath, the light the tongue, the coals the eye, the sparks the ear. On that altar the Devas offer food. From that oblation rises seed.

'The altar, O Gautama, is woman. On that altar the Devas offer seed. From that oblation rises man. He lives so long as he lives, and then when he dies,

'They take him to the fire, the funeral pile, and then the altar-fire is indeed fire, the fuel fuel, the smoke smoke, the light light, the coals coals, the sparks sparks. In that very altar-fire the Devas offer man, and from that oblation man rises, brilliant in colour.

'Those who thus know this, even Grihasthas, and those who in the forest worship faith and the True Brahman Hiranyagarbha, go to light, from light to day, from day to the increasing half, from the increasing half to the six months when the sun goes to the north, from those six months to the world of the Devas (Devaloka), from the world of the Devas to the sun, from the sun to the place of lightning. When they have thus reached the place of lightning a spirit comes near them, and leads them to the worlds of the Brahman. In these worlds of Brahman they dwell exalted for ages. There is no returning for them.

'But they who conquer the worlds, future states, by means of sacrifice, charity, and austerity, go to smoke, from smoke to night, from night to the decreasing half of the moon, from the decreasing half of the moon to the six months when the sun goes to the south, from these months to the world of the fathers, from the world of the fathers to the moon. Having reached the moon, they become food, and then the Devas feed on them there, as sacrificers feed on Soma, as it increases and decreases. But when this, the result of their good works on earth, ceases, they return again to that ether, from ether to the air, from the air to rain, from rain to the earth. And when they have reached the earth, they become food, they are offered again in the altar-fire, which is man, and thence are born in the fire of woman. Thus they rise up towards the worlds, and go the same round as before.

'Those, however, who know neither of these two paths, become worms, birds, and creeping things.

•

'If a man wishes to reach greatness, wealth for performing sacrifices, he performs the Upasad rule during twelve days, i.e., he lives on small quantities of milk, beginning on an auspicious day of the light half of the moon during the northern progress of the sun, collecting at the same time in a cup or a dish made of Udumbara wood all sorts of herbs, including fruits. He sweeps the floor near the house-altar, sprinkles it, lays the fire, spreads grass round it according to rule, prepares the clarified butter, and on a day, presided over by a male star, after having properly mixed the Mantha (mortar), the herbs, fruits, milk, honey, etc., he sacrifices, pours butter into the fire, saying. 'O Jatavedas, whatever adverse gods there are in thee, who defeat the desires of men, to them I offer this portion; may they, being pleased, please me with all desires.' Svaha!

'That cross deity who lies down, thinking that all things are kept asunder by her, I worship thee as propitous with this stream of ghee. Svaha!

'He then says, 'Svaha to the First, Svaha to the Best, pours ghee into the fire, and throws what remains into the Mantha.

'He then says, Svaha to Breath, Svaha to her who is the richest, pours ghee into the fire, and throws what remains into the mortar.

'He then says, Svaha to Speech, Svaha to the Support, pours ghee into the fire and throws what remains into the imortar.

'He then says, Svaha to the Eye, Svaha to Success, pours ghee into the fire and throws what remains into the mortar.

'He then says, Svaha to the Ear, Svaha to the Home, pours ghee into the fire, and throws what remains into the mortar.

'He then says, Svaha to the Mind, Svaha to Offspring, pours ghee into the fire, and throws what remains into the mortar.

'He then says, Svaha to Seed, pours ghee into the fire, and throws what remains into the mortar.

'He then says, Svaha to Agni (fire), pours ghee into the fire, and throws what remains into the mortar.

'He then says, Svaha to Soma, pours ghee into the fire, and throws what remains into the mortar.

'He then says, Bhuh (earth), Svaha, pours ghee into the fire, and throws what remains into the mortar.

'He then says, Bhuvah (sky), Svaha, pours ghee into the fire, and throws what remains into the mortar.

'He then says, Svah (heaven), Svaha, pours ghee into the fire, and throws what remains into the mortar.

'He then says, Bhur, Bhuvah, Svah, Svaha, pours ghee into the fire, and throws what remains into the mortar.

'He then says, Svaha to Brahmins (the priesthood), pours ghee into the fire, and throws what remains into the mortar.

'He then says, Svaha to Kshatra (the knighthood), pours ghee into the fire, and throws what remains into the mortar.

'He then says, Svaha to the Future, pours ghee into the fire, and throws what remains into the mortar.

'He then says, Svaha to the Universe, pours ghee into the fire, and throws what remains into the mortar.

'He then says, Svaha to all things, pours ghee into the fire, and throws what remains into the mortar.

'He then says, Svaha to Prajapati, pours ghee into the fire, and throws what remains into the mortar.

'Then he touches the Mantha, the mortar, which is dedicated to Prana, breath, saying: Thou art fleet as breath. Thou art burning as fire. Thou art full as Brahman. Thou art firm as the sky. Thou art the abode of all as the earth. Thou hast been saluted with Hin at the beginning of the sacrifice by the Prastori. Thou art saluted with Him in the middle of the sacrifice. Thou hast been celebrated by the Adhvaryu at the beginning of the sacrifice. Thou art celebrated again by the agnidhra in the middle of the sacrifice. Thou art bright in the wet cloud. Thou art great. Thou art powerful. Thou art food as Soma. Thou art light as Agni, fire, absorption of all things.'

'Then he holds the Mantha forth, saying: 'Thou knowest all, we know thy greatness. He is indeed a king, a ruler, the highest lord. May that king, that ruler make me the highest lord.

'Then he eats it, saying: *'Tat savitur varenyam*—We meditate on that adorable light—The winds drop honey for the righteous, the rivers drop honey, may our plants be sweet as honey! Bhuh (earth) Svaha!

'Bhargo devasya dhimahi of the divine Savitri— May the night be honey in the morning, may the air above the earth, may heaven, our father, be honey! Bhuvah (sky) Svaha!

'Dhiyo yo nah prachodayat—who should rouse our thoughts—May the tree be full of honey, may the sun be full of honey, may our cows be sweet like honey! Svah (heaven) Svaha!'

'He repeats the whole Savitri verse, and all the verses about the honey, thinking, May I be all this! Bhuh, Bhuvah, Svah, Svaha! Having thus swallowed all, he washes his hands, and sits down behind the altar, turning his head to the East. In the morning he worships Aditya (the sun), with the hymn, "Thou art the best lotus of the four quarters, may I become the best lotus among men." Then returning as he came, he sits down behind the altar and recites the genealogical list.

Uddalaka Aruni told this Mantha-doctrine to his pupil Vajasaneya Yajnavalkya, and said: 'If a man were to pour it on a dry stick, branches would grow, and leaves spring forth.'

Let no one tell this to any one, except to a son or to a pupil.

• • •

26. The Golden Book of Upanishads
27. Learn Rajayoga from Vivekananda
28. Colossus Vivekananda Select
29. Intellect India
30. Culture India
31. Mahatma Gandhi The Bhagavadgita
32. Shirdi Sai Baba
33. The Ramayana For Every Home **(New)**
34. The Mahabharata For Every Home **(New)**
35. Sai - The Age of Cosmic Family
36. Sathya Sai and His Miraculous Powers
37. To Bloom Like a Lotus
38. The History of Sikh Gurus
39. Indian Mythology
40. Human Rights in Islam